"A stranger and I met behind stage at an event where we were both scheduled to speak for fifteen minutes to a group of law enforcement people. The stranger turned to me and said he had no idea what he would say. When he did speak, he received a standing ovation, and I knew then and there that this stranger would be my keynote speaker at the upcoming International Crime Stoppers Conference in Wyoming.

Little did I know it would take intervention from Wyoming's United States Senator for him to get permission to cross the US/Canadian border. What had happened was this: a police chief had just made friends with a convicted felon named Serge LeClerc. No one meeting Serge would ever expect this well-mannered and educated man to have lived the childhood he describes in this book. No one could ever fathom the challenges he faced in prison. This is a story of a regular guy whose destination was hell, but as you will read in this book, Serge shows you that life is not a destination, but a journey."

Richard Paul, Chief of Police (retired), Gillette, Wyoming; Chair, Wyoming State Advisory Council on Juvenile Justice

"Life has not been great, but it can be! Serge's openness and sincerity will speak to many who have not even come close to living on the edge of disaster, as he has. Serge is a pardoned convicted felon who realized that being a 'career criminal' was a dead end. To survive meant he had to change, and he did. As someone who has 'been there, done that', he has become an advocate for good. Today he is my friend and my brother."

John Neely, Deputy Warden, Correctional Services Canada (retired)

"I first heard Serge LeClerc speak at an International Crime Stoppers Conference in Kelowna, B. C., Canada. He is a compelling and provocative speaker who is capable of influencing peoples' lives for the better in just a few brief moments. When he speaks, you want to listen, and so you do. His survival in a world of crime for a good deal of his life is only surpassed by his knowledge, experience, wisdom, and his unrelenting need to prevent people from doing what he himself did. I hold this man in the highest regard and with the greatest of respect."

P.G. (Pete) Netherway, Inspector, RCMP (retired); CEO of Kamloops & District Crime Stoppers Society (retired)

"I met Serge LeClerc fifteen years ago during a Prison Fellowship International board meeting in Toronto. Serge was there to share his remarkable story, his journey from a twisted life of crime and violence to finding a new way of being. As fifteen men and women from around the world listened to Serge tell his riveting story, we knew we were witnessing a miracle of transformation.

Over the years, I have seen Serge's passion and conviction touch the lives of many people in and out of trouble. He is a uniquely gifted communicator with a powerful personal message that is rooted in the depths of human experience."

Ronald W. Nikkel, President, Prison Fellowship International, Washington, DC

"Serge LeClerc greatly impacted the success of Crime Stoppers in Saskatoon where we first met. Through his potent message, police leaders throughout North America have gained better insight and understanding into how drug trafficking and criminal gang activities impact our communities. My friendship with Serge has grown through a long and trusted relationship that has given me a deeper understanding of the meaning of true friendship and the importance of 'knowing' a person before you judge them."

Dave Scott, Saskatoon Chief of Police (retired); National Parole Board, Prairie Region, Saskatoon, Saskatchewan

"When you've been a police officer for forty years, you think you've probably encountered everything. I thought that way, and then I met Serge LeClerc. He told me he had a soft spot in his heart for police officers and prison guards. I found that hard to believe because I was well aware of his past. Someone on Canada's Most Wanted List isn't generally the kind of guy who has a soft spot for police officers. But indeed, we became close friends.

As you read Serge's story, you will see that everything is possible. Read... and believe."

Henry E. (Hank) Harley, Chief of Police, Tillsonburg, Ontario (retired); Superintendent of Niagara Regional Police, Ontario (retired); Executive Director, Canadian Christian Peace Officers Association

It is with deep respect and gratitude that I acknowledge the following individuals, for without their ongoing encouragement and support, the story of my life's journey would have remained an oral version:

George Glover, Teen Challenge Inc.
Ted and Marie Merriman
Bert and Darlene Harman
Drew and Karen Byers

This book is dedicated to my dear wife Noreen for the life we have shared together. She had the insight to take the chance of saying " I do" when she knew about my past transgressions. She has shown great courage and has believed in me always.

This book is also dedicated to all those who have allowed my words and my experiences to be a part of their life's journey.

UNTWISTED
An Extraordinary Journey of
Overcoming and Redemption

The Autobiography
of Serge LeClerc
with Darlene Polachic

Untwisted

Published by Career 7 Associates Inc.,
Produced and marketed by Denis M. Smail
denis@sergetalks.com

Speaking engagements and additional copies of Untwisted can be arranged through www.sergetalks.com

Cover design: Omni Studios / Tim Purvis

Photography: Stuart Kasdorf Photographics

Interior production: Blairmore Media Inc.

ISBN 978-0-9782284-0-8

Printed in Canada

AUTHORS' NOTES

When recounting a life as colorful and eventful as Serge LeClerc's, it is sometimes difficult to bring all the pertinent details to mind. That became apparent during the preliminary manuscript review process when Serge discovered he had left out an entire prison sentence. The error was soon corrected.

In an effort to ensure complete accuracy in this account, we have used Serge's official criminal record as a guideline for the body of the story, and consulted RCMP records, his national pardon, and other documented material for substantive information.

As a result, Serge's story comes to you well-documented and well-supported. The endorsements you will read are from a sampling of the law enforcement professionals who recommended Serge for a national pardon. Their recommendations came only after a thorough investigation into his life, his criminal record, and his humanitarian endeavors following his final release from prison.

What you are about to read may stretch your sense of credibility, but let us assure you, every word is true, though some of the names have been changed to protect the guilty.

Serge LeClerc
and
Darlene Polachic

Prologue

It was a summer evening in 1985. I was a convict at St. Vincent de Paul, a super maximum security penitentiary in Quebec, Canada.

The cells were securely locked for the night. The guards had completed their hourly check to make sure each prisoner was present and accounted for. As convicts like to say, "They treat you like swine and count you like pearls."

St. Vincent de Paul was Canada's second oldest penitentiary. It housed 1248 convicts.

The penitentiary's original design involved six ranges that radiated like wheel spokes from a central dome. The ranges were four stories high, and on each level there was a double row of back-to-back cells, twenty-six to a side, with a narrow three-foot corridor between the rows. Only the guards used this corridor, and it could only be accessed through an internal doorway from the central dome.

Each cell had a peephole window in the back wall, and every hour on the hour a guard would walk down the narrow corridor, slide back the peephole door, and check to make sure each prisoner was in his place.

The fronts of the cells were fully barred. They faced the outer walls of the spoke and opened onto a four-foot-wide railed walkway. About thirty feet beyond the rails was a bank of twelve-foot high window panels that looked out onto the cell block yard. At night, when the world outside was black, the windows became mirrors that reflected what was going on inside the cells.

The cells themselves had five-inch thick walls and measured about six-by-nine feet. Each was furnished with a bed topped with a very thin mattress, a small table, a folding chair, a toilet, and a sink. A metal-shaded light fixture hung from the ceiling. A night light was left on at all times so the guards could see you during the hourly night checks. You were also required to sleep in such a way that the light shone down on you.

The front of the cell was a door made of heavy steel bars. You could put your hands through the bars and around the narrow wall dividing the cells, thus enabling you to play chess with the guy next to you, pass books, or have a quiet conversation.

In each range, there were run-rails in front of the cells with two big brass wheels at one end. When the wheels were turned to exactly the right position, the bars of each cell door would align with holes above the door, enabling all the doors in the range to be opened at the same time. Each door had its own individual lock lever which also had to be released in order for the door to be opened, and prior to sliding the rails into place, a range runner would run down the corridor and release the lock levers. Convicts had to be ready and waiting to push their door open. If you weren't ready, you were out of luck and had to rely on a fellow-convict to click your door lever as he went by.

The archaic heating system at St. Vincent de Paul constantly clanged and banged. Boiler radiators against the ground level walls heated all four stories of the prison range. This meant the interior was freezing in winter and unbearably hot in summer. The plumbing was equally ancient, with pipes that clanked and creaked, and seatless porcelain toilets.

Following a major prison riot in the early 1980s, which pretty much razed the prison to the ground, it was decided that St. Vincent de Paul would become one of two SHUs, or Special Handling Units, to house Canada's most dangerous convicts. Three of the spokes were salvaged and refurbished, but only the two lower ranges were opened. This created a much smaller, more secure prison for only 312 convicts. Everything else stayed the same.

There was something almost medieval about St. Vincent de Paul. It was a depressing mass of iron and concrete that had already seen a century of use. Sounds echoed continuously in the towering corridors—harsh voices, curses, iron grating on iron. At night, in the dense silence, you could hear the pain of the current occupants and the profound agony of a myriad of restless souls who had spent interminable months and years there before.

Life in the SHU was very regimented. Guards wakened you at 6:30 in the morning and you had to be up and ready to open your door in order to go down and get your breakfast which was passed to you on a steel tray through a slot. You immediately took the tray back to your cell where they locked you in and you ate your breakfast. An hour later, they unlocked your cell so you could go and return the tray. By this time, it was about nine o'clock in the morning.

In the SHU, unless you worked in the mailbag shop or attended school, you remained locked in your cell until lunch time. The guys who worked returned to their cells at noon and the breakfast routine was repeated for lunch.

During each of these processes, you were carefully counted. Every time you left your cell or returned to it, you were counted. Each time you went to the shop, you were counted. At every doorway you passed through, you were counted.

An hour after lunch, you were allowed out of your cell to go to the yard for a couple of hours to lift weights or pound the heavy bag. Then you went back to your cell.

At supper time the guards unlocked your cell door, you collected your tray, returned to your cell, and ate your supper. An hour later, you were allowed out to return your tray.

You went back to your cell and waited a couple of hours until they cranked your door open again so you could go outside for two more hours. In summer, as long as it was daylight, you could go outside and work out; in winter, you might be confined to the common room, an area where you could go and play games or cards.

You could also go to the shower which was basically a big concrete room with rows of spigots and drains in the floor. The shower could be a dangerous place. I witnessed a killing there, and saw a man get his belly split open. For security, there was a gun cage at the end of the row where a guard with a shotgun kept watch.

Everywhere you went in the penitentiary, there were gun cages. Guards broke up fights by shooting one shot in the air and the next one into somebody.

By nine o'clock, you were back in your cell and locked up for the night.

My cell was mid-way down the range on the second tier.

Next to me was a young man named Glen. He had robbed three pizza joints with an unloaded shotgun. The whole take was about $500, but Glen was desperate. He needed the money to buy crystal meth. During his trial, he tried to escape from the courtroom holding cells by crawling into the heating ducts, but they caught him and gave him nine years.

Glen was sent to the reception unit at Millhaven Penitentiary where another convict raped him. When they let Glen out of his cell, he got a knife from a range cleaner and buried it in the chest of the guy who raped him. The courts added another sawbuck[1] onto his sentence and shipped him to Quebec, to the SHU in St. Vincent de Paul, reserved for the worst and most violent offenders. He was nineteen years old, doing twenty years in a super maximum security prison.

Glen and I became pretty good pals. Both of us were English, which made us a minority in the French prison. The other connection was that Glen came from a town with which I was very familiar. During the period of time when he committed his crimes, it was my drug labs and my drug dealers that supplied his area with drugs.

Over the seven or eight months since Glen had come in, he and I talked about a lot of things. He was a nice young man, but he had many problems. Glen was born to a prostitute and had a half-dozen half-brothers and –sisters, but no father. He had been in multiple foster homes, was raped as a kid, and lived on the streets. It was not a pretty story, but one that can be retold by the majority of people in prison.

On this particular evening, the guards had made their hourly rounds and retreated to the glass-enclosed dome area on the ground floor to put in time until the next hourly inspection rolled around. The range was in secure lock-down.

I was surprised to hear the sound of fabric ripping in Glen's cell.

"Glen," I said. "What are you doing?"

He didn't answer, but when I looked toward the windows, I could see in the reflection that Glen was tearing his bedsheets into strips and braiding them together.

I spoke to him again, but he ignored me and kept on working. It

---

[1] Sawbuck - ten years

didn't take a genius to figure out what he was doing.

"Come on, Glen," I said. "You shouldn't be doing this. Whatever you're feeling will pass. Tomorrow is another day."

He didn't even look up.

I didn't know what to do. My convict instincts told me I didn't want to get him into trouble. I didn't want the guards coming in and gassing him, or knocking him out, or putting him into the psychiatric ward. On the other hand, it was obvious that he planned to hang himself.

I watched helplessly as Glen placed his folding chair under the light fixture that was mounted with a metal brace to the nine-foot ceiling. He climbed onto the chair and tied the rope he had made to the brace.

I began screaming for the guards. But they were in the dome, a good distance away at ground floor level. Of course, they couldn't hear me. The dome was fortified with bullet-proof glass, locked doors, and shotgun holes.

Eventually convicts on the various levels began smashing their metal cups on the bars to get the guards' attention, but by the time they got all the multiple locks open and reached Glen's cell, thirty minutes had passed and he was dead.

I was badly shaken by the incident. It made me rethink my own life and everything I had done to this point. I liked Glen, and in a way, I felt responsible for his death. If it hadn't been for my drugs, Glen might not have embarked on the journey into crime that led to his death. Contemplating all this made me profoundly depressed. I was at my nadir. I had never felt lower. I saw no reason to continue living, and for the first time in my life, I considered committing suicide, too.

I decided I would do it the most painful way I could imagine—by starvation.

But death by starvation is nowhere near instantaneous. I had plenty of time to lie on my hard prison cot and ponder my life and my sorry past...

ONE

Solely by my mother's account, I was the product of rape. She was Cree and Micmac on her mother's side and German and French on her father's.

Her immediate family lived around coastal New Brunswick, but the larger family stretches out from the Micmac reserves on the east coast of New Brunswick all the way to the Crees in Northern Quebec.

My mother was born into a family with a lot of alcohol abuse. Because she was the only girl in a family of alcohol abusers and residential school survivors, for her own safety, her maternal grandmother took her away from her parental home and brought her up in the traditional Cree way.

I once saw a picture of this woman, my great-grandmother. She was probably in her nineties, raw-boned and leathery, a small little gal and as Indian as she could be, sitting in a rowboat smoking a corn cob pipe.

When my mother was thirteen, her grandmother died and she was forced to return to her parents' home. Shortly afterward, she ran away.

Being young, she was sadly vulnerable to all sorts of difficulties and dangers. She was raped and became pregnant with me.

It is interesting that my mother decided against going back to her family home to have her baby. Despite her tender age, she knew intuitively that if she went back home, the likelihood was strong her child would become enslaved in the lifestyle of alcoholism and abuse that prevailed there. So she stayed on her own as a runaway.

I was born in an abandoned building. As far as I can figure out, it was a motel-type of building, perhaps a collection of seasonal cabins that people would have rented during the summer. Apparently the place had gone bankrupt and was now abandoned.

My mother lived in one of the cabins and scrounged for food. There must have been a lake nearby and ice fishing going on because my mother would go around and collect the fish that were discarded or left behind. At one point during the pregnancy, she got severe food poisoning from eating some of the discarded fish, and almost died. She suffered endless vomiting for days and feared she would lose her baby.

It appears there was another young First Nations woman, also pregnant, living in the room or cabin next door. When my mother went into labor, she began banging on the wall in a prearranged signal that she needed help. It was this girl who brought me into the world and cut the umbilical cord with a pair of scissors. They were like two babies having babes of their own.

I don't know exactly where the abandoned building was, and I'm not certain of my exact date of birth because it was never registered with the government. In later life, I was able to track down my baptismal certificate from a Catholic church in New Brunswick. Going by the baptismal certificate, my best guess is I was born October 24 of either 1948 or 1949. I chose 1949.

I know very little about my mother's early life other than the fact that she was very strong, very resourceful, and obviously had a will to survive. For a time after I was born, she worked as a housekeeper for a Lebanese family. She remembers them as being very nice people with a big family. My mother and I had living quarters in their house, and she saved all the money she made.

I couldn't have been much more than a year old when my young mother decided to take the money she had saved and migrate to Toronto. I don't know what she was thinking, because Toronto was an English city, which she couldn't speak, and could neither read nor write. Perhaps she just wanted to be as far away as possible from her former life. Or was it the rumor of gold-paved streets that lured my mother to Toronto? It was generally believed that no matter where you came from, you were guaranteed to 'make it' in Toronto.

My earliest recollections centre around living in a rooming house on the corner of Sherbourne and Gerard, right next to George's Spaghetti House. The rooming house was run by an Oriental family, and according to my mother, before I was five years old, I could speak French, Cree, and Chinese—but no English. We had a bed-sitting room that was basically one large room equipped with a two-burner hotplate.

Two memories of that time stand out. One is taping a tablespoon to a stick and leaning out a second floor window to scoop pigeon eggs from a nest below. Had I fallen out, I would probably have splattered like an egg myself. Don't ask me what I did with the eggs.

The second memory is taking the doorknobs off all the apartment doors in the rooming house. Understandably, it caused a fair kafuffle in the building.

On one occasion, I apparently went out on my own for the whole day and came back naked with a little girl in tow. When my mother asked where my clothes were, I told her I had thrown them down the sewer. I clearly remember my punishment: being made to kneel in the corner on dried peas.

From the rooming house, we moved to a little house with a dirt yard. It was directly across the street from Sherbourne Park. I would go to the park and hang out at the library which also served as a community center and the armory. I remember climbing on a pair of big metal lions that guarded the entrance steps to the building, and seeing a lot of drunks and homeless people sleeping under the bushes in the park.

Our next move was to the fringes of Regent Park. This was 'The Projects'—Canada's experiment with the American-styled 'Let's-put-'em-all-in-one-place' agenda. Regent Park could only be described as a concrete jungle of four-storey, flat-roofed apartments with probably twenty suites to a building. Two dozen or so of these apartment blocks were squeezed together on five or six acres of land with only concrete between them—no trees, no flowers, no grass.

Because the land on which the development stood had formerly been a cabbage farm near the Don River at the east end of Toronto, the Regent Park area became known as Cabbagetown. The City purchased the farm when it needed a place to put its poor people.

Cabbagetown was where migrants and new immigrants came. It was where the docks and the waste processing facility were located. It was a smelly place with an almost Bowery-type of environment. Cabbagetown was a melting pot for Germans, Ukrainians, Scots, and Irish—predominantly white, with the odd black. There were few Orientals, no East Indians, and no Aboriginals.

The years we spent in Cabbagetown were amongst the happiest of my life. We were all equal in Cabbagetown because all of us battled the common enemy of poverty. It didn't matter what color you were, what culture you belonged to, or where you came from. Shared poverty has that calming and leveling effect. It drew us all together.

Cabbagetown was not a dangerous place—if you were a resident, but it was a rough neighborhood with cobblestone streets and tough Irish beat cops who knew everybody by name.

The row houses we lived in were interconnected by dirt tunnels that we kids dug through the adjoining basements. Using the tunnels, a person could go from one end of the street to the other without detection. The parents didn't stop us from digging these tunnels, because if the police came to the door with an arrest warrant for the man of the house, it was very convenient for him to slip into the tunnels and disappear.

Outsiders were not appreciated in Cabbagetown. We didn't steal from anyone else in The Projects, nor did we let anyone come in and steal from us. The police had learned from hard experience never to park on the street; they knew full well the Cabbagetown kids would be on the rooftops dropping stones and bricks on their patrol car.

It was a district that took care of its own. You knew every shopkeeper on the cobblestone street by name, and they knew you. Families purchased meal plans from restaurants. If you didn't purchase your meal plan immediately after the welfare cheque came, chances were good that someone would drink the money away.

We had ice vendors who came with horse and cart to deliver big blocks of ice to the door for your icebox. We kids were always on hand to get a sliver of ice from the vendor to suck on.

This was also the era when vegetable people came to the door; milkmen delivered milk, eggs, and cheese; and knife-sharpeners came down the street with their big whet wheels. It wasn't unusual to see men on the street with music boxes and monkeys, and itinerant photographers who would take your picture on a pony.

And then there were the Sheeney Men, Jewish men with long black coats, black hats, and curls, who came down the street with their horse-drawn wagons calling, "Rags and bones, rags and bones." You could go to their wagons and trade things. Mothers with clothing their kids had outgrown could go out to the Sheeney Man and trade, maybe two shirts for one. The Sheeney Men had depots and yards where they took their wagonloads of merchandise at the end of the day.

Backyards often housed the family's chickens and clotheslines strung with garments that flapped in the wind.

People sat on the front stoop in the evenings and paid attention to everybody else's business. They conducted conversations with each other by yelling across the street. It was nothing to see an Irish mother beating her kid on the head with a broom. Nor was it unusual for that same Irish mother to beat me on the head with a broom.

Cabbagetown was the kind of place where a kid could walk into anyone's home and sit down with them for dinner. I often did that because my mother worked two jobs, a day job and a night job as a dishwasher at a diner called Lou's, where she eventually advanced to the position of waitress. The owner, Lou, had two sons, but I never met them because Lou wouldn't think of bringing his family into a neighborhood as tough as ours.

I didn't go to kindergarten. I went directly into Grade One at the age of six after the truant officer paid us a call. The visit frightened my mother deeply. She didn't know I needed to be enrolled in school and thought she had done something terribly wrong.

After school, I would go to Lou's and wait for my mother. I often had my supper there. I remember a waitress named Loretta who worked with my mother. Loretta chain-smoked and drank a lot, and had an apartment above the restaurant. She was a very nice lady and I used to stay with her when my mother was busy. I called her Auntie Loretta. Her husband was Marcel. He was a little guy. Both Loretta and Marcel were what I know today to be alcoholics.

Between Lou, Loretta, and Marcel, everybody had a piece of me, and there is no negativity attached to my memories from those days.

On Sunday afternoons, my mother would take me to a little store-front church, a Baptist inner-city mission under the bridge that spanned the Don River. They used to do puppet shows for us kids at the mission. The one I recall most clearly is the Jesus puppet.

The mission gave out sandwiches and soup, and on Sunday afternoons we would take a pot of something my mother had cooked up—maybe pork feet and shells—and deliver it to a couple of families on the street who were going through tough times.

I was considered lucky in the neighborhood because I didn't have a father. Many of my chums had fathers who were alcoholics or drug addicts. They took the welfare check or the grocery money and the kids went hungry. In my home, we always had food and the basic essentials.

I don't remember having much of a relationship with my mother, nor do I recall her ever being affectionate. On the other hand, she was a good provider and a great cook. Our home was always clean and I had clean clothes to wear. My mother taught me proper hygiene and the habit of wearing clean clothes, and she also tried her best to teach me good morals.

My mother was neither a drinker nor a doper, and I was considered lucky in my neighborhood because my mother didn't beat me. She yelled at me a lot and often pulled my ear. When she lost her temper, she would take a swing at me, not caring where her hand landed or if she had something in it at the time. I learned to be quick on my feet.

In spite of all that, my mother was not a mean-spirited woman. I think I frustrated her a lot. She was little more than a child herself, thrust into a confusing world of adult decisions and responsibilities.

I hardly ever saw my mother during the week. She went to work in the morning before I got up, and I was in bed and asleep when she came home. On Sundays, we spent the whole day together. It was during those times that my mother tried to teach me that I had value and worth. She encouraged me to believe I could be anything I wanted to be. She knew that as a 'half-breed' I would have a harder time in life than most. She taught me that I should always do the right thing.

Because I was left pretty much to my own devices, I became a solitary child, entertaining and caring for myself.

The street car was free for kids in those days, and my mother claims I was four when I began riding to Riversdale and the Don River. I do recall a lot of happy times swimming in the Don and roaming the streets. I also remember going to the park and talking to people there. Fortunately, we lived in an era when, by and large, people looked out for children.

My play included a good deal of reading, and I spent a lot of time reading books at the library. I don't know when or how I learned to read—it certainly wasn't from my mother—but I can't remember a time when I could not read. I have a vivid recollection of eating a bowl of Cheerios and milk in the little house with the dirt yard and reading what was on the box.

I also remember a little movie theatre and a second hand store or pawn shop that I used to visit. I was fearless, outgoing, gregarious, and extremely social. My friends' parents loved me. Even when I was a teenage gang leader, they would say to their sons, "Why can't you be like Serge?"

I hung out a lot with my friends' families. One friend, Kenny, came from an Irish family with thirteen children. I would go to see Kenny and think nothing of sitting down with them for dinner. The food wasn't as good as my mother's, but in retrospect, I think I probably went more for the warmth, the family environment, and the company, than the food.

I had no family outside of my mother, though I do have a vague recollection of my grandmother, a big woman, coming to Toronto once and staying with us. I believe she came to the city for an eye operation. Grandmother couldn't speak English and although I understood French, I didn't speak the language so we couldn't communicate. A strange little banty of a man came to get my grandmother. I presume he was my grandfather.

Memories of school are somewhat patchy. My only real recollection is getting the strap in Grade Two. I remember the nun being very angry because I kept pulling my hand away and she would hit herself on the leg with the strap.

My vivid memories begin when I was eight years old and probably in Grade Three. I made a bad choice that would affect me for the rest of my life: I played hookey from school.

I wasn't the only one to skip school. There was a group of boys in the school who I thought were pretty cool. They were older than me, and I thought it would be great to be part of their gang. Since I knew one of the boys, I asked him if I could join.

"Sure," he said, "you're a pretty cool kid. But you have to do the things we do."

I said, "Okay, what do you do?"

"Every Friday afternoon we skip school and go Uptown. We do a little shoplifting to get some money for the weekend."

"Okay," I said.

"Are you in?"

"Sure."

That evening, when I was by myself eating supper, I thought about what we were going to do and I knew I didn't want to do it. I knew if we were caught, it would hurt my mother terribly. I decided I would tell the boy the next day that I would not go.

At noon on Friday, the boy said, "We're going. Are you coming?"

I said, "Yes."

In making that choice, I launched myself on a destructive path that would result in years of untold pain and damage to myself and thousands of others.

We jumped on the streetcar and rode Uptown for some shoplifting. I was the lookout. The next thing I knew, the police were there and everybody was running. Being the youngest, with the shortest legs, I got caught. Everyone else got away.

I was arrested for truancy and taken to 311 Jarvis Street, the secure custody unit of the Juvenile Detention Centre.

I was eight years old, and I was terrified. And with good reason. This was the early 1950s, and under the Canadian Juvenile Delinquency Act, there were a number of punishable status offenses. They included having sex under sixteen, drinking under twenty-one, hanging around pool halls under eighteen, playing hookey from school, and being incorrigible, though I'm not exactly sure what 'being incorrigible' entailed.

It also needs to be said that in this era of the early Fifties, it was generally accepted that First Nations people were little more than savages and definitely inferior to the white population. It was during this time that Native children were ripped out of their cultures and placed in residential schools in an effort to assimilate them into 'civilized' society. In my case, the idea that a child had been created from the union of a First Nations woman and a Caucasian man was disgusting to many.

There was another strike against me. In the opinion of the courts, the politicians, and the social engineers of the day, if a male child from a single mother got into trouble, the child was obviously being improperly parented and must be taken away. If the single mother was poor, or of First Nations blood, there was an even greater stigma. If she was poor, she must be lazy. If she was single, it meant she was a tramp, a drinker, and definitely incapable of properly caring for a child.

Therefore, it was the responsibility of the state and the government to intervene and protect the child from this incompetent parent.

The practice of the courts was to place the delinquent boy in a training or reform school for an undetermined length of time. Prior to the revamping of the Juvenile Delinquency Act, any young offender charged with a status offense was given an indefinite sentence, meaning the child could be kept in reform school from age seven until he was twenty-one. Only the chief jailer or director of the training school had the authority to make the decision regarding when the young person would be released. He could not appeal; he had no advocate. No lawyer spoke on his behalf. Basically, the law gave the jailer unlimited and unmitigated power over the child.

Since my mother was single, and illiterate, we were placed in another category altogether.

Upon being arrested and taken to 311 Jarvis, I was locked in a secure room in the detention centre. My memories of the place are as clear and as painful as if it were yesterday.

The room had a concrete floor. Its furnishings were a steel bed, a table, and a concrete seat with a slab of wood on the top. The big steel doors were locked tight. There was a window with safety glass looking out on an inner courtyard where the kids were allowed to exercise. I saw some boys playing with a basketball, but I was not allowed outside because I had to appear in court on Monday.

I remember pounding, punching, smashing, kicking the door, screaming to be let out, but nobody came. Eventually, exhausted, terrified, and cried out, I fell asleep on the cold cement floor.

On Monday, they took me to court. For a little eight-year-old, the courtroom was an extremely frightening place. People in long, flowing black robes were running in every direction, and above everyone was the judge, also dressed in black, seated on a raised dais. He looked like a big black raven, and he scared the life out of me.

The only other person in the courtroom was my mother. She sat on the opposite side, but I was not allowed to go near her. She had a baseball bat, a ball, and a glove on her lap. I don't know why; maybe she wanted to demonstrate to the court that she was a good parent. I kept looking at her and wondering what the heck she was doing with all that stuff.

I don't remember much that was said that day, but several things will never leave my mind. One was hearing the authorities call my mother an 'unfit mother.' They called me a bastard and inferred that my mixed blood were somehow big factors in my delinquent behavior.

I remember being very angry at my mother because she didn't speak up and defend herself. I was also angry that she didn't tell them she was not an unfit mother. In retrospect, I realize she probably felt as powerless and as disadvantaged as I did, and thoroughly intimidated by the black-robed judge sitting on the pedestal.

The judge asked my mother if we were Protestant or Catholic.

"Catholic," she said.

It was a simple and honest response, but a tragic one for me. Being Catholic meant I was destined for St. John's Training School for Boys.

Had my mother said we were Protestant, I would have been sent to Bowmanville Training School. Bowmanville was a tough and brutal place, but brutality and corporal punishment were what you could expect if you were deemed a juvenile delinquent. Obviously, you were a bad kid who needed a hard, firm hand.

St. John's Training School was located near Uxbridge, Ontario, about an hour's drive from Toronto. It was operated and staffed by the Toronto Christian Brothers, a branch of the Irish Province of Christian Brothers who had a long-standing tradition of administering harsh corporal punishment.

In the history of Ontario, St. John's Training School became synonymous with violence, brutality, sexual abuse, rape, aggravated physical beatings, and assaults. It was probably the most violent training school in the entire country. Children were physically crippled at the hands of the Christian Brothers, and there are claims that some were killed. Incarceration there as a youth inevitably led to unrestrained drug abuse and suicide as young men grew into adulthood. I don't know anyone who survived St. John's Training School and was not horribly scarred for life by the experience.

Later on in my life, I would meet many former St. John's students in prisons, penitentiaries, and drug circles where we sat around together and got high on heroin and crystal meth.

Allegations of widespread sexual abuse at St. John's Training School during the Forties, Fifties, and Sixties surfaced in the 1980s. In 1990, the Ontario Provincial Police conducted a full-scale investigation and laid two hundred charges against thirty Christian Brothers. There would have been more, but some of the Brothers had already died. Seven hundred former students came forward with claims of abuse, saying they were punched, kicked, clubbed, denigrated, groped, and sodomized during the years they spent at the school. Ninety-eight percent of the claims were determined to be legitimate.

One witness was sentenced to St. John's for stealing four dollars worth of food from a grocery store because his father was gone and his mother was an alcoholic.

"I got four years in St. John's for my crime," he told the inquiry. "I ran after I was sexually molested by one of the priests. With hands tied to the front of the bed and my feet to the back and a pillow underneath to prevent damage to the spine, they beat me. We bear these scars on our hearts and will take them to our graves."

Another testified, "I ran away eleven times. After the third time, I was beaten so badly they brought me to the infirmary and the Brother in charge there cried… I showed the OPP (Ontario Provincial Police) the scars left by the blisters and cuts that took six weeks to heal from the infected wounds and they cried… But they wouldn't charge him.

"I gave confession and told the priest about a Brother who sexually assaulted me and he came out of the confessional and took my hand and took me directly to the Brother and told him what I had confessed…. Then the priest sexually assaulted me."

"I saw many young children beaten up and strapped," reported yet another. "I saw Brother ———— wake up young children and take them to a room to sexually assault them. I saw children handcuffed to a pillar in the basement. They would be pushed and kicked. I saw Brother ———— use a pool table stick to hit children if they would not have anal sex with him. Children were given cold showers, then strapped. If I told any Brothers that another Brother tried to have sex with me, I would be strapped."

This was St. John's. This was where I was headed at the tender age of eight.

Two

For the trip to St. John's Training School, I was put in a vehicle with a mesh screen separating me from the driver. I remember traveling down a road and going out into the country. It was a new experience for me. I had never been out of the city before.

St. John's Training School was an ugly place. That was my first impression as we drove through the big steel gates. It had a rural, farm-like setting, but there was nothing peaceful or pastoral about it. The compound consisted of several austere, brown brick buildings and a barn. Much of the complex was surrounded by a chain-link fence. The rest was farm property adjacent to a small town where many of the staff lived.

I was immediately taken to the office of the Head Brother in charge of my assigned dormitory. There I had my hair shaved off, was issued a suit of clothing (blue shirt and pants, both about six inches too long, and black tennis shoes), given a blanket roll, and pointed to my bed.

Having never been hit or screamed at by an adult male to this point in my life, St. John's Training School came as a new and terrifying experience. I instinctively rebelled against this environment that placed so much emphasis on shouting, hitting, and beating.

The regimen of intimidation and brutality came not only from the Christian Brothers who ran the place, but from the older, tougher boys, as well. They were used by the Brothers to control the younger, smaller children. It was what the older boys had to do in order to survive themselves.

As a small eight year old boy, I was quickly earmarked for 'special treatment,' particularly when word got out that I was the product of rape, a bastard with no father.

The first bit of trouble happened the day I arrived at St. John's. I was sitting at dinner that first evening and a boy leaned across the table and said, "You're new here. You're fish[2]. You'd better make sure you're in the showers tonight after lights out." He was informing me they expected me to give them sexual favors.

I looked back at him and said, "Or what?"

"You just be there or we'll give you the Blanket Treatment."

The Blanket Treatment meant they would sneak up on you while you were sleeping and either pull your blankets over you or throw another blanket over top of you, specifically over your head, and pin you down so you could not escape or fight back. Then they would beat you about the body with bars of soap concealed in socks. They wouldn't kill you or incapacitate you because that would draw attention from the staff; the beating was meant to intimidate you and make you compliant.

Having grown up in Toronto's Cabbagetown/Regent Park, I was used to taking care of myself. Every day I dealt with drunks in the gutter and drug addicts with needles in their arms. I saw my friends eating ketchup sandwiches because their fathers were on a drunken binge. Almost by osmosis, I had developed a different way of thinking about life, a way of conducting myself that put me in control. I had learned to be street-wise, and I knew from growing up in the Inner City that I could comply and became a victim, or I could attack. My strategy was to make them scared of me, make them think I was fearless, and that if they were going to interfere with me, they would have to pay a price.

That was the attitude I took that first day at St. John's Training School, and it was the kind of action that would become a pattern for the next thirty-two years of my life.

I immediately went on the offensive. I reached across the table and stabbed the boy in the face with a fork.

Off to solitary confinement I went.

Solitary confinement at St. John's Training School was a hallway

---

[2] Fish - newcomer, new prisoner

with four or five rooms the size of broom closets on each side. I was stripped naked and thrown into one of these rooms. It was so small I couldn't lie down straight; I had to curl myself around the corner. There was no window, no light. It was pitch black inside. The door was made of solid hardwood slats. The only furnishing was a plastic bucket for a toilet.

At night, the staff threw in a pillow and a blanket which they snatched away in the morning. I was given one glass of milk and a piece of toast in the morning, and later in the day I got a chunk of bean cake which was popular in all the juvenile correction institutions. They took all the leftover vegetables from meals, baked them in a pan, and cut the tough paste into squares. Bean cake had no taste whatsoever, and probably no nutritional value, either. But it did fill the stomach. Sometimes they gave me a cup of tea, as well.

I was kept in the nude in solitary confinement for seven days. This was meant to correct me. Of course, it only made me angrier.

The same day they let me out of solitary, I ran away. I don't remember the circumstance, whether we were let out for recreation or if we were going from the dormitory to the school building. In any case, I turned left instead of right and made a bee-line out of the compound.

I was only eight, and I had no idea where I was going other than home to my mother. I may have been angry at her for not speaking out at the trial, but she was the only person I knew to run to.

It took me three days of walking and hitchhiking to make it back to Toronto. The first night I didn't get very far. I think I slept in a barn or some type of out-building. When I got hungry, I would knock on a door somewhere along the way and tell the people I'd lost my bus ticket or my lunch money. "Could I please have an apple?" I'd say. No one refused a pathetic little eight-year-old.

Once I reached the outskirts of Toronto, I was in familiar territory and knew how to navigate. I caught a street car to Regent Park and home.

Had I been older, I would have realized that going back to The District was not a smart idea. The authorities had already been notified that I was a runaway from St. John's Training School and they figured the first place I would go was to my mother's. When I got there, the police were waiting for me. Within an hour, I was re-arrested and taken back to the St. John's where I was punished again.

Thus began an odyssey of punishment, escape, and re-arrest. I probably ran away from St. John's Training School twenty times in the next two years. On each occasion I would run to a different part of Toronto where it took the authorities longer and longer to find me.

During those times, I became acquainted with the various street gangs in the city, and often made contact with relatives of boys I had met in St. John's.

It has always been easy for me to interact with people and establish relationships, and I had quickly developed a group of friends at the Training School. I was never a bully, and until I got into heavy drug use, there wasn't a bit of nastiness in my make-up. I was not a liar, and people seemed to gravitate to me, maybe because I instinctively championed the underdog, something that often got me into more trouble than championing myself.

Each time I ran away, the punishment when I returned to St. John's was more severe.

Discipline at the training school was immediate and harsh. When I was nine years old, I had my jaw broken for speaking in chapel. Actually, I whispered to the boy next to me. The next thing I knew, I was flat on my back on the floor, bleeding from the mouth. A six-foot, two hundred-pound Christian Brother had smashed me in the face to quiet me.

For most of that day I floated in and out of consciousness until they eventually took me to a hospital and wired my jaw shut. After that, I was taken back to St. John's where I was immediately put in solitary confinement.

I have often wondered how it was that I could be taken to a public hospital and treated for a broken jaw without anyone questioning how it happened. Obviously, the hospital staff saw nothing suspicious in the injury. I suppose, with Christian Brothers in charge of the children, the idea of abuse was the furthest thing from anyone's mind. After all, teachers, social workers, and people from the town came to the Training School all the time. So did the police, especially when they were returning me to the school. No one seemed to notice or suspect that anything wrong was taking place.

Abuse was rampant, not only at St. John's, but in other institutions like St. Joseph's, a reform school in Ontario that, later on, was also at the heart of investigations into abuse by the Christian Brothers. Mt. Cashel in Newfoundland was yet another infamous institution run by the same order. Granville Training School for Young Women in the Cambridge area was run by civilians, but rape was prevalent there, too, including rape with broom handles. Like St. John's Training School, the inevitable legacy for survivors was suicide, imprisonment, drug use, alcoholism, prostitution, and the like.

All this took place at a time when society was somehow innocent of the fact that predators and pedophiles existed. There has been much publicity in recent years about the wholesale abuse of First Nations children in residential schools, but abuse wasn't confined only to First Nations schools. Whenever you place children in a situation where they have no power, no advocacy, and no ability to speak, where adults have complete authority over them, you will find a place to which pedophiles and predators gravitate. It is in these situations that they can have full control of the innocent and the power to gratify their sexual and emotional desires at the expense of the powerless.

After having my jaw broken in chapel, I flatly refused to attend services anymore. I spent more time in solitary confinement for that than most kids did for getting into more serious trouble.

Every Sunday the Brothers would say, "You're going to chapel."

I would say, "No. You people hurt me while I was in chapel, so I'm not going to give you the satisfaction of seeing me go back. I don't care what it costs me."

They would try to force me, I would kick and scream, and they would throw me into solitary confinement again.

That stubborn streak in my makeup definitely made life more painful for me at St. John's, and at times it could have been perceived as cutting off my nose to spite my face, but in the long run I believe it allowed me to survive. It built a streak of stubbornness in me that just would not bend. And certainly, in St. John's Training School, it kept me from being a victim of sexual abuse.

Later on, in the adult corrections system, that same unbending stubbornness made guards and convicts terrified of me. Many times people much bigger and tougher avoided messing with me because they knew how stubborn I was. They knew if they came at me, they had better be prepared to kill me. You either left me alone, or you went the full mile with me, something that saved me a lot of abuse and quite possibly, even my life.

I was lucky. I did not get raped at St. John's Training School, but I certainly heard the cries in the night of those who did. It wasn't only the staff who did the abusing. The older students did it, too—the ones the Christian Brothers used as bully boys to intimidate and control the younger ones and recruit them for sex. I think the reason I avoided the sexual abuse was because they thought I was crazy. I fought anyone who came near me.

There was one Brother at this place who had a special form of punishment for me because I was something of a thorn in his flesh. He was a big man, the Head Brother in charge of my barracks, the man directly in charge of me. Every time I escaped, he had the Administration's wrath coming down on him because he couldn't manage this eight-, nine-, ten-year-old kid.

I don't remember his name, maybe because I ran away so often that I was out of St. John's as much as I was in. Or maybe because the whole trauma associated with the place made my memory blank out names and even faces. They all wore the black cassock, and even now they all blur together in my mind into a common image of a big, black, evil raven. Many years after being in the training school, I talked with a friend, who was severely abused at St. John's, about our experiences there. It was this friend who told me the names of the Brothers, including the one who liked to beat me with a sawed-off goalie stick.

I wasn't the only boy who received this special kind of punishment from him, but it seemed that I received it more than anyone else during my time there.

He would begin by stripping me naked in front of the other boys. As a child, especially an underdeveloped male child with no body hair, there is nothing more humiliating than being stripped naked in front of your peers and prevented from covering your private parts. I couldn't do that because my hands were otherwise occupied holding two buckets of sand.

I would be instructed to hold the buckets at arm's length straight out from my sides at shoulder level. The Brother stood behind me with a sawed-off hockey goalie stick from which he had removed the blade and drilled a series of holes through the wide paddle part.

Keep in mind, this was still the era in which the strap was given as punishment, even in adult prison. The strap they used there was made of leather, generally one inch thick and six inches wide with holes drilled through it. The strap was administered across the buttocks. In reformatory, there was a structure something like a forward leaning crucifix to which you were tied with your pants pulled down.

The guards would shuffle their feet so you couldn't hear the sound of the strap coming. They applied it two-handed. It was probably from this form of punishment that the Brother got his idea for the wooden paddle.

The deal with the pails was if you couldn't hold them at shoulder height for the prescribed length of time, you got beaten with the hockey stick. The time really wasn't a factor, because no matter how hard you tried, you could never beat the clock. The Brother was the only one with a watch, and he set the time limit.

I would stand there knowing what was coming, and pretty soon a sweat would break out. The perspiration would start running down my back and tickle as it went down. My arms began to tremble and a terrible burning developed in my shoulders. Eventually, my arms would droop past the arbitrary level. Only he knew what that level was, and I couldn't look to see how far my arms were drooping because I had learned from experience that I could keep my arms up longer if I braced my back, kept my head up, and my neck stiff.

All of a sudden, I would hear the whistle of the hockey stick paddle as it whipped through the air behind me. The whistle was made by air rushing through the holes. I would brace myself as he hit me across the buttocks and the back of the legs, knocking me to my knees.

I immediately got back up again because if I didn't, I could expect even harder blows across my back and shoulders.

Usually the routine was repeated at least three times until the Time Game, as he called it, was over. That happened when his arm got tired or I collapsed and was unable to get up again.

The drilled holes in the hockey stick pulled like little suction cups causing blood blisters across my back and buttocks. I still carry the scars from those blood blisters, but the biggest scars I received came from his mouth. He called me Squaw, Garbage, Loser, Bastard, and many other derogatory names, and every time this so-called representative of God scarred me with his mouth, it went deep into my soul. The more he called me bad, the more I acted out. He would 'punish' me and I would await my chance to go-boy[3] again.

I ran away often, and each time it became more difficult for the police to find me because as time went on, I discovered different areas

---

[3] Go-boy - run away

of the city in which to hide.

One of my most interesting hideaways was a big wooden electrical spool in a railway shuttle yard at the top of Spadina Road where it curves at Dupont Street. The railway yard had a whole pile of these wooden spools, each one about four feet in diameter.

I spent one entire Saturday, when no one was at work, rearranging the spools to make a safe, secret hiding place for myself. I propped the spools and moved them around until I had a little rabbit warren of a maze for an entrance to the middle spool. I took out a slat so I could crawl into the innermost part. There I put blankets and pillows that I stole from unlocked cars, and a candle to keep me toasty warm. I hid there for about a month.

There was a bakery nearby on Dupont Street, and I ate from the dumpster behind it. You would be amazed at the quantity of discarded cakes, buns, and cupcakes that were deemed unfit for grocery store shelves.

I also stole vegetables from gardens and had my stretch of dumpsters behind restaurants on Upper Yonge Street. There I would find half eaten steaks, pork chops, and potatoes. My favorite restaurant was The Brown Derby.

On another occasion I spent time somewhere on Yonge Street sleeping on the roof of a building that had a roof vent. It kicked out hot air and kept me nice and warm all night. I got to the roof by climbing the fire escape.

I also frequented the subway tunnels. In those days, the Toronto Subway closed at a certain hour. I would go down into the tunnels and come out around the Rosedale area where I discovered a wonderful wooden terrace that afforded a great place underneath to sleep.

I often made use of abandoned houses. Sometimes I would find them completely furnished, possibly belonging to an estate. One was in the West End of Toronto near where my mother had moved.

I thought I had died and gone to Heaven when they began building the new Toronto City Hall. It had a multi-level heated garage underneath with a multitude of cubbyholes where I could hide. All I needed was a couple of blankets under a stairwell and I was safe and warm.

I loved the Jewish Market (now known as Kensington Market) where you could get wonderful ethnic food in the days before stores began to sell such fare. The Market took up four streets. You could buy everything from dogs, live chickens, and rabbits to clothing and food.

I would crawl over the fence at three or four in the morning to steal food.

Occasionally, I would sneak into a school during the day and pretend I was a regular student in the classroom. Often they gave me books which I loved to read.

I spent a lot of my time reading at the public library and always had a book in my back pocket. It was not unusual for me to get on the subway and ride all day—just reading. I would also read at night by candle light. Whenever the police discovered one of my squats, they always found a stash of books and magazines. I loved reading about the Vikings, especially stories that included the Norse god Thor. I read all the Grimms' Tales and the Greek myths about Hercules and Zeus.

Another thing I loved (and still do) was movies. During my runaway days, I spent whole days in movie theatres. First, I would buy a loaf of warm bread from the bakery. Then I would go to the grocery store for butter (I generally stole that). Then I'd go to the theatre and eat while I watched one, two, and sometimes three movies in succession. Adventure films were my favorites; I loved to lose myself in the world of fantasy.

Museums and art galleries were other beloved haunts. I knew every entrance, every corner of the Royal Ontario Museum. The part I liked best was the basement which housed a First Nations exhibit and a mock-up of a campfire scene. My second favorite place was the Armory Floor with its display of old swords and firearms. I was fascinated, as well, with the exhibits of animals, fowl, and snakes—beautiful, free-roaming creatures that one never saw in the city.

It may have been the thousands of hours I spent in the museum that spawned my life-long appreciation of art and beautiful things. To this day, I love good paintings, flowers, gardening, fine pieces of art, and music. I never learned to play an instrument, but as a young adult I would often lose myself in music—listening to it or dancing to it in clubs. It was nothing for me in my late teenage years to drive across the border to Buffalo, New York, with my black friends simply to spend an evening there listening to music in the black clubs.

Another favorite haunt during my runaway days was the Toronto Exhibition Grounds. I especially enjoyed the Royal Winter Fair. I would sneak onto the grounds via the railroad tracks and head immediately for the food booths and the free food.

It was during Exhibition time that I honed my pick-pocketing skills.

In the crush of the crowds, it was ridiculously easy; people would be buying things and leaving their purses wide open. I collected enough money that way to last me for three or four months.

In the off-season, I found a couple of very good squats[4] on the Exhibition Grounds. One was in the control building for the roller coaster on which I spent many a happy hour playing and climbing along the track.

Nearby, in a bank beneath the railroad tracks, I discovered a big steel door with a lock that I soon dispatched. Inside was a little room equipped with a cot and lantern which were probably used by railroad linemen in former years. Naturally, I spent some time there.

For a while I had a squat in an army tank at the Fort York Armories. Fort York is the reconstructed site of the original settlement of Toronto. The site had old wooden palisades and bunk houses complete with soldiers' uniforms.

Looking back, I see myself as something of a modern-day Oliver Twist or a Huckleberry Finn. When I was hungry, I dug in the dumpsters. If I needed clothes, I stole them off clotheslines or shoplifted them from stores. By the time I reached adulthood, I had become a very accomplished booster[5].

My biggest money-making operation in those days was checking newspaper dispensers for coins that hadn't quite fallen into the collection box. I would walk down Queen Street from east to west, all the way to High Park and then back again the other side, a distance of about ten miles. It took the whole day, but I would end up with a pocket full of change which I spent on meals, clothing, and shoes. The next day I would do the same thing on King Street.

I became a panhandler before people panhandled. I would knock on doors and spin a little tale of woe: "I've lost my street car ticket and it's too late for me to get home. Could I please have a quarter for a sandwich?"

Toronto's population was probably less than a million people in those days, and I got to know the city intimately as I roamed it from one end to the other. In the process, I met a lot of different kids. Some would skip school and hang out with me, though they made sure they

---

[4] Squat - a temporary place to sleep

[5] Booster - a shoplifter

were back in time to go home after school.

Sometimes I would take three or four of them shoplifting. We would go to a store where I would send two of them to the back to knock something over. While the proprietor was hurrying to see what had happened, I tapped the tills[6], scooped up a handful of money, and ran.

On one of my escapes, I went to my mother's place. By this time, she had moved out of the East End of Toronto to place nearer the West End. With all my running away, I guess she figured she would never see me again if she stayed in Cabbagetown. I was sitting on her front porch, waiting while she went inside to make me something to eat, when I spotted the police coming. I took off.

"Yes," my mother said, "Serge was here on the porch just a little while ago. Someone must have abducted him. I'm sure he didn't run away. Why would he run away when I was making food for him?" It was her way of protecting me, trying to mitigate my trouble.

I spent one whole summer on the grounds of Casa Loma. The castle—and it really is a castle—was built by a multi-millionaire for his wife in the early part of the last century. It sits on top of a hill surrounded by a castle wall made of big boulders. I climbed over the wall and into the lower yard which was overgrown with lush vegetation and a forest of trees.

My explorations uncovered a tunnel that led to a small house on the grounds, possibly the groundskeeper's dwelling in former days. I pried open the tunnel door and found a nice little cubby hole inside about five feet long which I furnished with a candle, blankets, and pillows stolen from visitors' cars. At night, I collected the coins people threw in the huge courtyard fountain. It is so big, I had to dive to get the coins, and this served as my bath time, as well.

Food was no problem; there was a large dairy across the street. Those were the days when dairymen delivered milk, bread, eggs, and cheese to the door. Some days I would go ahead of the dairyman, at four or five in the morning, and collect the money from milk bottles. Other times I went after the dairyman had made his deliveries and collected the milk, eggs, and cheese.

I learned very quickly how to eat raw eggs. You poke a hole in the

---

[6] Tap the tills - steal money from the cash register

end of the egg with a nail, put the egg to your mouth, poke a hole in the other end, and suck hard.

At the age of ten, after spending two years at St. John's Training School, I hit the front page of the Toronto newspaper for the first of many times. The authorities caught me selling cigarettes on a street corner after stealing a station wagon from behind a drugstore. The vehicle was loaded with cartons of cigarettes. The newspapers made a big thing of it: 'Ten-year-old living beneath the porch of an empty mansion on St. George Street [one of the most prestigious streets in Toronto] hot-wires and steals car.'

The house was near the university and the Royal Museum where I spent so much of my time. Beneath its porch, I had pillows and blankets and a lot of other loot I had acquired, including an expensive bust I removed from the Royal Museum without setting off the alarm system.

I also had the stolen cigarettes. Inside each package were two brand new pennies. I think the packages were destined for vending machines and the pennies were probably the change due the buyer. Anyway, I sold the cigarettes on the street for ten cents a package and used the brand new pennies to buy pop and chips. Eventually, a store proprietor figured it all out and phoned the police.

Zap! I was caught.

Making the front page of the Toronto Telegram caused St. John's Training School a good deal of embarrassment. Once again, I had escaped. Once again, they hadn't been able to control this little, under-sized, ten-year-old kid. As the police drove me back to the school, I knew I would have to face the head of my barracks, the Brother with his infamous form of punishment. Only this time, I knew the punishment would be much more severe.

When we arrived at St. John's, they removed my handcuffs and I got out of the paddy wagon. Every other time, we went directly inside to see the head of the barracks. He and the authorities would hold this little court session and I would be sent off to solitary confinement. This time they put me in a little side room to wait.

It was all the opportunity I needed.

The moment the door closed, I crawled out the window and headed for the stable where the cows and horses were housed and the harnesses and garden tools were kept. How many times had I been sent there to clean out the manure? Enough to be very familiar with the stable and its contents. I knew exactly what I was looking for.

I quickly grabbed a big pitchfork and tried to break off a tine. For a ten-year-old weighing all of seventy pounds, this was no easy task. I eventually wedged the handle of the fork into a crack in one of the stalls and pushed on the tine with all my might. When it snapped, there was nothing bracing me and I fell forward, cutting myself on the broken metal. It caused a deep gash across the base of my thumb that laid the palm of my right hand wide open. The wound began to bleed profusely.

I ran up to my sleeping cubicle in the barracks, tore a strip off my flannel pajamas and wrapped it around my hand. Strangely, the barracks was empty at the time; the other boys must have been working or in school.

The rough bandage was soon slippery with blood, but I didn't care. Nor did I notice the pain. I had a job to do.

The Brother who liked to beat me with his sawed-off goalie stick was in his office. He was a big man, about six-and-a-half feet tall, not particularly fat, but raw-boned and very strong.

I didn't stop to think about what he would surely do to me. Taking a deep breath, I opened the door and before the Christian Brother could rise from his chair, I rushed across the room and buried six inches of the broken pitchfork tine in his belly.

THREE

I regained consciousness on the way to 311 Jarvis Street and the Juvenile Detention Centre.

Why they would be taking me there was rather confusing to me at the time, because I thought what I had done was perfectly normal given the treatment I had experienced at the hands of this Christian Brother.

The courts did not agree.

"The boy must be brain-damaged," they said. "For a ten-year-old boy to be so violent as to attack a grown man, he is definitely brain-damaged."

A disastrous psychological process had begun in me. I had developed an attitude that is common to many people when they are messing up their lives, when they're making wrong choices and getting involved with drugs and alcohol, or suffering a lot of pain. It is the 'I don't care' attitude which becomes a protective armor. We try to pretend that nothing bothers us, that we don't care. And at the tender age of ten, I was already an expert at it.

Often, when children who are involved with their parents' divorces hear someone say, "You must be feeling a lot of pain with all that's going on with your parents," they respond, "I don't care." Of course they care. 'I don't care' is something they do to protect themselves from the personal internal burdens they carry and the turmoil going on the outside.

When I walked into court with my Cabbagetown swagger, I had already become an expert at 'I don't care.'

The judge said, "You are brain-damaged. I'm sending you to a maximum security reformatory."

I said, "I don't care."

In fact, I cared so little that as I left the courtroom, I said to myself, "Brain-damaged, eh? That's kinda cool. Brain-damaged... Gee, I betcha' there aren't too many people who are brain-damaged." And I wore the title almost as a badge.

Fortunately for me, the authorities said I was too violent for St. John's Training School and they sent me to a place called Ontario Training School.

OTS was a maximum security centre for older boys. It was hooked onto the Guelph Adult Reformatory. At ten years of age, I was the youngest boy there.

Ontario Training School was a tough place filled with tough kids. It was situated in the middle of the countryside outside the city of Guelph and surrounded by barbed wire. Guards on horses secured both the training school and the reformatory.

My first encounter at OTS was with a guard who let me know in no uncertain terms that he had my number. I had a go-boy[7] reputation, but there would be no go-boy here, he told me. He assured me the place was escape-proof and that no ten-year-old would get the best of him.

Admittedly, OTS was hard and brutal, but there was none of the sexual abuse that existed at St. John's. There was physical brutality from older, tougher boys who abused the younger ones and took their goods off them, but that was understandable since everyone in OTS was seriously dysfunctional. Many came out of situations of extreme abuse and poverty.

For a little ten-year-old like me, life at OTS was hard. We were required to do physical labor, generally on a cleaning crew or in the laundry, but living conditions were much better than what I had known at St. John's. Each of us had a cell-like enclosure in a dormitory, and the staff was consistent. You didn't have to worry about them raping you at night. If you did what you were told, you got along fine. If you

---

[7] Go-boy - (noun or verb) run away from juvenile prison

gave them any lip, they slapped you in the head and didn't hesitate to knock you down. But they were predictable and very easy to deal with, as opposed to St. John's where the Brothers were completely erratic and violence and brutality could flare up at any moment for no apparent reason.

I remember one incident at St. John's where we were lining up to go into one of the ugly brown brick buildings. A kid was talking to me and without any warning whatsoever, one of the Brothers took the boy's head and smashed it into the brick wall. I remember looking at the wall afterward and seeing pieces of the boy's skin and his hair on the rough bricks. He didn't deserve that kind of treatment, but the action was typical of the unpredictability and violence that was the norm at St. John's. In retrospect, I believe it was probably used as an intimidation tool to keep the boys off balance so they wouldn't resist the sexual abuse.

None of that brutality and violence existed at OTS, which may account for the fact that my memories of the place are largely a blur. Or it may have been that I was functioning on cruise control, quite likely suffering Post-Traumatic Stress Syndrome after my time at St. John's.

I do remember fighting with the older boys. Because I was much smaller and younger than all the rest, I spent a good deal of time defending myself, and for that, I would be sent to solitary confinement.

Solitary at OTS was more like a cell than the dark, Draconian closets of St. John's, but it was solitary confinement nevertheless.

Another reason I don't recall many details about OTS was because I spent a lot of my time there as a runaway despite the dire pronouncement of the guard that first day.

Two years after being sentenced to Ontario Training School, I escaped for the third time.

To create a diversion, I started a fire in the gymnasium by dousing the sports equipment with gas I had siphoned from a truck. I put a match to it, and while everyone was rushing about dealing with the fire, I jumped in the truck, drove it through the security fence and about ten miles down the road to Highway #401, only to find the Ontario Provincial Police there waiting for me. They surrounded the truck when I lost control of it and crashed into the median. I came out with my hands up and surrendered. I was twelve at the time.

They took me back to court and declared I was irreparably brain-damaged. They said they could control neither my behavior nor my violence, and the only solution was to put me in a group home for unwanted children.

I believe that indictment caused me more pain than anything I had experienced to that point in my life. I was unwanted, undesirable, and unworthy. There was no thought of returning me to my mother. The government had tried, without success, to straighten me out, and now they were sending me to a home for children that no one else wanted to deal with.

I was twelve when they put me in a group home on Boulton Avenue in East End Toronto just above Queen Street. It was a corner house adjacent to a parking lot.

There were a number of other children there, as well, being kept in a regular home by a mother and her grown son who would have been in his late twenties or early thirties. They were East End people doing what they could to bring in some extra income, probably being paid by the city to operate a group home.

I don't know what I did the first day I got there—maybe swore at the son or something—but they stripped me down to my underwear, stood me on the kitchen table, and the son took a leather belt to me. I guess he put me on the table so he could get a good strong shoulder level swing at me. He gave me four or five good whacks across my buttocks. Then I was sent upstairs to bed.

I immediately escaped through the second floor bathroom window wearing only my jockey shorts. The policy at the group home was to take away your clothes and locked them up on the first floor so you couldn't sneak out at night and run away. I don't know if they did it every night; I didn't stay long enough to find out.

I dropped from the second floor bathroom window to the parking lot below and started running.

After dashing through a few backyards, I found some laundry hanging on a clothes line. I took some clothing, put it on, and headed for the West End of Toronto with which I was much more familiar.

I ended up at my mother's house and spent the next two-and-a-half years bouncing in and out of her home, trying to maintain some form of normalcy in my life. I attended school for a little while, at least for one or two grades, but basically I did whatever I wanted whenever I wanted to do it.

At thirteen, I devised a lucrative scam that gave me more money than I knew what to do with.

There was always a group of kids hanging out with me, and among them was Stinky Maguire. (We called him Stinky because he really was. I don't know what his problem was, whether he ate a dozen eggs a day or what, but Stinky had a serious gas problem.) Stinky's parents reminded me of the couple in the Andy Capp comic strip: a very wide mother and a pencil-thin father.

Stinky Maguire's father was a nefarious fellow who helped us pull off the scam. We stole bicycles and he cut them apart and made bicycles-built-for-two with the pieces. In cutting the bikes apart, the serial number was lost, so they were untraceable. We would paint the converted bikes and advertise them for sale in the newspaper. This was in the days before bicycles-built-for-two were trendy. Had I patented the idea, I could have become a legitimate millionaire.

We probably stole two hundred bikes from everywhere in the city—except our own district.

At thirteen, I got the first of my five tattoos. For me, I believe it was a rite of passage to manhood. I chose a peacock because I arrogantly believed I was 'as pretty as a peacock.' I considered the tattoo to be a piece of art that I could carry around with me.

At thirteen, I also had my first sexual experience. I moved in with a hooker who was about ten years older than me. I don't remember her name, but I do recall she had a little blonde-haired daughter who was about five at the time.

Through my relationship with the hooker, I got a first-hand look at the human face of prostitution, and I acquired a deep hatred for pimps[8]. I became known as a protector of girls on the stroll. I learned that no girl ever wakes up one morning and thinks: 'My life's goal is to become a prostitute.' No, it is always a survival thing.

I lived with the hooker off and on during those years, with my mother off and on, or with friends. I also had a place of my own that nobody knew about. It was where I went when I needed solitude and down time.

I think I was born generous. As a young teenager, when I walked down the streets of The District, I was continually surrounded by little

---

[8] Pimp - a person who solicits clients for a prostitute

kids. They knew I always had a pocketful of nickels which I gave out liberally. In those days, five cents could get you a pop or an ice cream; two could get you into a movie.

That same generosity was expressed in the way I protected prostitutes and underdogs. I hated bullies with a passion, and liked nothing better than beating them up because they were mean-spirited people who enjoyed making life miserable for others. I believe that fervency was developed in St. John's Training School and later in OTS where I was forever championing the underdog. Often at St. John's, I would intervene for a little kid and get a beating from the staff for my efforts, but I was willing to take the beating if it got their attention off the other kid. Later on, as my life became more and more twisted, being a champion for the underdog was one of the few things that allowed me to maintain my sanity and sense of self-worth.

In my early teens I got involved in gang action and soon became a gang leader. What I lacked in size, I made up for with viciousness and weapons. Though this was an era when guns were almost unheard of, I carried a handgun. I also carried a straight razor up my sleeve, so perhaps it is easy to see how I assumed leadership in The District.

In addition, I was an amateur boxer and gained a strong reputation as a street fighter. I trained and worked out at a number of community centers including Hart House which is part of the University of Toronto's sports complex. My trainer was Tony Canzano who later became the Boxing Commissioner for Canada.

Boxing served as a survival skill for me, but I found I loved the sport. I had excellent eye/hand co-ordination, and even won a couple of Golden Glove Awards.

My life in those days followed a pattern. For most of the night, I hung out with my guys at a 24-hour hamburger joint on the corner of Queen and Bathhurst called The Deco. That became my territory, my place. With The Deco on one corner and taverns on the other three, the location was quite a hot spot.

Early evening would find us at The Gorevale Restaurant until it closed around 2 a.m. The Gorevale was further west on Shaw and Queen, and served as neutral territory between the two tough districts in West End Toronto where there was a lot of poverty and gang action. The Gorevale was my headquarters in the neutral zone, and it was there I met a lot of guys from the Parkdale area.

My gang and I made a lot of money in those days from stealing.

I had a lucrative B&E[9] operation going where I would break into a place through the roof with a drill and bit, then come down and steal whatever they had inside: clothing, suits, televisions, hi-fis. We took the stuff out the back door and loaded it into trucks.

To transport the stolen goods, I bought a garbage truck and redid the back hinge so it would open up and we could pack the loot inside. It was an ingenious plan. Whoever stops a garbage truck?

We also stole transport trailers from loading docks. I knew a fellow named Bronco who worked as a dock man. He would tip me off whenever a good load was coming in. Maybe the trailer would be filled with silverware or bolts of cloth. We had a fence just outside Toronto who paid me cash—as much as $5000—for each load. We simply drove the rig into his barn, collected the cash, and left. He got rid of the rig and the merchandise.

At one point, I rented the top floor of a mini-warehouse building and started running gambling games. This was the inner city part of the West End and we had plenty of people coming to gamble: boxers, drinkers, and lots of Irish, Ukrainian, and Polish immigrants.

The first time I walked into the warehouse, I noticed some odd-looking contraptions on the ground floor level.

"What are those?" I asked the owner.

"They're stills," he said. He used them to manufacture and distill dry cleaning fluid for the commercial dry cleaning industry. It was a legitimate business operation and he explained the process to me.

"I've seen movies where they make whiskey out of contraptions like this," I said.

"Yeah, those stills are exactly like these, and you do it exactly the same way."

In no time, I had built myself a couple of stills and was running potato mash through them, adding caramel coloring to the distilled liquid to make it look like whiskey.

By the time I was fifteen, I was running a string of alcohol stills, selling raw potato mash to the majority of bars in the city of Toronto. They bought my whiskey for one-third of what they had to pay Seagrams, and no one knew the difference because it was sold as bar stock, anyway.

---

[9] B & E - break and enter

I also sold whiskey to a number of blind pigs[10] and bootleggers[11]. There was a vigorous bootlegging industry in Toronto in those days and I supplied quite a few of them, as well as having a couple of my own bootleggers.

I had been drinking alcohol since the age of thirteen. By fifteen I was also doing drugs, sticking needles into my arms to lose myself in a strange netherworld in which you are neither dead nor alive.

I was becoming a very good criminal with good criminal contacts. I was an expert at picking locks, breaking and entering places, and peeling safes[12].

I also had some extortion rackets operating. There were a number of the stores in the district, and around ten o'clock at night one of our crew would walk past a store and throw a brick through the window. The next day, I would stop by and say to the owner, "For a fee, I can make sure that never happens again."

They knew exactly what was going on, but they would pay the twenty dollars or so a week anyway to make sure we wouldn't break their windows again or burglarize their store. Multiply that by seventy or eighty stores and we collected a tidy sum each week.

The merchants were safe because our gang controlled that area. But there were many other gangs in Toronto like the Parkdale Crew, the Dundas Crew who were all Italians, and the College Crew which had a lot of Jewish kids in it.

We were an inner city type of gang, not ethnic, though there were a number of Irish in the group. Mostly we were all poor whites. We didn't have a name. In fact, I didn't even go by the name LeClerc then. (That's because I didn't know my last name.) I was simply known as Serge.

There were dozens of members in my street gang. Many were in their twenties. Why, you ask, would a twenty-year-old take orders from a little fifteen-year-old kid? One reason was my 'I don't care' attitude. I didn't care, and I made sure everybody else knew it. I didn't care who he was, how big he was, how many people he had in his family, how tough he was, or how tough he looked, if he came against me, he

---

[10] Blind pigs - afterhours booze houses
[11] Bootleggers - illegal suppliers of alcohol
[12] Peeling safes - breaking into safes

had better be ready to kill me because I was quite prepared to kill him. I didn't particularly care about dying. That's what happens when life has no meaning; you really don't think or care about death. And when death means nothing, living has no particular value, either.

The second reason people took orders from me was because I had discovered the wonderful world of money and I had a natural talent for making it. I bought my first house at the age of fifteen and paid $63,000 cash for it. Yes, you can buy a house at fifteen. All you need is the money.

Early on, I learned the truth of the adage: 'Money corrupts.' I found that even though people thought I was garbage, they called me 'Mister' because I had money. I discovered that people worship money. I discovered that there really was a god and it was on the hundred dollar bill. I discovered that the world revolved around money and that I could buy lawyers. In fact, I could do whatever I wanted because money gave me power and people followed me and obeyed me because I had money.

I had developed many criminal contacts throughout the city and eventually began taking my crew to The Junction where there was another big gang. The Junction guys were the ones who started up some of the big motorcycle gangs that are still operating today.

In further expanding my territory to The Village, Yorkville, and uptown Yonge Street, I crossed a number of influential boundaries that opened the door to a whole new world of criminal activity.

I also acquired contacts in Montreal, and my crew and I liked to go there to party. In Montreal, even if you were underage—as I was—you could get into any club you wanted. I had two favorites: the Americana and the Playgirl Club.

It was in Montreal that I met up with an American clique that was into robbing banks. I tied in with them and some Quebec guys, and we did some Montreal-style bank heists. In a Montreal-style robbery, you took over the whole bank. You didn't just rob one teller, you robbed the whole bank. You set it up or 'keyed in' in the morning just before or just after the Brinks armored truck had unloaded the day's money supply. Our goal was to get in before they double day-locked the bank vault so we could clean out everything in the vault and the tills.

On this one particular occasion, I was the gunman, armed with a sawed-off M1 with two taped-together banana clips. We had customized the gun by filing off the retainer pin so when you pressed the trigger, it became an automatic instead of a single-shot weapon. Upon entering the bank, it was my job to fire shots into the ceiling or into the air.

On this occasion, we were in the bank a bit too long, and by the time we made it outside, the police were pulling up. There was none of this "Stop in the name of the law" stuff you see in movies. They came out of their squad cars firing. We fired back.

I got shot twice. The first bullet went into my left hip, ricocheted off the bone and came out my left buttock. It knocked me back about six feet and lifted me into the air. I went down shooting, spraying bullets all over the place, shooting out windows in buildings as far as a block away.

The second bullet went in the front of my left thigh and exited through the inside of my leg.

My partners grabbed me and dragged me to the car. All the while, I was still spraying bullets in every direction.

We got away, and my partners brought in someone to treat my wounds. I don't know who it was, maybe a veterinarian or somebody. Whoever it was, the wound got cleaned and we figured that was that.

Unfortunately, a fragment of cloth from my trousers was carried in with the bullet and became lodged against the bone. The wound soon became infected.

My partners did their best for me. They got some penicillin and pain pills, but the problem was much more serious than that. Within a week, my thigh was swollen almost to the size of my waist and gangrene was setting in. The leg was blue and green, and starting to smell. Pus oozed from the wound in putrid ropes.

Some of the guys in the Montreal gang were American, so they made some connections and transported me to an underground abortion clinic in Vermont. By this time, I was delusional and running a dangerously high fever.

The doctor at this illegal clinic was a little man with a big hook nose and Coke bottle glasses. He opened the wound and went in with forceps to remove the scrap of fabric. Then he started me on an intravenous antibiotic drip.

Shaking his head, he said to my partner, "We may have to amputate the leg to save him."

Even in my delusional state, I understood the implications of that.

"No, you won't," I said. "Here's the deal. If you take the leg off, my partner is going to shoot you in the head. Got that? You either save me with my leg on, or I die with my leg on, but this leg ain't comin' off."

We stayed a while in Vermont, then headed back to Ontario and dug in around the Cornwall and Thousand Islands area. It took about three months before I fully recuperated.

The experience persuaded me to give bank robbing a pass, and I eventually returned to Toronto.

FOUR

It was the 1960s, and I was about eighteen when a group of men approached me. The spokesperson was named Ian.

"I work with a man in California named Dr. Timothy Leary," he said. "Dr. Leary has come up with the chemical formula for manufacturing 'acid'—LSD. I know how to do that, and I want to set up some laboratories in Canada.

"You have plenty of contacts and a really good enterprise going," he continued. "You're the man, Serge. We know all about you. You control a large part of Toronto—all the West End and a good part of the East End. Between your alcohol and fencing all your stolen goods, you have an impressive distribution network. What if I give you another product?"

"Really?" I said. I was very skeptical. "What's the product?"

"Drugs."

I laughed. I knew all about the drug scene that existed at that point. There was no marijuana, no hashish. It was all heroin and pills—uppers and downers. Truckers used bennies[13] or uppers; prostitutes and grifters[14] took the downers or bombers. It was a very negative scene with no money to be made. Besides, I didn't want to mess with the Inner City.

---

[13] Bennies - amphetamines

[14] Grifter - a criminal involved in fraud, counterfeiting, or pyramid schemes

"Trust me," I said. "You can't make any money with drugs. The people who use them are prostitutes, pimps, petty criminals, and bums on heroin; it's for mooches, garbage people."

Ian tried another tactic. He began telling me about the United States and what was going on there.

"You read the newspapers?" he asked.

"I don't read the newspaper," I said. "I read books."

"Surely you watch TV."

"No, I don't watch TV. There's nothing on TV that interests me." The truth was I didn't have much opportunity to watch television. I was into gambling so heavily that I was lucky if I saw daylight three or four times in a month. Then Ian commenced to give me a lecture on the Vietnam War. It meant nothing to me because I had no idea where Vietnam was. I knew about the United States and Canada, but that was the extent of my world knowledge.

"The young men in the United States don't want to fight in the War," Ian said. "There are draft dodgers, and protests, and a revolution happening down there with the young people. The kids are letting their hair grow long. The music is changing, and so is the way they dress. They want to make love, not war. They're shedding the values of a generation and they want to party hearty."

All of this was news to me, especially the part about dress. I was into suits and ties, straight-laced shoes, and overcoats. I saw myself as a gangster like the ones I saw in the movies, and I dressed like one. What he was talking about sounded like something out of a story book. It was completely foreign to me. Besides, what did I care about hippies and flower children running around in Volkswagens singing protest songs? My music was Rock and Roll, black music, Elvis Presley, and the Blues. In The District, we were strait-laced and anti-drug. This wasn't for us.

I was very, very skeptical.

"Kids in Canada are watching all this on TV," he went on, "and they want to be cool like the Americans."

"Really?" I said again. I didn't believe a word of it.

"Let me show you," he persisted. "Give me a week and I will prove it to you."

I was an entrepreneur. It wasn't like I had a nine-to-five job and couldn't take time off from work, so I said, "Okay, I've always got time for something that looks like a money-making enterprise."

"You'll give me a week?"

"Sure..." I was known as a man who kept his word, and in giving my word here, I was promising him a week of my time to show me this scam. For his part, he was agreeing not to approach any other crew with the opportunity.

The next morning Ian drove me to a high school in a nice middle-class suburb of Toronto. I had never been to a high school before, and certainly not to one in suburbia. I was out of The District and out of my comfort zone. There were no streetcars or buses here, nothing with which I was familiar.

"Let's get out of here," I said.

"You gave me your word," Ian countered.

"Yeah," I said, "but somebody's gonna phone the cops and we'll get busted. This is not a good idea. C'mon, let's get out of here."

"You said you'd give me a week. Now watch."

"Okay."

Everybody smoked in those days, and schools generally had smoking pits adjacent to the school grounds for student smokers. Because I was a boxer, I did not smoke, and the last thing I wanted to do was be around a bunch of smokers, especially these kids with their penny loafers and straight white teeth and their hair neatly combed in the Pat Boone style. Everything about me was the antithesis of the Pat Boone-style. I was way out of my element.

The first day Ian handed out weed[15] to some of the kids in the smoking pit. Marijuana was a new thing and a big time drug. I watched while Ian rolled up the weed for these kids and showed them how to smoke it. They soon got giggly.

The next day we went again and Ian did the same thing.

On Wednesday, Ian started handing out little capsules.

I said, "What's in the capsules?"

"LSD—acid."

I knew about LSD. People who took LSD saw walls melting; it made them jump off buildings. "We shouldn't be playing with this stuff," I said.

"It's okay, Serge. There's only a little bit in here, and it's mixed with icing sugar. You watch."

---

[15] Weed or Grass - marijuana

On Thursday he told students, "We're only going to be here one more day. If you want to buy some of this acid or marijuana, it'll be five dollars a hit."

Later that day I said to my guys, "He's crazy. Nobody's going to buy this garbage."

On Friday, Ian was flooded with buyers. I noticed that three would come together; one kid would buy and then split it up with his friends. It seemed that everyone was turning several others on to the drugs.

I went back and called my boys together. "This is big business," I said. "We're in."

It was still hard for me to believe this could happen because we in the Inner City lived by a very different kind of philosophy. When we saw our friends screwing up, we tried to stop them. We said, "Hey, you're drinking too much. You're doing a little too much dope. Man, you are messing up. You've got to pull it together." Yet here were these middle-class kids, who had everything in the world going for them, encouraging their friends to jump headlong into risky and uncharted waters.

But then, what did I know about middle-class kids? I had a Grade Five education. I had never met anyone from my district who went to high school, never mind college. Here were these kids with so many advantages using their money to buy dope.

Well, I may have been brain-damaged, but I wasn't stupid. I said, "This is a big money-making enterprise. All we have to do is get three or four kids in each school and they'll do the pushing for us."

Thus I embarked on an odyssey that would make me the first and ultimately one of the most powerful drug dealers in all of Eastern Canada.

I brought drugs into The District, and that caused quite a rift because drugs were not that well accepted there. People stopped talking to me, especially some of the older crowd. There was a stigma attached to dealing drugs, but I didn't care. This wasn't a popularity contest, and I saw it as a way to make some serious money.

Since it was a relatively new game, we had to feel our way along. I began selling marijuana in matchboxes, as Ian had done. We charged ten dollars for a small matchbox of weed and twenty dollars for a large one.

When we first began peddling LSD, we had no idea how to sell it. We manufactured LSD powder from chemicals we got from the University of Toronto. It was a case of just winging it and putting together our own formulas.

As the authorities made certain drugs illegal, we invented new ones. That is how methamphetamines (crystal meth) and MDA or methylenedioxy-methamphetamine (also known as the Love Drug) came into being. Common names for crystal meth are meth, speed, crank, and crystal. We made it in our laboratory. It was a much more sophisticated drug than the one used today, and a lot safer for users, even though it still brought on the same hallucinogenic state.

We made the transition from marijuana and LSD (lysergic acid diethylamide) to MDA, a mixture of LSD and crystal meth. MDA was the precursor of MDMA or Ecstasy, which has just one molecule different from MDA.

We started dealing in the West End, but I quickly realized that what I had seen happening in the high school was not being echoed in The District. Obviously, the students in suburbia were watching television and were more plugged in to this counter-culture movement. I figured they must be more in tune with the idea of rebelling against parents and The Establishment and doing their own thing. That sort of thing didn't resonate with us in the Inner City.

I decided to use my contacts and see what was happening in the rest of the city. It was about that time that I broke with the majority of my people in The District and moved Uptown, taking a select handful of gang members with me.

I very quickly learned that the centre of all the action Uptown was Yorkville Village in the heart of Toronto. Yorkville Village was created when the street was closed off to motor traffic and houses and buildings in the immediate district were turned into clubs and boutiques. This is where the hip crowd gathered. On Friday and Saturday nights, it was flooded with people.

These were the days when Neil Young played on street corners, when Gordon Lightfoot was in The Riverboat, and Jose Feliciano played at the Mousehole. Bands like Steppen Wolfe and singers like Janis Joplin were in their heyday. A whole new era of clubs and discos was opening up, and the club scene very quickly became the drug scene.

It was also the beginning of biker gangs like the Vagabonds and the Paradise Riders. That wave came on the heels of the American draft dodgers who ran to Canada and gravitated to Toronto's Yorkville

Village and Rochedale College where the dominant talk was about the Vietnam War, the Protest Movement, and the Psychedelic Revolution. It was here that I centered most of my drug-selling activities.

With the money I made, I bought a house on nearby Madison Avenue and made investments in several businesses and other pieces of real estate. I went into partnership with a whole new crew of guys, amongst them a gang of bikers known as the Paradise Riders. The sergeant-at-arms and his brother became my business partners. Along with a fourth person, we pretty well dominated the market for speed and acid.

My partners were, by and large, guys just like me who came out of the different districts. I had known many in the crew before they became bikers, especially the ones who started the Vagabonds and the Paradise Riders, the precursors of Hell's Angels and Satan's Choice. Now I was into formal gang action, networking with associates and the many contacts I had made during my early years as a runaway, crossing the lines into other districts. All of this stood me in very good stead as our drug empire expanded.

In introducing marijuana and speed to The District, it was inevitable that I would start using it myself. Very quickly, I graduated to using it intravenously, as did many of my guys.

I began to change. I started hanging out in the clubs, and changing my style of dress. Instead of being the neat, clean-cut, 'American Gangster' sort of kid in a pin-striped suit, I switched to cowboy boots, jeans, black shirts, leather jackets, and long hair. I took up riding motorcycles. My mentality began to change, too, as I got more and more wrapped up with drugs and the twisted world of the drug culture. I became more and more violent.

Before, in the West End, I was into what might be called traditional 'corner boy' crime: gambling, bootlegging, and B&Es, but there was no drug use. Now, as a drug dealer and a heavy user myself, I was in another realm altogether. My crime went from multi-dimensional crime to a single criminal activity—drug dealing.

I became well-known in the Village. It didn't matter which club I went to, whether it was the In Crowd, Devil's Den, Chez Monique, or Charlie Brown's, there were always people there I knew.

Toronto had only two or three gay clubs at the time, and when I found out that the gay population was way ahead of the curve in terms of drug use, I began supplying drugs to the gay scene by putting pushers in each club. It was a fairly innovative move since straight people never went near gay clubs or gay people in those days. But it was a lucrative market that I would hold onto for many, many years during my criminal career. I even owned a piece of the clubs.

While I was buying houses, businesses, cars, and motorcycles, I was steadily spiraling out of control with my personal drug use. I became a hardcore intravenous crystal meth user. I would use crystal meth to get high, then mainline heroin to bring myself down, then take speed to bring me up again. It was a vicious and dangerous circle, and quite frankly, it fractured my personality.

Drugs were so new that we had nothing on which to gauge our use. We didn't realize that doing too much acid could fry your brain. In fact, when we first began distributing acid, we bought gelatin capsules at the drugstore, mixed liquid LSD with the powder, and recapped them. Sometimes people got a little too much concentrated LSD and the walls began to melt on them.

We didn't know the pitfalls, and many of us, including myself, ended up contracting Hepatitis C from shared needles. In those years, it was very difficult to get needles. In the United States, especially in Upper New York State, if you were caught with a glass set of works[16], you were automatically sentenced to five years in prison. As a result, we learned to do it with eyedroppers until we found a way to acquire syringes.

The more strung out I got, the more outrageous I became. It was nothing for me to shoot a full syringe of crystal meth into my body, followed by a full syringe of downers so I could do it all over again to experience the high. Sometimes I didn't sleep for weeks at a time. There was no limit to the amount of drugs I would use, no consciousness of the destruction it might wreak on my body and my brain, no cognitive thought that this behavior could kill me. I knew there was such a thing as overdosing because people overdosed on heroin all the time. I just didn't know it could happen with speed and acid. I have absolutely no idea why my brain did not melt inside my skull, and how I made it through that part of my life without permanent brain damage.

In retrospect, I believe I was functioning in a dimension some-

---

[16] Glass set of works - non-disposable glass hypodermic syringe

where between drug-induced insanity and psychosis. For a large part of the time, I was completely out of touch with reality. Hallucinations were routine, especially at night. I saw 'people' hiding behind bushes and garbage cans and in shadows so frequently that I didn't pay attention to them any more. On one occasion, I walked off a second storey roof and landed on my back. My buddies picked me up, took me inside, and I immediately did some more dope.

There was one episode where my partners and I went to see a guy who owed us a lot of money. When we caught him, I proceeded to pistol-whip him, then we took off. The police stopped us about five blocks away. I had dropped the gun in a sewer, but for some reason, I still had the bullets in my pocket. Out of the three of us, I was the only one they could pin anything on because I had the .38s in my pocket. I was higher than a Georgia pine when they took me to the police station, but I remember thinking: "Here's what I'm going to do. I'm going to smash my head against the cell walls and split it open. Then they'll have to take me to the hospital and I'll run away."

The plan didn't work out quite that way, although I did split my head open in several places. I became so psychotic that the police were afraid to come into the cell. (By this point, I also had a reputation for extreme violence and unpredictable behavior.) The officers ended up letting my partners into the cell to bring me milkshakes and hopefully, to calm me down.

Eventually I was transported to a hospital where the staff put me on an intravenous valium drip to try to bring me down. It didn't work.

The doctor said, "If we give him any more of this stuff, it will stop his heart. He has so much crystal meth in his system, his blood is crystallizing. It looks like syrup. We've taken blood samples and you can actually see crystals in it."

In fact, there was so much crystal meth in my body that crystals came out of my tear ducts and broke through my skin in different spots, especially inside my mouth.

"We're not saying he's going to die if he doesn't stop," the doctor told police. "We're telling you we don't know how he is still alive."

They released me, but of course, I didn't stop. I continued using drugs to the degree where I was completely irrational and fearless to the point of stupidity. There was no limit to what I would do.

Everyone thought I was crazy. Guys who knew me well said they always knew when a switch had clicked inside my head. I would go silent; my face would turn white with no trace of emotion. As long as I was screaming or bellowing, they knew things were cool. But when I went silent, I was apt to do something irrational like beat someone up, or stab them, or shoot them for no reason at all. I believe those episodes were due in large part to the immense rage that I carried around with me in those days.

In my drug-induced state, it was hard to differentiate between what was real and what was not, so I kind of ignored it all. My life disintegrated to the point where I couldn't even drive anymore, and people stopped doing business with me because they were afraid of me.

One bad drug deal here and another there lost me all three of my houses, my motorcycles, my cars, and my money, as well as a lucrative silent partnership in a fire extinguisher business. Basically, I lost two-and-a-half years of my life.

It wasn't until I broke into a house just to raid the refrigerator that I realized I was at rock bottom. Intuitively, I knew I needed to dry out.

I said to my partner, "Give me a room in your house and lock me in. Let me out in two or three days."

He locked me in the room with five gallons of water and a plastic bucket. All I did was sleep. I probably hadn't slept at all for about a month prior. When they finally let me out, I devoured a dozen hamburgers, cheeseburgers, and milkshakes, then went back inside and slept again.

When I was feeling more like myself again, two guys came to me and said, "Hey, Serge, we've got this scam happening. You used to do this with us before; why don't you join us again?"

The scam was breaking into businesses, usually in industrial malls in the suburbs, and stealing blank checks out of the middle and bottom of their company cheque books. We would use their own perforating machines to make out the cheques for varying amounts. They were big cheques—made out to Susie Jones or Barbara Smith, all fictitious women's names, but names for which we had identification cards. On Fridays, we would take some women to the grocery stores—Dominion or Loblaws—and give them the cheques and the corresponding ID cards. The women would buy twenty dollars worth of groceries, sign over a ninety dollar cheque, and get back seventy dollars cash.

I had run a crew that made a lot of money with that kind of scam, so when these guys asked if I'd be interested in partnering with them again, I said, "Sure, let's go."

We broke into a company office in Milton, just outside of Toronto, removed some checks, and printed them up. However, when we came out of the building and got into the car, lights came on all around us. The police were waiting. Obviously they knew what was going on.

The two other men took off running. I just stood there. I thought, "They can't pin anything on me."

There were two cops, and boy, did they lay a beating on me. They choked me out, broke my nose, and tried to thrash the names of the other two guys out of me, but I refused to talk.

Ultimately they brought out the dogs and tracked down my partners-in-crime. The three of us were taken to Halton County Jail and charged with B&E and a number of other offenses.

The other two fellows had already done penitentiary time, and one was actually on parole. I, on the other hand, had no adult criminal record, so I said, "I'll swallow the beef[17] and plead guilty. You guys plead not guilty. They can't hook you into this, and that'll be the end of it."

Being as cocky as I was, I didn't realize they would jam me[18] with a very heavy sentence for what was a relatively minor offense. At least, to my mind it was minor.

I got twenty-one months, an unusually harsh sentence for B&E, considering that a life sentence for killing somebody was only twenty years. The other reason I felt it was out of proportion was because my only criminal record as an adult consisted of convictions for attempted theft, possession of stolen property, a previous B&E, and possession of a weapon—all of which had been withdrawn.

The charges were withdrawn because I always made deals with the police. I'd say, "You want to charge me with possession of a handgun? Well, I know where you can get twenty-five handguns off the street. Wouldn't you like to do that? Aren't those twenty-five handguns better than throwing me in jail for a couple of years?" The bargaining always worked, and as a result, I had only one adult conviction to that point, an attempted theft in 1968. Everything else was dropped.

My hope this time was that the sentence would be suspended, or if they did give me jail time, it would be minimal. I certainly hadn't figured on twenty-one months. What's more, because I had a concealed

---

[17] Swallow the beef - take the rap or the punishment
[18] Jam - sink, finish

weapon—a straight razor—and some dope on me, they added another twenty-eight days to my twenty-one month sentence.

When the Oakville Police checked with the Toronto Police, they discovered there were some other unsettled convictions on my record. So while they jammed me in Oakville, they also withdrew a lot, like two more charges of possession of weapons dangerous to the public, seven B&Es, six charges of impersonation, six charges of stolen property, and public mischief. In all, there were more withdrawals than convictions.

I was nineteen or twenty at the time and old enough to go to adult prison, so off I went to serve the twenty-two month sentence in Guelph Reformatory—this time, on the adult side.

FIVE

Reformatories and penitentiaries in those days were correctional institutions for people aged sixteen and up. Whether you went to a reformatory or a penitentiary depended entirely upon your sentence, not your crime. On the other hand, the crime dictated the sentence. For instance, young offenders could get a life sentence in the federal prison system at fifteen years of age if they committed a murder.

It was the times. It was a reflection of society in the era of the Fifties and Sixties. If you were a bad person, you did prison time. There was no talk of rehabilitation. That fallacy came in when the social engineers designed the Charter of Rights without first understanding the concept of rehabilitation.

The very word 'rehabilitation' means 'to change to a former state.' So if you were a dysfunctional inner-city kid (and almost everyone in the prisons came from a lower socio-economic class), rehabilitation to a former state was not at all what you needed.

For me, Guelph Reformatory was not an unfamiliar place. It was attached to the Ontario Training School where I had spent time previously and broken out after setting the gymnasium on fire. The adult section, in which I would now be incarcerated, was very different from the juvenile training school part.

The prisons of those days no longer exist today. In some weird way, the Charles Dickens line: 'It was the best of times; it was the worst of times' seems a remarkably apt description of the prison environment of the mid-1960s.

In my entire prison career, Guelph Reformatory was probably the best prison to which I was sentenced, though I was not aware of it at the time. The fact is, I wasn't aware of much. I was still fried from two-and-a-half years of complete hedonism and over-the-top drug use. Let's just say I wasn't the sharpest pencil in the box. My auto-pilot was on the lowest setting possible: basic survival.

They put me on a bus to take me to Guelph Reformatory which was a large prison complex on the outskirts of the city of Guelph. There was no wall around the Reformatory, but the perimeter was fenced.

The internal structure of Guelph was a blend of securities. Some of it was dorms; some was maximum security where you were locked in your cell. There were different work crews within and without the institution, and probably about a thousand people in the reformatory population. We ate in a dining hall, which is exactly opposite to most maximum security institutions where you eat in your cell.

My stay at Guelph was short, probably no more than ninety days. Being as seriously unbalanced as I was, within three days of arriving I became extremely violent and punched somebody out. That was followed by a series of fights with other convicts and then a attack on a guard, after which I spit at the warden. If they said, "Turn left," I turned right. As a result, I spent a good part of the ninety days in a solitary confinement cell rather than being housed in a dormitory as I would otherwise have been.

Having already made my mark as a crime figure, there was a crew of people in Guelph that I knew, and I fell in with them. It just so happened that they were the crew that was running the prison.

I need to make something perfectly clear. Guards do not run prisons. Convicts run prisons. Inmate cliques run prisons. Guards keep convicts inside prisons. There is no possible way guards can run prisons, if only because of the sheer number ratio. There are perhaps thirty-five guards on each shift attempting to keep several hundred convicts in check.

When I got out of solitary, I went to the Work Board and asked for the worst job they had. They called it the buller gang. It was where they put all the trouble makers. The buller gang cut logs outside the prison property, hauled them in, steamed off the bark, and cut them up. It was dirty, messy, cold work, and they guarded you on horseback.

Why did I ask for the buller gang? Because I knew they were going to put me on it anyway. And besides, most of the guys I knew were on the buller gang.

As it turned out, I didn't do much work on the buller gang. I spent more time sleeping on the cold cement floor of a solitary confinement cell thanks to my violent and aggressive behavior.

The administration realized very quickly that I was a lunatic and sent me on to Millbrook Reformatory, a provincial maximum security institution located in central Ontario near the town of Millbrook.

Millbrook was an experimental prison adapted from an American model. It was the first maximum security prison in Ontario and, quite frankly, it was more secure than the federal penitentiaries of the day. It became the model for Millhaven Penitentiary, Edmonton Maximum Security Facility, and Archambault Penitentiary in Quebec.

Millbrook was designed on the pod system. Pods are units at the end of hallways that radiate out from a secure central dome like spokes from a wheel hub. Each pod is isolated from the others, and if a riot should break out, a pod can quickly and effectively be isolated simply by closing down any access to the hallway.

Millbrook was where they sent all the drug addicts and trouble-makers from the other reformatories in Ontario, which qualified me on two counts. It was also where they sent the violently and criminally insane. Basically, it was a catch-basin for all the undesirables in the province.

The other convicts in Millbrook were those with sentences of two-years-less-a-day. Any sentence of less than two years was served in a provincial institution. If you got an even two-year sentence or anything higher, you went to a federal penitentiary. However, in a provincial institution, you could serve successive back-to-back sentences of two-years-less-a-day as long as the second two-years-less-a-day was an 'indefinite sentence' in which it was left up to the Parole Board to decide whether you should serve it or not.

In the late 1960s there was no such thing as prison reform, no ombudsman, no watchdogs, no Charter of Rights as pertained to the prison system. The authorities basically did to you what they wanted when they wanted to do it.

What that amounted to at Millbrook was this: we were in the middle of nowhere, in a maximum security unit with no inspectors coming to see how we were being treated, and with no complaints or grievance system to which we could appeal.

And what happened at Millbrook in terms of prisoner treatment was frankly out-of-hand. It was only a provincial facility, but the way they handled prisoners—the total lock-down and the brutality of the guards—was far more severe than anything in the federal system. There is nothing then or now to compare to it. It was Draconian. It was punitive. It was brutal. Quite frankly, it was a place that completed my journey into insanity.

They took me to Millbrook in a paddy wagon, handcuffed, chained, and shackled. Around my waist I had a chain belt that was attached to irons anchored to a ring in the floor of the vehicle. I had never experienced treatment like this before.

When we arrived at Millbrook, they put me in a cell in the reception area, and after the necessary paperwork had been filled out, the people who brought me left. I had no idea what to expect next.

I was ordered to strip and they ran me down the corridor, buck-naked, to solitary confinement with guards clubbing me with sticks all along the way.

I was thrown into the back end of solitary and left there overnight, nude, with no blankets, no pillow, no mattress, no furniture, nothing—only a cold cement floor.

The room itself was concrete-walled, about six feet by nine feet, with a solid steel door fitted with a one-inch thick safety glass window. The door had a slot in it and it was through this slot that a guard handed me a toothbrush the next morning and a tin cup filled with soapy water.

"Wash the floor," he growled. "If you do a good job, you'll get breakfast."

It was the staff's way of making you compliant. They started by giving you breakfast, then clothing around the second or third day. Eventually you got a mattress, a pillow, and a blanket, but that could take up to four weeks. If you misbehaved, big men came in with riot batons and tear gas and gassed you. The prison called them the Riot Squad; to convicts, they were the Goon Squad.

I complied, but not right away. The first day, I took a swing at one of the Goon Squad and for my efforts, was tear gassed, choked out, knocked out, and beaten up pretty badly.

I spent four or five weeks in the back end of solitary confinement. Eventually they moved me up to front end which meant a move of about six cells. Here, instead of a mattress on the floor, I had a mattress on a steel bed frame attached to the wall, and a desk.

In back end, you were never allowed out of your cell; in front end, you could have a shower and even go out to the exercise yard—depending on the guards and what day of the week it was.

If you behaved yourself, after four more weeks you were moved from front end solitary confinement to a regular range or cell block that had individual cells on each side of a corridor.

I eventually made it out of front end, but was thrown right back in after mixing it up with another convict. I doubt if I was on the range for more than ten days. The fight had to do with pecking order.

In prisons, pecking order is a well-established fact. Sex offenders and pedophiles are at the bottom of the pile; the remainder of the order has to do with your crime, your reputation, and your fighting ability.

There are things you do to secure your place in the pecking order. In the central corridors where we were allowed to go in the evening, there were steel benches similar to picnic tables attached to the floor. You established where you sat to play cards or whatever. To throw their weight around, someone might elbow you off the bench. Or, when you were standing in line to get your dinner tray, they might bump ahead of you. Of course, that kind of treatment did not sit well with me, and I refused to let it go.

The fellow who challenged me was a bully who ran the range and figured, since I was fish, I was an easy mark. He knew nothing about me and didn't realize he was way out of his league. He didn't know that with me, the normal rules did not apply because I knew no fear. There was no establishing a pecking order over me. You might as well be prepared to kill me because I was certainly prepared to kill you.

His other mistake was being a bully. Remember, I hated bullies, and still do. Maybe it came from the heroes I read about in books, or maybe from my own way of being. Perhaps it was the way my mother raised me. I do know that much of my hatred for bullies originated in St. John's Training School.

This particular bully went to get the knife he had made by shoving razor blades into a melted toothbrush handle. I went to get my own weapons: a piece of metal and an iron padlock. The padlock was from the wooden footlocker that each convict has in his cell for personal possessions; the guards have the master key.

I put my padlock in a woolen sock, tied a knot at the end of the sock and hid it behind my back as I approached the other convict. Before he knew what was happening, I went on the offensive. I swung the sock over my head and hit him on the top of the skull. The padlock bounced like a marble. Then I leaned him up against the corridor wall and began stabbing him with the piece of metal. When he slumped, I braced him up and kept on assaulting him. A couple of times, the shard of metal bent and I had to stop and straighten it out before going at him again.

During this process, the guards appeared. I was so intent on stabbing this guy, that when one guard grabbed me from behind, I thought it was another convict. I whirled around and hit him, damaging him somewhat, possibly breaking his jaw.

It was down to solitary confinement again.

What does one do during those long and tedious hours in solitary confinement?

Absolutely nothing.

You pace. You do sit ups. You do push ups. You do isometric exercises, pushing against the walls.

I sang a lot, songs like 'The Shadow of Your Smile,' 'The Girl From Ipanema,' 'I Left My Heart In San Francisco,' and all the Dean Martin and Frank Sinatra tunes. I still remember the words.

In back end solitary there were no books, no radio, no television. Mind you, even if you weren't in solitary, there was no television or radio. The mainline population—that's anyone outside The Hole, as we called solitary confinement—was allowed only three books per month.

You do bizarre things in solitary. You take your bread and bean cake and make marbles from it. You compress white bread until it is hard and almost like chalk, and you use the bread to draw a circle on the floor. Then you play the old marble game with your bread marbles.

I even had pets. A green praying mantis and a brown praying mantis came into my cell. I had never seen anything like them before. I wondered what the heck they were. I made a cage for the insects and watched them for hours on end until one chewed the head off the other. Much later in my life I learned that once a male and female praying mantis mate, the female kills the male by biting off his head.

Other than those few isolated incidents, my time in solitary con-

finement is largely a blur. It was boredom. That's what all of prison is:
sheer boredom. Hour runs into hour, day runs into day, into day, into
day, into day....

There were very strict rules in Millbrook. You could go to solitary
confinement for not having your shoelaces tied up. Everywhere you
walked, you were required to have your right shoulder touching the
wall. When they opened up your cell door, you immediately got up and
put your nose in the right-hand corner of the cell.

If they asked you to come out of your cell, they cracked your door
electronically. This was the first prison in Canada with the electronic
lock system that could be activated from the Bubble, a safety-glass en-
closed central dome.

When they unlocked your cell door and called your name over the
speaker, you had to come out immediately. You took two steps for-
ward, one step to the right and one and a half steps backward so you
were standing with your back against the wall. You stayed there until
you were told to move.

Yet despite all the high-tech advancements, Millbrook still had
guards on horseback patrolling the property and the riot squad was at
the ready to charge into your cell with tear gas. The guards were very
brutal, and there were a lot of convict suicides as a result of the treat-
ment received. I can recall at least two incidences where people died at
the hands of guards, though the official word was they had somehow
killed themselves.

You were either extremely compliant and did everything you were
told to do, or you were a hardhead like me and embarked on a cam-
paign to underscore your reputation as a hardhead. The upside was
that among the convicts, you were considered too dangerous to mess
with. If they came at you, they knew you would fight. The guards came
to know this, too.

I don't know how many months I spent in solitary confinement. It
was a predictable pattern that came with the territory. The authorities
gassed you, beat you, put you in the back end for a few months. You'd
just get up to front end, and they would bring you before the disciplin-
ary board. You spit and swore at them and they put you back in, maybe
for six months this time. You soon lost track of time.

Eventually, they decided to put me to work in the marker plant
where all of Ontario's vehicle license plates were manufactured.

I refused. I had met people who lost fingers and thumbs, even hands, doing such work. Besides, I knew the machines at Millbrook had come from Guelph Reformatory where they were considered too antiquated and unsafe for use. The machines were known as 'The Bloody Mary' and 'The Masher'.

The Work Board said, "You are going to work in the marker plant."

I said, "No, I'm not. I don't work around machines." Back to the Hole I went for another few months.

When I got out, they took me before the Work Board again. "You don't have to go to the marker plant," they said.

"Good."

"Instead, you're going to work in the tailor shop where they make mail bags. The guy in the mailbag shop said you can use the stitcher and sew labels on the bags."

I said, "I don't work around machines."

They gave me an ultimatum: "Either you do what you're told, or you go back to solitary."

My first day on the job, I took a ball-peen hammer and smashed the machines.

They came in, gassed me, beat me up, and sent me back to solitary confinement.

By that time, I had probably been in Millbrook for about a year. Most of it was spent in solitary.

When they let me out this time, they put me in a special lock-down range where I was able to spend more time in my cell.

One day they came and said, "How would you like to work in the book binding shop?"

I said, "Nah, I don't want to do book binding."

"This is a special project," they said. "The shop is making Braille books for the blind. They have this copper plate and a machine that makes indentations in it for dots. You would bind the books."

I thought that was fairly cool, so I did that for a while until I got into trouble again. This time it was a fight with Crazy Al McKennan. For whatever reason, I beat the bark off him, and back to the Hole I went.

When I got out of solitary after that episode, they didn't bother trying to get me gainfully employed. Instead, they left me pretty much in the range where I had access to books and was entitled to three hours a day in the exercise yard.

I did my full twenty-two month sentence, most of it in solitary confinement. As a matter of fact, I was released from solitary confinement directly onto the street.

I believe I was on the street in Toronto for a grand total of fifty-five days. I immediately began doing drugs again and got so strung out on methamphetamines, I don't think I slept at all during the fifty-five days.

I was back to carrying a gun and got involved in a couple of bank robberies and a jeweler store heist. I knew the police would be looking for me, so I left Toronto and spent some time in Montreal.

Sure enough, when I came back, there was a warrant out for my arrest with a 'Do not approach; this man is known to be armed and very dangerous' caution attached. I knew nothing of this and walked into my apartment.

There they were.

Actually, the police had come to arrested some other people who were in the apartment, one with a murder charge. When I opened up the door and saw the cops inside with guns drawn, I immediately closed the door. But they had already spotted me.

I booted it out of the building, not realizing there were more officers outside who had seen me go in and now had the building surrounded.

There was a minor shoot-out—minor in the sense that nobody got killed or wounded, although a lot of shots were fired. I headed for the backyard, shooting behind me as I went.

I'll never forget the wooden fence. It was solid, and a good twelve feet high. I have no idea how I got over it, but I did. I bounced to the ground on the other side and dashed down the street.

The police were close behind, shooting at me while I shot right back at them. I wasn't paying attention to what was in front, and I ran smack into a police car, right up the front of it, landing on the windshield.

Of course, they grabbed me and gave me a thorough beating.

I was sent to Toronto's Don Jail and held there in the old death cells. It took a long time for them to process me. I think I spent about a year there in total, during which time I got into a number of fights, often with the guards, and acquired a reputation for being a crazy, dangerous nutbar.

Finally the sentence came down. As was my habit, I made a deal to diminish the sentence. I don't believe any of the charges in my criminal career ever went through the complete court system. We always made a deal: If I pled guilty to one particular charge, they would agree to drop the others. This is not unusual in the justice system, and with good reason. If it weren't for plea bargaining, the system would bog down completely.

I never liked people who whined when they got caught. My attitude was: "Hey, I'm guilty; you got me; I'll do the time; let's figure out what we can do here to make the time as short as possible and save everybody a lot of headaches."

In this case, on top of the armed robbery and possession and use of a firearm, I had racked up a number of other charges including possession of narcotics, B&E, and theft. I made a deal in which they dropped many of the charges and gave me four years of penitentiary time.

The sentence came down in late spring, just in time for me to walk into Kingston Penitentiary for the 1971 prison riots.

SIX

The city of Kingston was a hub for prisons in Ontario. Right within the city were Kingston Penitentiary, Collins Bay Penitentiary, plus a penitentiary for women. Outside was Joyceville Penitentiary and later, on the other side, Millhaven Penitentiary.

In 1971, Kingston Penitentiary was the only maximum security facility in Ontario. It was old. The doors slammed. Guards walked around with guns.

When you came through the doors as a prisoner, they processed you like cattle, shaving off your facial hair and clipping the hair on your head right down to nothing, stripping you naked and spraying you with bug spray, then forcing you to walk through purple dye to disinfect your feet. It was a pretty whacked-out place for someone coming into a federal prison for the first time.

The other problem with Kingston Penitentiary was the serious overcrowding. Plans were in the works to shut it down in favor of a new maximum security prison, Millhaven, that was being built at Bath, Ontario, a forty-minute drive away. The guards at Kingston were resisting the move, maintaining it was not a good thing. The truth was, they had no desire to relocate to Bath, nor were they interested in a long commute.

The convicts weren't eager for the transfer, either. Rumors were floating around about what Millhaven would be like and how secure it was going to be. The word was there were cameras in every cell which meant privacy was non-existent. As it turned out, most of the rumors were false.

There was another factor in play. Being a convict in prison has a strange effect on an individual. You become familiar with your surroundings and your situation. You settle into a comfort zone where change is very difficult. The strict, regimented routine of the day becomes predictable and secure, and the prospect of a move and an upset in routine is very threatening. It was especially so for convicts at Kingston Penitentiary, and caused a good deal of nervousness and tension.

That, combined with the discontent of the guards, made the old Kingston prison a powder keg just waiting to explode.

In every penitentiary there are cliques or crews of people with common affiliations. Cliques give individuals connection and power. There are cliques of bikers, cliques of individuals from a specific ethnic or racial group, even from particular geographic areas. There are also cliques formed around the issue of sentences or similar crimes. The lifers hang together, as do the armed robbers, the drug dealers, and murderers. The majority of murderers in Kingston at that time were domestic killers who had murdered their wives.

In every institution, there is also a clique of young Turks or gladiators[19] between the ages of eighteen and thirty who are into homebrews and drugs, and are just one step away from being insane. They are violent, knife-carrying rebels-with-attitude, aggressive anti-authoritarians who perpetually cause trouble just for the sake of causing trouble. It is how they do their time; it is how they keep their sanity in prison. Needless to say, they can be very dangerous.

It was this particular clique that was agitating as tensions mounted in Kingston Penitentiary in 1971.

The serious overcrowding at the prison didn't help matters. Thirty-five guards on each shift tried to keep order among a thousand convicts in an antiquated facility. To do this, very stringent restrictions were imposed. For instance, in winter, convicts were not allowed outside for fear one might take a sheet with him as camouflage against the snow, and escape. The only time you went outside was if you were going to the tailor shop, the shoe shop, or the mailbag shop. And then, it was

---

[19] Turks and gladiators- young warriors who want to make a reputation for themselves by fighting

only during daylight hours and under full scrutiny.

With no outdoor recreation, an evening regimen was in place where half the prison population stayed in their cells while the other half went to the gymnasium. The next night it was reversed. It was a predictable and established routine.

One night, as half the prison was coming back from the gymnasium, a guard had words with the crew of nutbar Turks and one went after him.

The guard threw down his keys to the dome and shouted, "Riot," whereupon the two guards in the dome ran for their lives through the outside entrance to the staff area, also screaming, "Riot! Riot!" They locked the door behind them, leaving the prisoners with the keys and in full control of the dome and the prison. So in reality, it was guards, not prisoners, who triggered the infamous riot.

Naturally, the doors were quickly opened and the whole prison population broke out. Six or seven guards were grabbed as hostages and after that it was complete chaos.

Different factions got involved in the action. There was one group that wanted to kill the hostages. Some of the older prisoners, including Eddy Day and Billy Chevy and his crew, were bound to protect them.

Because I was new in the penitentiary, I wasn't directly involved in any of this, although I did know the clique of Turks. Fortunately, I was closer to the guys protecting the guards.

For three days, the convicts controlled the prison. It was complete insanity. Walls between cells were knocked down; doors were ripped open.

The protective custody range where the sex offenders were housed was broken into and the sex offenders brought out. A couple were killed. One was known as The Camel. He had raped and murdered two girls. If I remember correctly, he killed them with a can opener. The other guy they killed had abused his children. He sat them in boiling water. His wife was in a penitentiary for women. Here again, if I remember rightly, her fellow-convicts doused her with boiling spaghetti sauce.

During the riot, everyone from protective custody was dragged to the dome area where, over the three-day period, they were repeatedly beaten. They had hoods pulled over their heads and then the Turks would walk in, smash them across the nose with a metal bar, cut their legs open, and urinate on the open wounds. The rest of the prison population just stood in the open doors around the dome and watched it all.

While all this was going on, others got into their homebrews and glue-sniffing. The drag queens broke into the priests' offices and began running around in clerical robes. It was a scene out of Dante's *Inferno*.

Negotiations got underway to try and mitigate the riot. The army arrived and set up on the prison walls. We could see them up there with their machine guns and .50 caliber rifles.

In the end, the negotiations went through and the convicts gave themselves up.

We were put on buses and transported to Millhaven Penitentiary, even though construction there was not quite complete and full services were lacking. We lived on sandwiches for months.

When we stepped out of the buses, we faced a gauntlet of guards in riot gear with the shields, helmets, hoods, riot clubs, and the works. We, of course, were shackled and handcuffed, and by the time we got through the gauntlet, every one of us was beaten terribly. I had ribs broken and one of my lungs perforated.

The ringleaders of the riot were put into solitary confinement; some were tortured. We were all in lockdown twenty-four hours a day.

There was a major inquiry conducted following the Kingston Riot. Both the circumstances leading up to the riot and the Kingston Penitentiary itself were well documented by a former inmate, Roger Caron, in his book entitled *Bingo,* ('Bingo' is prison lingo for 'riot') and in the Swackhammer Report which came out of a governmental investigation into the incident.

Toward fall, they began shipping us out of Millhaven. I was sent to Collins Bay Penitentiary. Quite frankly, it was a welcome move. After Kingston, Collins Bay seemed like a normal prison.

In the hierarchy of prisons, Collins Bay occupied a special niche. It may have been the only prison in Canada at the time with a Level 5 security. Level 4 is classified as medium security; Level 6 is maximum; Level 7 is super-maximum. At Level 5, Collins Bay was a maximum/medium security facility.

It was an interesting prison, still run under the old system before the Charter of Rights. Many of the guards were retired Army. The rules were very strict, but fair.

Collins Bay operated on the silent system: no televisions or radios in the cell; prisoners were not allowed to speak from cell to cell. You walked through hallways quietly. Everywhere you went, your shoulder had to touch the right-hand wall. Prisoners were not allowed to have moustaches or beards, and the hair had to be cut above the ears. Your shoelaces must be tied at all times, and your shirt tucked in.

The prison uniform consisted of grey pants with your number on the back right-hand pocket. (You were never addressed or identified by your name, only by your prison number.) The number was also over the left-hand pocket of your pin-striped shirt. Everyone wore pea jackets with their ID number across the back and on the left pocket. The jackets, which we called jo-jos, came in brown, blue, and black. The brown ones were most sought after because they were scarce; blue was the next most desirable. We also wore pillbox hats with our number emblazoned across the front.

Because this was the pre-Charter era, there were no drugs in Collins Bay. Homebrews were at a minimum and so were killings and serious violence. Given the amount of drugs I was doing at the time, I believe that going to prison probably saved my life. It didn't rehabilitate me, but it did get me temporarily clear of drugs.

In Collins Bay, you were allowed to go out in the yard every second night in summer. In winter, we were taken to the gymnasium. There was only one television in the facility and that was on the stage in the gymnasium. Each of us had our own table to sit at and drink tea or coffee and watch TV.

Each prisoner was issued a tea and coffee box so he could make a hot drink for himself in his cell. Hot water was available in a big urn in the washroom, and convicts referred to as "Range Runners" also made a daily hot water run to the cells.

I got a job in the electronics shop and immediately embarked on a money-making scam manufacturing dunkers. Dunkers were gadgets you plugged into the electrical socket in your cell and dipped into a cup of water to make it boil. With a dunker, you could have hot water any time of the day or night.

I made the dunkers from two tablespoons by cutting off the handles, leaving a little bit of a nipple at the top of each one, and hammering the curved bowls flat. Then I drilled a hole through the middle, bolted them together with a washer and screw, and attached a piece of electrical cord with one wire connected to each nipple. And voilà!

A dunker. Even though my invention blew the breakers in the prison more than once, dunkers became a valuable and desired commodity.

The staff person who ran the electrical shop was interesting. He was great big black fellow from Trinidad or Jamaica. I liked him, and I sensed he liked me. Guards were as much prisoners as the convicts were, and over time, you acquired a certain respect for each other. This fellow went to bat for me on a couple of occasions.

There was a simplicity and inexplicable innocence in those days that no longer exists. Life in prison was less complicated. You knew where you stood and what you needed to do to make it through.

A life sentence was twenty years, but with good behavior, you could cut that down by thirty-six days a year. It was called 'good time,' and it meant exactly that. Every month, with good behavior, you could earn three days which were taken off the end of your sentence. In a year, that added up to thirty-six days, and on a twenty-year sentence it represented a significant chunk of time. Parole was hard to get, so if you got a nickel parole[20], it really meant something.

The mentality in prison was different, too. Convicts were put to work in the shops—the shoe shop, the tailor shop, and vocational shops. The authorities actually believed they could rehabilitate you by teaching you a trade.

At one time, the prison system was self-supporting. Each institution had its own farm to supply dairy products and meat. Convicts worked at raising and preserving the food that supplied the system; they also sewed the prison uniforms and built the furniture. Different prisons had their specialties. Joyceville in Ontario, for instance, canned food for all the institutions in the system.

There was very little violence among prisoners in those days. Prison was more of a game. It was your job to see if you could get away with things, like making dunkers and running scams, and it was the job of the guards to catch you. There was less aggression and violence, and more of a convict code within the prison structure that required you to be a solid, stand-up guy, a person of your word who did the right thing.

American inmates used to express admiration for Canadian convicts. We were known as having a certain class. We didn't inform, and

[20] Nickel parole - five years

there was a code of ethics regarding how we treated one another within the prison milieu. In a sense, it was like being in a prisoner-of-war camp environment. The guards weren't malicious or mean-spirited. They played by the rules, too, and that resulted in a certain civility. Prison was safe, sane, very structured, and highly disciplined.

With good behavior, I got myself a day parole from Collins Bay Penitentiary to the Portsmouth Centre, the first half-way house in Ontario and perhaps the first one in Canada. It was located in Kingston in a building that used to be the warden's house, but was now a supervised residence for convicts out on day-parole.

They got me enrolled in St. Lawrence College, but I was soon wired to the teeth with heroin and methadone and walked out of the halfway house. I made my way back to Toronto where I immediately embarked on another crime spree.

I ran up eighteen, twenty, maybe thirty charges for all sorts of felonies under a number of aliases. The police would arrest me and let me go on bail, and I would simply switch identities—become someone else—and keep on doing what I was doing.

My favorite alias was Terrance Aloysius Carr. That was my Irish identity. I felt the name had a nice ring to it. My partner called himself Anthony Carr and we posed as brothers. I also had Italian aliases: Sergio Romano and Serge Mattucci. And at any given time I might go by the French-Canadian name of Serge Tessier, Serge Benoit, Terrance Benoit, Benoit LeClair, or Serge LeClair.

I got involved with a B&E crew as a heel man[21]. I went into places like factories and dressing rooms in sports facilities where I would rifle through people's lockers, and apartments.

On Tuesdays, Wednesdays, and Thursdays, from 9:30 to 11:30 a.m. and from 1:30 to 3:00 p.m., we broke into apartments, mostly duplexes and triplexes, and emptied them of anything of value. The tenants were away at work, so we just picked the locks and walked in. I'm sure I did several hundred such break-ins. On Mondays, we went to different hotels and Army & Navy clubs where we fenced our stolen goods.

Another scam we operated involved an ace gaff, a tool that opens circular locks like those on coin-operated washing machines. We unloaded a lot of change from public laundromats, as well as machines in

---

[21] Heel man - prowl man who is a daytime sneak thief looking for opportunities to steal

apartment buildings. We also went to Montreal where we got a flat fee for shutting off alarms for B&E crews there.

My partner in all this was Hank who ended up getting a life sentence for killing someone and then killing a guard and a kitchen staff worker in Collins Bay Penitentiary. Prior to that, Hank and I were a two-man crime wave.

I was back with my old crew and into old-style criminal activity: stealing, fencing, and scamming in every way possible—the kind of crimes I had done before becoming a drug dealer. I wasn't dealing drugs now, but I was still going to the clubs and using them myself.

In late 1973, I was arrested again. I got three and a half years, though a whole bunch of charges were dropped including six counts of fraudulent impersonation, five charges of stolen property, and about thirty-odd charges of B&E.

I made a deal in court. I said, "Okay, you got me. Now what can we do here?" I think I pleaded guilty to one break and enter, one possession of stolen property, and one breach of recognizance.

Of course, I still had the parole violation, so back to prison I went.

SEVEN

Shortly after I began my new prison sentence, penitentiaries began to change. The Charter of Rights was put into place and the world I knew began to change—for the better and for the worse.

Left-wing politicians like the Commissioner of Penitentiaries and the Justice Minister of the day had led the charge to reform the existing Canadian justice system and replace it with ideologies reminiscent of Plato's *Republic*. They didn't realize that was probably the worst possible approach they could take to prison reform. In essence, they were letting the lunatics loose.

The Charter of Rights made prisons immeasurably more violent and dangerous, and among other things, laid them wide open for unchecked drug use.

Under the new ideology, prisoners could not be called convicts anymore; they had to be inmates. Nor were they referred to by number. Everyone must be called by his name.

I wouldn't let the guards call me by name. I only answered to my number: 7777. If I liked the guard, I would say, "I'll give you a break. You can call me 'Four Sevens' for short."

Nor would I use the term 'resident' or 'inmate.' To this day, prisoners are convicts to me.

Numbers were removed from uniforms which had also changed. Now we wore green pants and light green polyester shirts. Coats with linings were issued to replace the pea jackets, and for recreational wear we were given golf shirts and khaki pants.

Of course, being the rebel I was, I kept my old prison clothes and refused to wear the new uniform. The guards chased me everywhere trying to get the old uniform off me. They even raided my cell trying to find the old prison garb, but I had it stashed. Instead of putting it through the regular laundry, I had a guy doing my laundry for me. As a result, I was one of the last convicts to wear the old uniform—just because I wanted to be ornery and anti-establishment. I sometimes wonder if, in holding onto the old uniform, I was somehow trying to keep the prison from proceeding on the degenerative downward skid toward the insanity that it was in.

Under the new regulations, a convict could now have a beard, a moustache, and hair as long as he wanted. Open visits were allowed because they were more humane. Even conjugal visits could be arranged. Of course, once they were allowed, the place was flooded with drugs.

Conjugal visits meant a convict could have visits from his legal or common-law wife or homosexual partner. Most penitentiaries provide two or three motorhomes in a fenced-in area within the walls. The motorhome is stocked with food, and the occupants can order more: chicken, steak, lobster, whatever they want. They are also allowed to bring in food. So, for two or two-and-a-half days on a weekend, a convict can have all the sex he wants, watch television, and play DVDs and video games with his kids. At a prescribed time each day, a guard comes outside and stands by the gate; the convict shows himself and is marked as counted. Conjugal visits are allowed once every two to three months on a rotating basis.

I had no interest in conjugal visits. I had the philosophy that if you were a criminal, you shouldn't be married. You shouldn't bring women or children into that kind of life. In fact, I had a strong disgust for men who brought their families into prison to visit. I considered it very low class. I figured if you were going to be a criminal, you should be a good one and do it full time, but if you were going to have the responsibility of being a father, then get a job and be a proper father.

I had never allowed myself to become seriously involved with anyone, though a number of women lived with me at one time or another throughout my criminal career. As soon as they wanted to get serious, I found a way to break it off. Going in and out of prison made that easy. I'd say, "No you can't come and visit me. It's over."

I had this thing about class and tended to judge people from that perspective. Deep down I longed to be middle-class and was careful to practise the social graces that I associated with being middle-class. I learned proper etiquette and how to eat and dress from books and watching actors like Cary Grant in movies. I wanted people to think of me as a classy guy.

I didn't necessarily want to be liked, but I did want to be respected, so I always strove to be a classy criminal. The people I did business with followed a certain criminal code that said you never ripped off a friend or stole his girl. Or, if one of your guys got arrested on a bust, you took care of his family and his lawyer. You never ratted[22] on anyone. If you were going to be a rat, you had no business being a criminal. My view on regular citizens was this: If a citizen saw me committing a crime and reported me to the police, they were doing their job, and shame on me for letting them see me do it.

The new Charter of Rights brought another big change in the introduction of the grievance system and prisoners' rights, something that broke down the entire prison culture. Daily life became egregiously violent. Now you had convicts arguing with guards and guards being alienated. Guard/convict relationships based on mutual respect were a thing of the past. The guard was now the enemy, and the justice system was soon bogged down with convicts initiating court action against guards with charges of cruel and unusual punishment.

Strange wannabe do-gooders came into the prisons and started inmate committees and citizen advisory groups. Convicts were now meeting with the warden and demanding all sorts of things.

Under the new system, the longest you could spend in solitary confinement was thirty days, after which your case had to be reviewed. As well, anyone in solitary confinement had to be allowed out of their cell for three hours every day. Once they put television sets in the solitary cells, the threat of solitary confinement was no threat at all. I began to book in whenever I wanted a rest. All you had to do was sit around, watch television, and read.

Convicts also had the right to go out of their cells each night. That led to more of everything: more violence, more drugs, more knives, and more insanity.

As the breakdown of the traditional prison culture continued,

---

[22] Ratted - informed on

something else was happening on a parallel plane. There was greater access to networking and outside contacts. Under the old system, guards were able to keep tabs on who you talked to and who you hung out with; all that information went to the parole board. Now there was so much movement and so many drugs coming in that the guards began to pull away for their own safety.

Power bases developed according to the quantity of drugs an individual convict could get in, how much money he had, and how many mules[23] he had operating. I never had visitors, but I didn't hesitate to enlist others, especially the women who came in for visits. My personal feeling was that women who did this sort of thing lowered themselves, but it didn't stop me from using them.

Under the mule system, a convict would instruct his wife or girlfriend to put drugs in a balloon and conceal it in a body cavity. During the visit, the drugs would be passed on to the boyfriend who would swallow the drug-filled balloon or hide it in a body cavity of his own. The process was known as 'hooping.' The convict involved got a percentage of the money generated by the drug load.

We ran all sorts of scams in Collins Bay. We made lock-picking tools and learned to pick locks by practising with the home-made devices. We made silencers for guns in the machine shop. We had an underground radio station with obscene call letters, Station F.U.C.K., that broadcasted all around the immediate area.

Syndicates developed inside the prison that allowed enterprising individuals to accumulate significant sums of money. That created fertile ground for deep-rooted corruption, and staff members were often the objects of the corruption. One was an obese fellow who ran the clothes room. Some of us arranged for him to meet up with a couple of girls from Toronto. We had them videotaped together and then used the video to blackmail him into keeping us supplied with drugs and liquor. In return, we rewarded him with money and hookers.

To say the Charter of Rights and Freedoms changed the whole world of justice, law, and order is an understatement. It turned the whole system on its ear, and to this day, it has never recovered.

On the heels of the new Commission came new sentencing guidelines. The old ones were deemed to be cruel and unusual punishment,

---

[23] Mule - someone who brings drugs into prison from the Outside

and in great need of adjustment. A life sentence used to be twenty years of solid time. Most convicts did sixteen years and change on a life sentence because, with good behavior, you could get your three days per month of good time. If you got into disciplinary problems, not only did you go to solitary confinement, you lost your three days that month, and worse, they could take off thirty days a year of good time. There was far less recidivism in the old days because jails were tougher.

Now sentences were open-ended. Life meant a minimum of twenty-five years. Good time meant absolutely nothing. If you came in with a sawbuck[24], you immediately got a quarter of that as good time with mandatory supervision. In order to justify the mandatory supervision, judges now had to extend or bump up the sentences.

The new sentencing structure created chaos in prisons because penitentiary staff and guards no longer had the tools they needed to control the convicts, nor were there any more incentives for convicts to 'play the game.' As a result, the light at the end of the tunnel grew dimmer and convicts were seized with a kind of desperation that led to more violence which spilled onto the streets once they were released.

Under the reforms, people began talking about racism and human rights. There had never been any of this in the prison system before. Whether you were black, white, yellow, or red did not matter; everybody was treated the same—as criminals and prisoners. Now, whenever a black convict committed an offence, you could expect the race card to be played. And the more people used race as a weapon to avoid or shorten their due punishment, the higher the racial tension boiled. White convicts said, "What are you talking about? You're being treated exactly the same way we are. Your crime is the issue, not your race, your ethnicity, or your social status."

I went through a couple of race riots that were spawned by just such arguments. In the convicts' minds, privilege became entitlement. I, too, got caught up with the psychology of using rioting as a tool to get what I wanted, and was personally charged with instigating one. I think it was over something as silly as recreation. I went around to everyone and said, "It's nuts around here. We're going to start a riot." We tore the range apart, and when the opposite range heard about it, they

---

[24] Sawbuck - ten years

did the same thing. Soon the riot spread through the whole prison.

About this time, I was working as the head clerk for the vocational office at Collins Bay Penitentiary. (This was in keeping with the new idea that convicts could be rehabilitated if they were given counseling and psychological testing. Instead, the prison system actually took a giant step backwards and the incidence of convicts re-offending went through the roof.)

From my position in the office, I was able to investigate a little clique that had formed in Collins Bay Penitentiary. I was curious about them. There were only four people in the clique and they were all from Northern Manitoba. I couldn't help wondering what they were doing in this prison. One of them, I particularly disliked.

The clique first came to my attention when another convict mentioned having seen one of the four in the county jail— "on some kind of sex beef," he said.

You will recall that sex offenders and pedophiles are the lowest of the low in prison society and that it is every convict's sworn duty to punish or even kill them.

I went into the vocational office files to see what I could find. Sure enough, all four were sentenced for sex crimes. It appeared they were picking up hitchhikers, probably First Nations girls, and raping them. The men got caught, copped a plea, and ended up in Collins Bay Penitentiary.

I talked with a few people about them, and word got back to the Manitoba clique. The toughest of the four came after me. I knocked him out, dragged him into the shower, and jumped on his legs, breaking both of them—and my own thumb in the process.

Then I went down and got the second guy. I took him into the gymnasium showers and beat the bark off him.

The next morning at breakfast, I caught hold of the third guy. I bent him backward over the table and began beating him over the head with an HP Sauce bottle. With my broken thumb, it wasn't easy. I would whack him a couple of times and the bottle would fly out of my hand. I'd hold him down and grab another bottle and give him some more.

A guard came by and tried to stop the fight. He grabbed me from behind, and I flung him against the wall, breaking his arm.

Then several more guards converged on me, choked me out, and dragged me off to the Hole where I stayed for about six months.

The incident left the administration in a quandary. They didn't know what to do with me. They hesitated to get too heavy-handed because not only were these four guys sex offenders, but the administration was a little embarrassed that I had gotten into confidential, and supposedly inaccessible records.

The other thing in my favor was the fact that the staff person in charge of me was one of my hashish connections. He brought in dope for me and I had some pretty serious goods on him. He knew he was at risk, so he went to bat for me.

The administration ended up shipping me to Joyceville Penitentiary which was a Level 4 prison, one level down from Collins Bay in terms of security.

Joyceville was an interesting place. It was an old prison, but a very comfortable one. It and LeClerc (no connection) in Quebec were built on the same premise and housed older convicts. While Collins Bay was a gladiator school for young bloods, Joyceville housed the older crowd, usually second or third time non-violent offenders.

The prison itself had an open kind of concept with two cell block wings connected to a middle area for the guards. Each range had a common room where everyone ate their meals. There was a range cleaner, and a more relaxed atmosphere with less obvious security. It seemed rather ironic that they would send me to this medium security prison when I had just spent six months in the Hole for breaking one guard's arm, another guy's legs, and beating a third one senseless with an HP bottle, but who was I to complain?

Needless to say, I had a great time in Joyceville. In the relaxed atmosphere, I regained a little bit of sanity and matured as a human being. I met a lot of older, second and third time offenders, and established relationships which effectively expanded my network of contacts.

We still had drugs, but Joyceville was a place where they didn't do a lot of chemicals. Because it was a more mature crowd, there wasn't any violence, or stress, or fighting.

The staff would let us out in the morning and lock us up again at eleven o'clock at night. With the living unit concept that existed, there wasn't much additional contact with the staff. It was party time all day long, and I gained weight from all the good food we prepared in the common room.

I also went into aversion therapy in Joyceville. The place was filled with spiders, and I hated them with a vengeance. Come spring time,

Joyceville was alive with the nasty creatures.

I put tape around the door and windows of my cell to keep the spiders out, and I had a can of insecticide that I was constantly spraying around my cell.

The deputy warden said, "Serge, you've got to quit spraying. People are going to die if you spray any more of that stuff around here." And it was true; the fumes were so thick nobody wanted to walk down the corridor.

At his suggestion, I agreed to see a psychiatrist who said, "We need to bring someone in to do aversion therapy with you, and teach you some relaxation techniques."

I went through all sorts of bio-feedback, relaxation therapy, and aversion therapy for my arachnophobia. The final test was putting my hand into a glass cage that held a large tarantula. The space for my hand was enclosed in glass, so it was perfectly safe, but I didn't know that. I had to keep putting my hand in the cage until I could do it without any trauma.

I still don't like spiders, but I can now deal with them. If one lands on me, I can brush it off or kill it. I still practise the relaxation techniques I learned in Joyceville, taking deep breaths and visualizing myself under a tree by a babbling brook while the fluffy clouds drift overhead and the birds tweet sweetly in the trees.

The therapy didn't do a thing to change me as a criminal, but it sure made me a more relaxed one.

Eight

When my sentence was up, I left Joyceville and went back to Toronto. It wasn't long before I was arrested again on a very interesting charge: 'Conspiracy to commit robbery with person or persons unknown.'

It was actually a robbery charge, but as usual, I was able to bargain the police into dropping that charge and giving me two years for conspiring to commit the robbery, even though the robbery was deliberate and specific.

It all began when a certain drug dealer ripped off a good friend of ours, a woman I happened to have a thing for. He sold her bad drugs, so my men and I basically went to his place, beat him up, hog-tied him, took the payback for all the drugs he may or may not have had, and left.

The police found me in short order and I ended up in Toronto's Don Jail. Also incarcerated in the Don Jail was a fellow named Peppy who was there on drug laboratory and conspiracy charges. Peppy and I became very good friends. Even though we were in direct competition—he controlled the East End of Toronto and I controlled the West End and Uptown—we cemented a criminal friendship and partnership. We had different crews and networks, but many of them were cross-overs, including a number of mutual biker friends who had grown up with us.

I spent about two years in the Don Jail. I was there on remand, but it was a particularly long process because the police were trying to make the 'conspiracy to rob with person or persons unknown' charge stick and get me a ten-year sentence. They were having all sorts of trouble doing that because witnesses kept disappearing or failing to show up for the preliminary hearing.

I had been in the Don Jail before, just prior to going to Kingston Penitentiary in 1971. On that occasion I was put in the old turn-of-the-century Toronto Gaol section which had two different types of cells: single cells so narrow you had perhaps twelve inches between the bed and the wall, and four-person cells with two sets of bunk beds. In both types of cells you had a plastic bucket for a toilet and a bathroom at the end of the range.

There were also the death cells. The last prisoners to be held in those cells were Lennie Jackson and Steve Suchan, members of the infamous Boyd Gang who were hanged in the mid-1950s for killing a police officer, Eddie Wong.

The basement of the Don Jail was like a dungeon, and it was there that the solitary confinement cells were located. Predictably, I spent some time in solitary after getting into a fight.

Eventually a new section was built onto the Don Jail, and, as befitted someone of my stature as a top-flight criminal, this is where they put me during the remand period. Peppy and his brother Artie were there, too, as were members of Peppy's crew and associates like Simpleface, the sergeant-at-arms for the Paradise Riders biker gang. We had dribbled in on different charges and ended up in the same range. You could say they had all the nutbars together, but in this case, the nutbars were top criminals. For us, it was like Old Homecoming Week.

We corrupted everyone in that facility. The guards and staff people were afraid of us, and to keep us placated, they supplied our every demand. We had drugs coming up with our food and a continual stream of packages from contacts on the outside being dropped off by various guards.

One day, after I punched out a guard who hadn't delivered what he was supposed to, they moved me to the death cells. It was supposed to be a temporary thing, but when I wasn't moved back, Peppy, Artie, and Simpleface started a riot. That resulted in all four of us being relegated to the death cells.

In one sense, it was a score. There were four gigantic cells with floors, walls, and toilets made of steel. We had two windows—the same windows through which the Boyd Gang members had once escaped but were now covered with a double set of steel bars. Below the windows was a radiator on which we kept a pot of coffee warming. We had a table, a television, double locks on the doors, and one guard for the bunch of us. What more could we ask?

It was a good situation for the guards, too, since we were isolated and gave them no grief.

We spent several months in the death cells, smoking dope and doing valium. When the door was opened, the smoke literally billowed out into the corridor.

Eventually, Peppy and the others began going to their *voir-dire* trials which took them away from the cell every day for several months. (Voir-dire trials are preliminary hearings where all the evidence is examined to see if there is enough to take the person to trial.) Because Peppy and his bunch were being charged with a clandestine laboratory operation[25], it took months.

Meanwhile, I was back in the death cells holding the fort and demanding food of all kinds from the kitchen.

By the time we finished dealing with my own conspiracy charge, two years had passed. I was given a four-year sentence which meant I still had two more years of prison time to do plus what remained of the parole I had been on when released from Joyceville Penitentiary.

They sent me back to Kingston.

By this time, Kingston Penitentiary had semi-recovered from the 1971 riots and was serving a variety of functions. It was the reception unit or central clearing house where all prisoners went prior to being sent on to the appropriate prison. Kingston was also being used as protective custody for sex offenders and informers. In addition, there were two ranges where static population was housed. Static population is composed of convicts who work as cleaners, maintenance people, and kitchen helpers. Each status is grouped together and kept separate from the others.

Kingston had a central dome design with several four-storey ranges radiating out from it. The top two floors were still not operational, though improvements were being made. The protective custody area

---

[25] Clandestine drug laboratory - a secret illegal laboratory set up for the sole purpose of manufacturing illicit drugs

was in the oldest part of the prison where the cells were very small and there was no proper plumbing.

Soon after I arrived at Kingston Penitentiary, the deputy warden came to see me. We were no strangers. He had been my classification officer in Collins Bay Penitentiary, so he knew me well. (A classification officer has a caseload of convicts with whom he meets on a monthly basis. He gives advice regarding programs they should take and helps them fill out applications for day passes, paroles, or orders for court. The C.O.'s primary role is to work with the convict to achieve some level of rehabilitation.)

"I'd like you to do me a favor," the deputy warden said, "and I will do one for you in return. Here's the deal. We want to turn this prison into a full protective custody facility, but in the meantime, we need to get it back on its operational legs.

"I would like you to stay here in static population and become head of the inmate committee. You're one of the few people I know who can pull this off because of your status and your reputation. You have only two years remaining on your sentence. If you will give me one year here, you can pick wherever you want to go for your final year. I don't care where it is."

I said, "You've got a deal."

And so for a whole year, I was involved in pretty well everything that concerned the convicts. The only people I did not deal with were those in protective custody. No self-respecting convict had any dealings with them.

I started on the library, probably because it was closest to my heart. Being self-educated, I read everything I could get my hands on. I devoured books, reading five and six a week, and two or three newspapers each day. Putting the library back together was a challenge because many of the books had been burned during the riots.

Among the library rubble, I found an old fish tank. I persuaded the staff person in charge to get some fish for the tank. (It was probably my way of obtaining a pet.) In order to justify the tank and the fish, I started giving lectures on tropical fish to anyone who was willing to listen, even though I didn't know a thing about it outside of what I read in library books.

Kingston Penitentiary had a radio room with a good collection of records and tapes. Many of them were trashed during the riot, but I put everything back together again and became the radio operator. The convicts had earphones which they plugged into jacks in their cells. They had the option of listening to the radio room operator or listening to nothing. I started doing a radio show where I played music and some of the old comedy programs. On Friday nights, we had a request show with yours truly as the DJ.

Another initiative was the sports program. We established weight-training and a baseball league with me as the chief umpire. It probably wasn't the best position for me to assume; I beat one guy with my umpire's face mask for getting mouthy with me, but because of the work I was doing, I avoided going to solitary.

It was an interesting year. I didn't mind it at all. Little by little, working hand-in-hand with the deputy warden, I was able to put things back into operational condition and the prison resumed some structure and order.

There were other perks. I ate very well in Kingston thanks to a Brit, a master chef and baker who was in for a life sentence for killing his wife. He was in static population in Kingston while they figured out what to do with him. It was in Kingston Penitentiary that I tasted beef Wellington for the first time.

I was also in charge of the canteen where convicts came to spend their allowance of twenty-five cents a day, paid out every two weeks. They generally spent it on tobacco and chocolate bars.

During that year I got involved writing grievances for guys. Though I was not formally educated, I was very literate and I knew what to say and how to say it. As a result, I became a prisoner advocate. People came to me to write out their parole plans and help with their appeals.

In so doing, I made some pretty good friends in prison, and I think the guards came to respect me. I know the convicts certainly did.

When the year was up, they were ready to make Kingston Penitentiary a full protective custody facility and turn the place into the official reception unit.

The warden called me in. "Your year is up," he said. "Where do you want to go?"

I didn't hesitate. "Beaver Creek."

Beaver Creek is near Muskoka in Ontario's Lake Country. It was formerly a WWII Norwegian Air Force base and came equipped with its own swimming pool and mini-golf course. There were no fences at Beaver Creek, and only minimal security. I refer to it as the first Club

Fed.

The warden gave me a hard look. "I had a feeling that would be your choice."

I arrived at Beaver Creek tipping the scales at 260 pounds of hard muscle from bench-pressing a few hundred pounds every day. My head was shaved bald and when I got off the bus at Beaver Creek, the warden took one look at me and said, "We don't want you here."

"Too bad," I said. "I really don't care what you want. I'm here. Argue it out with Regional."

"You're not going to get any special treatment while you're here," he warned.

I said, "Mister, just being here is a score. I don't care if you don't give me a pass. In fact, I don't care what you give me, period. I'm here, you've got me, now leave me alone."

And that is basically what they did. The guards and the other inmates were afraid of me. A lot of them were fringe-type convicts: white collar criminals, first-time convicts, and a couple of people who needed to be in semi-protective custody.

I had a four-person room in one of the buildings all to myself because that's the way I wanted it.

They put me to work on the maintenance crew.

The head of the crew said, "Here's what I'm going to do. I will give you a list of things that need doing, and you're in charge of yourself. You can repair electrical fixtures, plaster holes, and fix plumbing, but if there's a job you can't do, just give me a call and we'll look after it together."

I was only on the job about one week when a lifer guy who had beaten somebody to death in Northern Ontario got on my case.

I said, "You and I are going to have it out. Meet me this afternoon in the maintenance building."

We had it out.

After I had beaten on him for a while, he ran inside a shop and closed the door which had a safety glass window reinforced with mesh. I was so angry I put my fist right through the safety glass. I cut my hand up pretty badly, but when word got out that I was so completely insane I had punched my way through safety glass, the guards and everybody else left me even more to myself.

There were maybe three out of the fifty convicts at Beaver Creek with whom I had contact. Mostly, I just stayed in the background, operating on my own schedule and moving around the property. I set up snares for rabbits and dealt with the overabundance of beavers. Part of my job was to break up the beaver dams to prevent the property from being flooded.

For the whole year, the warden kept trying to get me out of his prison, but he was unsuccessful because I wasn't doing anything wrong.

From my perspective, it was a pretty good life. I had all the drugs I wanted, I was smoking dope, lifting weights, and because I was getting prostitutes for the guy who ran the kitchen, I ate virtually whatever I wanted. Rather than serving a prison sentence, it seemed as if I had won a lottery or been given a year-long Caribbean cruise.

A minimum security penitentiary is an interesting phenomenon; I would say that no one in Canada with an annual income of fifty thousand dollars a year or less lives better than a convict in minimum security.

I was in Beaver Creek for the entire year. The only time I left the place was the occasion when I went golfing with a Catholic priest. I had never golfed before in my life. He stuck a cigar in his mouth, I stuck one in mine, and we went on the course. My language was about as raw as it could get, but I didn't care if he was a Catholic priest or not. I used every swear word I knew. He never took me golfing again.

My two and a half years at Kingston and Beaver Creek were interesting in a number of ways. Not only did I establish a reputation for leadership in the prison arena and the criminal world, but I also cemented and reinforced my criminal contacts throughout Ontario, Quebec, and beyond. Those friendships would come in very handy later on.

Those months were also the time where I learned to stick handle prison culture. Before, I had always been hardnosed, fighting, stabbing people, beating guards, spending my time in solitary confinement. Now I learned to finesse the system and it changed the whole pattern of how I served time in prison.

I already had the tools; I had learned them from the streets. But I was too raw, too headstrong to know how to use them to my advantage. In learning to handle the guards and the administration, I discovered how to survive in prison with a degree of comfort and sophistication.

I owe a great deal to that deputy warden, who went on to become a regional director in the prison system. I believe he intuitively recognized valuable skills and abilities in me and deliberately placed me in a position where I had no choice but to use them. I owe him a great debt and still think of him today with a great deal of fondness and respect.

NINE

Upon leaving Beaver Creek, I was very quickly back into action[26].

I moved to the Parkdale area of Toronto, rented a very nice apartment, and started dealing drugs to a lot of my contacts in different parts of the city. I had an excellent supplier and was soon making a lot of money.

After about six months, I went Uptown to catch up with my contacts in the gay clubs and found they had no dependable supplier. It was a void that I was ready and willing to fill.

I went into partnership with a fellow in a private club that had been the Paramount Theatre's headquarters. We made it into a classy, private club with a four-star dining room.

I ended up with six clubs in the Uptown gay community, half of which I owned as a silent partner. I was also getting into some serious weight[27] in terms of crystal meth.

Outside of drug dealing, I was a legitimate businessman. I established Denim World, a business that manufactured and sold jeans and screen-printed t-shirts. I made a lot of money at that, but at the same time, I was very much caught up with the criminal world. My feet, my head, my life were going a hundred miles an hour.

Then the wheels fell off.

---

[26] Action - criminal activity
[27] Serious weight - large amounts of drugs

I had some extra weight[28] that I needed to get rid of, and I decided to flog it to some select people.

One of the guys who came to see me was fresh out of prison and the RCMP and the Integrated Drug Squad were keeping an eye on him. This fellow parked his vehicle in front of my apartment, and when I came out of the building with another drug contact, Donnie, we discovered some men searching the fellow's car.

Like an idiot, I yelled, "Get out of there. What are you doing with my friend's car?"

The men turned out to be the Integrated Drug Squad. They immediately recognized Donnie, grabbed him and sat him on the hood of the car, pulled down his pants to mid-thigh level, and searched him. They knew immediately who I was, but they knew better than to search me.

Still, I was made[29], and I was made in the company of a major drug guy while claiming another drug dealer as my friend. It made me really angry, because not only did I have to move, but I also had to sever all ties with that crew.

First, though, I had to get rid of the drugs. What I needed was a front end[30] who would deliver the goods to my other contacts. The person I chose was J.J., someone I had known since the Seventies. J.J. was one of the guys from my old gang in The District. He was living with a girl named Jinx.

My proposition to J.J. was this: I would manage the Uptown action if he would manage the action with the other crowd. J.J. agreed and we set to work.

The three of us moved together to the East End and shared a huge four-bedroom apartment. J.J. and Jinx became almost like family to me. Off and on I would have different girlfriends move in with us, too.

I purchased several other apartments which I rented out or used as stashes. We were probably running $100,000 a week in action. Things seemed to be ticking right along.

But I had a weakness. I loved stealing. I loved the adrenalin rush that came with a good break-out. We would walk into a place, maybe a

---

[28] Weight - drugs

[29] Made - the police were onto me, were aware of my activities

[30] Front end - someone who deals out front for you so you don't have to deal directly

Canadian Tire or a department store, and hide. When everybody else was gone, we would crawl out of our hiding place (generally under a bed or something), gather up the stuff we wanted, re-rig the alarms, and break out.

I didn't need the action, but when a colleague came to see if I wanted to work with him on a deal, I said, "Sure." I knew the guy well. He was a thief, too—one of the fellows who got me vehicles. (I generally traded a quarter-pound or a half-pound of speed for a vehicle.)

"I've got a good store with suits," he said. "I need a few bucks. Do you want to come in on the job?"

"Yeah," I said.

By this time, J.J., Jinx, and I had moved to house on a classy cul-de-sac, up the street from the Port Credit chief of police, and the mother of several cops on the other side of us. She often had me babysit the grandkids. As far as everyone knew, I was a pillar of society. I figured I was safe from the cops.

My colleague and I were still working out the details for the suit store heist, when a mooch looking to buy some of my drugs came out of the blue and parked his car in front of my house on this cul-de-sac. He was the type of person to whom I would never have given the time of day. I told him I wasn't interested in doing business with him, but it was too late. The deed was done. Was he working for The Man[31]? Was he an informer, or just somebody so strung out the police were following him? I'll never know, but when he came to my house and I appeared on my porch, the police were watching, and my whereabouts was no longer a secret.

The suit store heist went ahead. J.J. went with us. We collected six or seven hundred suits, each one worth two to three hundred dollars. We had them all wrapped in sheets, ready to go to the fence[32], but thanks to my idiot visitor, the police were watching us.

They saw us loading merchandise into a vehicle, and because I was involved, they assumed we were moving drugs. They probably figured they were onto a major marijuana bust or something, but of course, it was a load of brand new suits. They grabbed us anyway.

J.J. was immediately arrested and denied bail.

From that point on, the police were all over my place, watching

---

[31] The Man - the police
[32] Fence - buyer and seller of illegal merchandise

everything I did. I was out of action and the pressure was on.

Jinx and I moved to the other end of the city, to the Lakeshore area of Toronto, but without J.J. there to keep me rational, I started using drugs again. I should have hung tight and stayed put, but the drugs kept me from thinking clearly.

Then I made a very stupid mistake. I decided to do one more quick sting[33].

I had word that a certain hotel owner would be going to the bank to collect $25,000 in cash. He owned a hotel near a big tire factory in the Etobicoke area and needed the $25,000 to cash the paychecks of factory workers who came to his establishment for booze. I decided to get a gun and rob this guy.

I got the gun, put a nylon stocking over my head, and held the guy up just as he was getting into his car. I grabbed the money and shoved him into his car which was parked in the lot behind his hotel. Unfortunately, I neglected to notice that there was a bus stop right beside it. I was exactly in the middle of trying to handcuff the guy to his steering wheel when a bus pulled up.

The man started screaming for help. I slammed the car door shut so the passengers and the bus driver wouldn't hear him. Pretty soon the bus closed its doors and drove away, but by this time, the fellow had locked his car door and was leaning on the horn.

I took off, heading for a laneway connecting to the next street over where I had left my car in a 'No Parking' zone on the wrong side of the street. I was about three-quarters of the way to the car when I felt someone grab my shoulder.

It was the hotel owner.

I spun around, and pointed the revolver at him. "Enough," I said. "You stay right there. Don't make me hurt you."

By this time, I had ripped the stocking off my head, so my face was clearly visible.

He kept moving toward me.

I aimed the gun at the centre of his body and fired. There was a puff of smoke. The man reeled, grabbed his chest, and fell against a wooden fence.

"Oh, no," I said to myself. "I've killed him. This is it. This is big

---

[33] Sting - criminal action

time, Serge."

I got in my car and started the engine, but the next thing I knew, the same guy was there, trying to get at me through the window. I was absolutely shocked. I was convinced I'd killed him.

I jammed him against the window frame with my arm and stepped on the gas. When the car got going too fast for him to keep up, I let him go and he rolled away onto the pavement.

Ten minutes later, I was at the house.

"I've got the money," I told Jinx, "but I have to go into hiding. I need you to take this gun and dump it in the lake." (Lake Ontario was about a hundred yards behind the house.)

I broke open the gun to remove the bullets, and as I did, I was astonished to see the tip of a bullet sticking out the end of the gun. Somehow, it had jammed in the barrel.

I tossed the gun to Jinx and took off.

The first thing I did was ditch the car. It was a Dodge Charger, and far too recognizable to be safe. Besides, there was every possibility that someone had observed the episode and taken the license number.

As it turned out, someone had. The police traced the car to me at Jinx's address and wiretapped all the public payphones within a three block radius of the house. They knew that Jinx would eventually make contact with me, and they were right.

When she called, we arranged to meet in a park where I would give her $10,000 and let her know where I was going. I knew I had to leave town quickly because after what had just happened, there was no question the police would be looking for me.

When I reached the rendezvous point, police officers came out from behind every bush and tree with guns aimed and ready. It was a pretty tense time and everyone was nervous. One sergeant had to lay his arm over the car door because his hands were shaking so much.

I just put my hands in the air and said, "Look, the hands are here. Take it easy. I don't have a gun. Relax."

But they weren't taking any chances. They knew me from the days when I was insane with drugs and completely out of control. There had been numerous 'Do Not Approach: known to be violent, armed, and dangerous' warnings out regarding me. Naturally, they expected a shootout.

I was taken into custody. They told me the evidence: an eye witness who recognized me, two people who had seen me get into my car and drag the man down the street, and my license plate number. Now they wanted the gun.

I said, "Let's make a deal. You know I'm a man of my word. I will tell you where the gun is when we have the deal locked in."

I didn't want them to have the gun any sooner than necessary because I was afraid they would see the jammed bullet and charge me with attempted murder. As it was, they charged me with the use of a firearm while committing an indictable offence. And, of course, I already had a B&E charge for the truckload of stolen suits that the police thought was marijuana.

I made one court appearance, entered a plea right away, and settled on a deal for nine years—two for break and enter and theft, six for robbery, and one year for use of a firearm while committing an indictable offence. It was all over the Toronto newspapers: 'Swift Justice: arrested Friday, pled guilty and sentenced to nine years on Monday.'

By the week's end I was back in Millhaven Penitentiary, starting a nine year sentence. To be honest, I considered myself very lucky; with all the evidence they had, they could have put me away indefinitely.

I had plenty of time in prison to think about the puzzling circumstance of the jammed bullet. I still think about it today. Having handled and fired weapons from the age of fifteen—everything from old Thompson machine guns and sawed off M1s with banana clips to automatics—I had never before heard of a gun jamming in this way. And it was a good gun, a .38 revolver, and revolvers don't jam. This particular revolver did not misfire. The tip of the bullet was still in the barrel. Somehow, something in that narrow, three-eights of an inch space stopped that bullet and saved a man from dying. It also saved me from a murder charge. Had the bullet hit its intended mark, I would still be in prison today serving a life sentence. Given my background and criminal record, there is no question I would have been charged with first degree murder in the commission of armed robbery. The sentence would have been twenty-five years minimum and I would have died in prison with no negative feelings about the fact that I had taken someone's life.

I didn't realize it at the time, but the incident was probably a turning point in my life. While it did not impact me directly then, it definitely set the stage for what would happen later on.

I spent some time in the Millhaven Penitentiary reception unit, and was then transferred to Collins Bay where I was immediately among friends. Many of my pals and associates were already incarcerated there including Peppy, the national president of Satan's Choice, and various childhood friends and fellow bandits from the East and West Ends of Toronto.

Because of my notorious reputation, I entered prison at the top of the prisoner hierarchy. I immediately got into one of the best cells on the best range. I had a television, a stereo, and all the drugs I wanted.

I was able to get these perks because the convict power elite pulled some strings and got concessions from the various keepers on my behalf. Such arrangement are always reciprocal. Often, guards will speak to the convict elite about a prisoner who is getting out of control, perhaps someone too strung out on drugs. They see tension developing, and rather than risking a strike or lockdown where someone is bound to get hurt (often the guards), they ask the power elite to exert some pressure. In return, those same convicts are able to go to a keeper and say, "Look here, Serge just came in. You know him. He's a good guy. He doesn't want any problems. We'd like to have him over in Cell Block Three with us. There's a cell down at the end. Why don't you give that to him?"

Thanks to pressure from my friends, I got a cell in the best range with my door open all day long.

Now I needed work.

The inmate committee I had headed up during my previous sentence was already locked up by one crew, and recreation was controlled by another. But there was the canteen.

To this point, the canteen at Collins Bay had been a kind of warehouse depot on a farm camp where you sent your canteen order to be filled. Every two weeks, you received your order in a bag. Everything was handled by guard personnel. Now they were considering putting a convict in charge, and what's more, they were going to set up an actual store front inside Collins Bay Penitentiary where the men could go any time during the week, and daily, if they wanted to. That was right up my alley.

I took over operation of the canteen along with a couple of old-time convicts, salty old crusts with good bookkeeping skills. It was a good position with lots of freedom. I was my own boss, which allowed me to run several good scams from the canteen.

For one thing, we sold hashish and took payment in new postage stamps. The stamps were sent out through Hobbycraft where convicts made purses and other nice craft items to give to their loved ones. Every time crafts went out of the prison, we slipped in a parcel of stamps destined for someone on the street who paid us money for them.

We moved out about $5000 worth of stamps every month with that scam. Since I was the guy monitoring and ordering the stamps, no one else was keeping track. And because everything seemed to be running smoothly, no one suspected there was anything nefarious going on. Everyone was happy, particularly the 750-member convict population who loved this open canteen concept.

The canteen became our crew's headquarters. I had a television in there and some couches and other amenities. We had birthday parties and smoked dope. It was pretty cool.

When the prison kitchen did an inventory and found they were missing a portable stove, they came to the canteen. "This is the only place the missing stove could be," they said. "Can we just see it so we can check it off on our inventory list?"

There were only two keys to the canteen. I had one; the other was locked in the chief keeper's safe. It had to be signed out because there was $30,000 worth of stock in the store. Naturally, I kept the place locked and secure. To get in or to even talk to me, the guards first had to knock on the door.

From my position in the canteen, I had a pretty good view of what was going on throughout the prison. I must point out here that jail culture in Canada is unique. The prison system is smaller and much more conservative than in the United States. There isn't as much rape and racial violence, or roving gangs. In the American system, sex offenders often go into the general prison population; in Canada, they go into protective custody because they are in serious jeopardy of being murdered.

That doesn't mean there is no sexual abuse in Canadian prisons. If you're a lifer, you recruit the younger prisoners coming in—the eighteen- and nineteen-year-olds—for sex. You do it craftily, though, without strong arm tactics. You start by getting them into your debt: you befriend them, get them high on dope, and then you say, "You owe me an ounce. That'll cost you a thousand bucks. What? You don't have any money? Well, tough. Pay me or I'll kill you. Or, you can give me your body."

I saw all of this from my vantage point in the central canteen and was continually paying off kids' debts so they wouldn't be forced into the sex thing. Sometimes the lifer didn't want the debts paid off. I would have to go into the yard with a weight belt strapped around my waist and a couple of knives sticking out of it and say to the lifer, "You've got a choice. You and I are going to war. If you go to war with me, you go to war with my crew. But if you forgive this kid's debt, I'll give you $500 and we'll call it a day."

Eventually my partner said, "Serge, this is nuts. You're going to get yourself killed. You've got a dozen kids hanging around you. They have to report to you and stay out of debt. We'll have to start calling you 'Mother.'"

In retrospect, I can't help thinking my actions in this regard were the beginnings of a social conscience for me. In some ways, my care for these young convicts was an echo of the days when I carried nickels for the little kids on the street.

Why was this suddenly happening to me? I believe I had reached a level of power where I literally could dictate whether someone else lived or died. It had taken me many years and a lot of time in solitary confinement for beating and stabbing people to earn that reputation. I had risen in the criminal hierarchy to the point where I was acknowledged as a power broker, a big money-maker, a man who was extremely dangerous and would go to the edge with you. In other words, I could have you killed without doing it myself and without having go to solitary confinement for the deed.

Ironically, I had all that power and was running a top crew of criminals, yet I was developing a social conscience. To me it says that, even then, I wasn't all bad. There was something redeemable inside me, something good left over from the moral direction my mother had tried to give me as a little child.

During my incarceration at Collins Bay, I again became an advocate for convicts and was the first prisoner in the history of the Canadian penal system to represent another convict in front of the parole board. I appeared at a hearing on behalf of Eight Ball. I don't remember his real name, but he had an 8-ball tattooed on his forehead. Eight Ball was brain-injured when he tried to escape from the Prince Albert Penitentiary and fell off a wall, cracking his head on the way down and landing on his feet. The impact drove his legs up into his body and he walked with a shuffle forever afterward.

The highlight of my stay at Collins Bay Penitentiary was taking over the organization of the Exceptional People's Olympiad in 1981.

The city of Kingston, where Collins Bay Penitentiary is located, has a number of large facilities for the developmentally handicapped. The Exceptional People's Olympiad was an annual competitive sporting event put on by penitentiary inmates for the students in those institutions.

The Olympiad was originally the brainchild of a French clique from Montreal, a powerful group of guys in Collins Bay who figured it would be a good 'make work' project. The event afforded the clique an office, screen-printed t-shirts and running shoes, and offered a fun weekend for everyone because the convicts participated as chaperones and judges in the various sporting events. The organizers also hoped it would get them early paroles.

Of course, everybody thought the Olympiad was a great idea, including the warden who could see some nice praise coming his way for having his convicts involved in such a worthy community initiative.

The Olympiads of previous years had been resounding successes, but now the French clique was gone, and the Exceptional People's Olympiad was in danger of falling by the wayside.

My partner Peppy came to me and said, "Serge, I was here when the French crew started this thing. I think you should take it on. Do you know what's involved? You get your own office and there are plenty of good scams we could run. Besides, the convicts get something of it, too. There's a big payoff for the whole population. What do you say, Serge? Why don't you take it on?"

"I understand there's another crew that wants it," I said.

"Yeah, but we don't want them to have it."

"Why?"

"It's Jimmy Cavanaugh and the Christian crew."

I said, "I see what you mean."

The Christian crew left a bad taste in my mouth. They had once brought Charles Colson to Collins Bay Penitentiary to speak. Charles Colson was part of U.S. President Richard Nixon's inner cabinet and was indicted in the Watergate Scandal. While in prison, he became a Christian and upon his release, started Prison Fellowship Ministries which now operates all around the world.

On his visit to Collins Bay, I went down to the auditorium with my crew and booed him. After generally disrupting things, we left. (I have since spoken with Charles Colson personally. Ironically, it was through the ministry he started that my life was eventually turned around 180 degrees.)

"If the Christian crew takes on this Olympiad, it will die because nobody will get involved," I mused aloud, weighing the alternatives. "Except for Jimmy Cavanaugh, nobody wants to have anything to do with the Christian crew."

I liked Jimmy, maybe because I knew something of his story. He got a life sentence at fifteen for attempting to kill a cop. Jimmy was a pretty tough guy who had, in fact, killed another convict in Millhaven, but he came to the point where he wanted something else in his life to fill the void and displace the hate. He decided to become a Christian. It was after that that Jimmy was crippled by a brain embolism. He thought he would never walk again, but he did. Jimmy was the real deal, and people respected him. But he was the only guy in that crew they did respect. A lot of the convicts in the Christian crew just played the game. They were a disreputable lot, scum at the low end of the food chain. I knew if they took on the Olympiad, the whole thing would collapse.

"If you take it on," my partner urged, "everyone will support it."

"Okay," I said.

If I still had doubts, his next remark cemented my resolve. "You could probably get an early parole out of it."

Early into the preparations for the Olympiad, there was word a riot was about to break out at Collins Bay. A couple of groups, the lifers and the ten-plus (guys doing more than ten years) were unhappy about something and threatened to riot. Since that would have jeopardized my plans for the Olympiad, I went around to see them.

"Listen, you guys," I said. "I've got an Exceptional People's Olympiad coming up here, and I don't care what your grievance is. If you guys put this riot together and shut the joint down, I will be very unhappy with you. If you cause me grief, I will cause you all kinds of grief afterwards. Listen to what I have to say: you will stop this."

It is interesting and somewhat ironic that when I went in to speak to the ten-plus group, the man who would become the national director of the John Howard Society, Graham Stewart, was sitting there. As a result of the incident, he became one of my references during my parole board hearing and related how I stopped an impending riot and was such a good influence on the penitentiary. In reality, I didn't care if they rioted or not. I just didn't want them screwing up my Olympiad.

We got the Exceptional People's Olympiad incorporated as a non-profit charity (the first time that ever happened in a Canadian penitentiary, before or since) and then I went to work raising funds for it. I had plenty of lucrative contacts. We got donations and financial support from all our criminal friends: the Jewish mob out of New York, the Irish and Italian mobs out of Montreal, the Italian mob from Toronto, and the Italian mob in Hamilton, as well as three motorcycle clubs: Satan's Choice, the Paradise Riders, and the Vagabonds.

We put together a construction crew made up of all the bikers in the penitentiary and built a full-sized professional running track. The gravel alone cost $60,000. I also had a stage and an official Olympic-styled podium built. We obtained an authentic Olympic torch for the Torch Run which we organized through the streets of Kingston.

It was a big deal. I called a press conference and everybody in the media came. No convict in the history of the Canadian Penitentiary Service had ever called a press conference before. It caused quite a stir within the administration. I set it up in the warden's boardroom. He freaked when all the reporters appeared.

"Who called this press conference?" he demanded.

"Serge, the chairman of the Olympiad committee," the reporters said.

"Oh."

We arranged for hockey stars Gump Worsley and Guy LaFleur to kick off the opening ceremonies. (Our first choice for keynote speaker was Maria Schreiver from the Kennedy family, but that didn't work out.) We got Gump and Guy through our contracts in Montreal; it was a case of the right people contacting their agents or their drivers.

I booked a Scottish pipe band and highland dancers to come in for the closing ceremony. When they tried to bring their swords in for the Sword Dance, Security got all up in arms. They couldn't believe what was going on.

"They have to have the swords," I said. "They can't do the dance without them. I give you my word. Nobody will get stabbed and all the swords will leave with the dancers. Just let them in."

They did.

About three hundred developmentally-challenged kids participated in the Olympiad. Each one got a t-shirt, a baseball cap, and new running shoes. There was pizza and candy floss everywhere. It was an unbelievable time—three full days of celebration. The athletes were treated like royalty. Each had his or her own convict 'godbrother,' as we called them, to coach and support them. All the convicts got three t-shirts each, a baseball cap, and a new pair of running shoes.

The event wound up with a huge awards banquet where we gave out trophies like the Satan's Choice Cup, the Vagabond Cup, and the Para-dice Cup. Families and the public came. Staff from all the different centers attended. There were dignitaries and politicians all over the place. Even the commissioner of penitentiaries came. So did the newspapers. Of course, we made sure there were plenty of photo opportunities.

Putting on the event like that involved a lot of hard work, and I lost thirty pounds in the process.

The biggest payoff was being granted a parole for my efforts. In March of 1982, after serving three years of a nine-year sentence, I was granted a full, maximum parole.

TEN

I stepped out onto the street ready to rock and roll.

During our time in Collins Bay, my partner Peppy and I had put together some elaborate plans. We had also put together a pretty good crew.

One of our key people was David, probably the world's largest exporter of hashish. He came out of the Punjab in India, near the Pakistan border. David was a doctor of laser surgery, educated in the London School of Economics. He came from a very wealthy family and was well-connected. In fact, his partner in India was part of the Indian prime minister's family.

David had a very serious contact for brown Pakistani heroin. (Heroin comes from the poppy plant, and there are two kinds: white, or China White, which comes out of the Golden Triangle in Thailand and Cambodia; and brown, which comes out of Pakistan.)

I met David in the Don Jail. He was in the same cell range being held on a charge of importing hashish oil. He was arrested going into Belgium when his driver/bodyguard gave the wrong passport. The authorities grabbed him and brought him into Canada. We became close friends.

David was given a fifteen-year prison sentence and sent to Millhaven to be classified. Through his lawyer, we made the recommendation that David should apply to go to Collins Bay Penitentiary so he could be with us. Our contacts in Millhaven reception unit oiled the process.

We knew David had an elaborate distribution network in Canada for hashish, and we were also aware of how much we could do in India through him. Our strategy became three-pronged: to get David back to the Punjab; to send Peppy to India to work with David and learn the trade; and to get me out of prison so I could manage the Canadian end of things until we got Peppy back into the country.

In order to get David on his way back to India, we first needed to get him transferred to a minimum-security farm camp. Since he was in for a non-violent offence and this was a first-time sentence for him, and because he was only five-foot-five and not a violent man, it was not too difficult to have him transferred to Beaver Creek. Naturally, he disappeared in very short order.

It should be noted that to make the arrangements for all these various movements from prison to prison, we were reaching into the federal government and touching members of parliament. It cost us $10,000 and a case of Chivas Regal[34], but we invariably got the job done.

David went to Amsterdam, Holland, where we had purchased a hotel to use as a destination. Here anyone from our organization could stay, switch passports, and move on. We had a collection of fake, stamped passports under different names for different destinations.

The second part of our strategy was to move Peppy as soon as he was allowed out of prison on a pass. Peppy had been convicted for a clandestine drug lab in Barry's Bay, Ontario, near Napanee. It was the largest drug bust in Canadian history to that point, and he received a nine-year sentence. However, because of his involvement in the Exceptional People's Olympiad, Peppy was now eligible for day passes.

On his first pass, we arranged for Peppy to go to my people in Montreal and hide out there for a while. Then we shipped him off to India.

One of the first things he did in India was remove his fingerprints. He did so by slicing into the pads of his fingers and inserting blue Draino granules under the skin. Then he bandaged up his fingers until they healed. It was a very painful process. He was on opium for several weeks, and was very, very sick, but the end result was a mess of scars

[34] Chivas Regal - a brand of scotch whiskey

where identifiable fingerprints used to be.

Peppy met up with David in the Punjab and started our first drug lab to manufacture crystal meth. We saw setting up a factory in India to be a huge opportunity because we could make immense quantities of drugs there for very little cost.

I finally got my parole and went immediately to Montreal to serve it.

"Do you have a job to go to?" the parole board inquired. I needed one in order to secure parole.

"Yes, I have a job," I said. It wasn't really a job; it was more like a scam with a good flim-flam artist who had the Canadian contract for a vending machine company. The machines dispensed candy, pop, detergent, and the like.

Vending and laundromat machines—anything with cash money going through—are very popular with criminals because the money collected is not be traceable.

On my release from Collins Bay, I rented an apartment and began pulling together a crew. Peppy's wife came, so did a couple of our key guys, J.C. and Larry. At the same time, I was looking up all my Quebec contacts and re-establishing and cementing old professional criminal relationships. Among them were the Irish crew, the Italian crew, and the Lebanese crew who were part of Peppy's gang. We amalgamated into one big crime family, about seventy strong.

Now that we were manufacturing massive amounts of speed[35] in India, all we needed were some good pipelines to get it into the country. One strategy we used was hiding product inside a shipment of replacement parts for Mercedes-Benz trucks. The parts were like huge rubber shock absorbers which we hollowed out and stuffed with meth. Each part could easily hold a pound of meth, and with the drug selling here for $10,000 a pound, it became a very valuable load, indeed.

We also smuggled drugs inside the hollow components of bamboo furniture.

A couple of loads sailed in from India on the 90-foot sloop we purchased. Because of weather, we could only go that route twice a year, but on each occasion we brought in five tons of hashish. We ran the sloop right up to the docks in Montreal where the Irish crew worked.

---

[35] Speed - methamphetamines or crystal meth

Even more efficient was bringing our drugs by the container load into the United States. Since our Philadelphia mob contacts controlled the airport there, we made arrangements to fly the containers to Philadelphia. Each one had about 5,000 kilos or 12,000 pounds of hashish inside, worth approximately $15,000 a pound.

Like all containers that originate in a foreign country, these ones were sent directly to a cargo warehouse for inspection. Our gaff[36] was to change the designation on the paperwork so the container was taken from the bonded warehouse and put on the domestic side as if it were simply being moved from one destination to another within the country. For that, we paid out one-third of the load to our people in the Philadelphia syndicate. They shipped the container to a warehouse in Canada; we sold the drugs at a good high price and gave them one-third of the money. It was a satisfactory working relationship all around.

We also smuggled drugs using David's established contact with an African diplomat. Because this person had diplomatic immunity, his luggage was never inspected. He would bring in five kilos of heroin at a time inside the walls of his suitcase. That pipeline cost us $10,000US, but each load he brought made us a quarter of a million dollars.

On one occasion, I picked up a delivery of heroin from the diplomat myself, and brought it to my apartment. Unfortunately, I forgot to wear gloves and a mask, and when I opened the package, the fine heroin powder flew all over the place. I got higher than a Georgia pine. It took me about three days to come down.

We only moved heroin a few times. I was edgy about handling something that could get us a life sentence. Designer drugs were much safer because they were still under the Food and Drug Act in those days and possession got you a maximum of ten years. That has since changed. In 2005, crystal meth was sectioned under the Narcotics Act. Now it, too, can get you a life sentence.

Suffice it to say, I was getting jittery, so once we made our nut[37] — around three quarters of a million dollars — I said, "No more heroin. We have hash and crystal meth coming in from India. We don't need the heroin anymore."

Eventually, Peppy came back from India and we were ready to set up a clandestine drug manufacturing laboratory in Canada. The details

---

[36] Gaff - trick or deceit

[37] Made our nut - covered operational costs

for doing so had fallen into place quite nicely.

Glassware and burners, essential for the manufacture of drugs, were very difficult to come by. You had to register them. It was one of the ways the RCMP monitored drug manufacturers, by identifying who had the sophisticated equipment and speculating on why they needed it.

We got our manufacturing equipment as a result of a batch of meth-gone-wrong. The chemist for an Italian syndicate in Montreal butchered a load of meth worth about $30 million. He couldn't get it to crystallize.

A mutual friend said, "I know some lab people who can fix this."

The mob guy contacted us.

"Sure, we can do it," I said.

"What will it cost us?"

I said, "If you're running a lab, you must have access to chemicals and glassware. That's what we need for our own lab."

And so, in correcting the load of speed, we tapped into a safe source of chemicals and equipment. As a bonus, because this mob guy was a major cocaine dealer, he also gave us an ounce of cocaine every week.

We bought the largest retail pharmaceutical outlet in Montreal and also purchased a pharmaceutical company in Britain so that we would have a ready supply of chemicals and capsules for our designer drugs. As well, we acquired lingerie companies and tanneries for the chemicals and dyes we needed to run the labs.

With everything in place, we went to work, and were soon generating about $130 million worth of drugs a year. It was an amazing period of time. We owned numerous liquidation companies; I personally owned forty-five laundromats through which we laundered the money we made.

Our operation grew to the point where there were multiple fingers in many different pies and we needed to establish a sharper delineation of duty. We designated Peppy to take care of the importing, manufacturing, and chemical side of things. Our front people for the lingerie companies and tanneries were three fellows with roots in the Middle East. They were also our bankers. One was a Jewish fellow who once ran for mayor of Autremont, the richest suburb of Montreal. The second man was Syrian, and the third was a Lebanese fellow we called Uncle because he was the uncle of Peppy's girlfriend. Uncle had been a mover and shaker for years in Dubai and other places, trafficking in emeralds and diamonds. He was always on the shady end of things, though never involved in overt criminal activities. His worldwide connections were very valuable to us.

My role as co-leader of the family was to set up a series of numbered companies. Uncle introduced us to a lawyer who helped us do all that.

It should be noted that organized crime cannot operate at this high level without accomplices who are willing to be involved. There must be business people, straight people, connected people in the banking world, the business community, and the legal system who are willing to be corrupted. We corrupted them all.

Our lawyer, for instance, was one of the top corporate lawyers in Quebec. One of his children was head of the Young Liberals. I would go in every few weeks to set up a new numbered company and sign the papers with a different name each time. It was a clear case of nudge, nudge...wink, wink. I didn't tell him what we were doing, but was I asking him to break any laws? Not really, although he was perfectly aware I was not who I said I was, and he couldn't help but suspect there was something nefarious going on. Of course, he was making huge sums of money off each transaction.

We had a numbered bank account in Liechtenstein that controlled three numbered companies in the Bank of Hong Kong. Each of those owned three more numbered companies that were registered to the Grand Cayman Islands. From the Grand Caymans, we used a bank in Montreal. I had the lawyer set up a whole array of numbered companies in Montreal and it was through these companies that we purchased vehicles and property. I owned a couple of houses, a five-bedroom chalet in the Piedmonts, several condos, even a farm with a mountain. No names appeared on any of the accounts or properties.

The hotel in Amsterdam and the pharmaceutical company in Britain were owned by a numbered company out of the Bank of Hong Kong. Anything in the United States came out of our bank accounts and holding companies in the Grand Caymans. We also used the numbered companies to wash and move money and pay the taxes. Ironically, we were among the biggest taxpayers in Quebec, out-generating Proctor & Gamble in Canada in terms of yearly earnings.

The forty-five laundromats, which were also owned by a numbered company, might earn $10,000 a week, but we declared revenues of

$75,000 a week and paid taxes on that amount. The company would turn around and use the money to buy a house or something else for us, or the money was reinvested.

My role with the finances stopped after opening up the numbered companies in Montreal. They were split into two categories: some for washing money, the rest for operations. The ones for washing money were channeled to Uncle. I gave him all the money that came to me and he flushed it through.

I was also the distribution network, handling all the drugs, and generally all the chemicals that came in. It was Peppy's job to manage the laboratory and make sure the product was manufactured. He sent it on to me and I would move it to our stashes. No one but me—not even Peppy—knew where the stashes were located.

I actually had several stashes for heroin, hashish, crystal meth, and the other designer drugs we made, like quaaludes and ecstasy. The main stash was in a highly secured building that had security guards, cameras, and double locks. It was open only from 9 a.m. to 8 p.m. Most of the offices and outlets were occupied by diamond importers and jewellery manufacturers. We rented our space through one of our numbered companies.

The actual trafficking was done through a network of distributors who were bikers, organized crime people, or a combination of organized crime families. We controlled Ontario's drug needs with two distributors, and Quebec's, with one. Through the person in Quebec we also supplied Upper New York, New York, and the people in Philadelphia. We had a lock on Florida, as well. Typically, we would deal with the president of one motorcycle club. How he distributed the drugs after that was immaterial to us.

The only one of our crew who met the distributors was me. When I went to see any of them, the meetings were prearranged up to a month in advance, but never through phone calls. We didn't believe in having telephones. The only time we talked to one another by phone was on special sidewinder phones fitted into custom-made attaché cases. They were not part of the regular telephone system; you had to have the other half of the magic pair in order to communicate. These special phones were equipped with scramblers so that whatever you said was garbled to anyone listening in.

We had all the latest high-tech electronic devices. When you came to talk to me, we swept you for bugs[38]. We swept our houses and

---

[38] Bugs - listening devices

apartments daily, as well as our vehicles. We had a bank of scanners that could pick up all the undercover radio channels the cops and the RCMP used, and we had it manned 24-hours a day.

I got so paranoid about being caught that I wouldn't fly in an airplane because of the RCMP presence at airports. To get from Montreal to meetings in Toronto, I would catch the overnight Red-Eye train. I would sleep all the way there, get up the next morning, have a half-hour meeting with someone, then get back on the train and go home. No money was exchanged, nor did I pass over any drugs. All I did was arrange the details for the next delivery of drugs and money.

Our reputation was such that we could do a $10 million drug deal without a sample. We guaranteed our product. You bought it, it was delivered, the product was the quality we said it would be. We learned very early on that, as with every other commodity traded in the world, you needed to have an impeccable reputation. Our reputation was based on the fact that we used only the best product, and we were very efficient and completely honorable in all our dealings.

The drugs themselves were delivered by runners. We would pack the load behind the inside door panels of a vehicle. We especially liked station wagons, and had a whole network for purchasing them.

The car became the load. One of our guys would drive a car to Montreal, for instance. It would be loaded with a hundred pounds of meth worth about a million dollars, and for all intent and purpose, he was just delivering a car. The paperwork for the vehicle was all in place. He would throw the keys to the recipient, hop on a plane, and come home. Once the drugs were removed, the recipient could do whatever he wanted with the car. Most were cut up and the pieces thrown in a junk yard to end the trail.

Like everyone else in our organization, the driver worked on a salary. If he moved nothing, he still got a salary; if he moved something, he got a bonus. Even the strong-arm guys—our collectors and security—were on salary.

The money we made was phenomenal, and I became a workaholic.

All the while, I was on a full national parole. I went to the parole office as required, sat with my parole officer for an hour, told him what he wanted to hear, then walked back to my Cadillac parked two or three blocks away. I had a staged apartment under my legitimate name where they could go and check if they wanted to, though I never went there myself.

Officially, I was on welfare. (I lost my 'job' with Jimmy when he had to pull the plug on the vending machine scam and go back to Ontario.) So now I was going to my parole officer to collect bus tickets "so I could look for another job." Had he bothered to check, he would have found the apartment in my name cost far more in rent that any welfare cheque could begin to cover.

For two and a half years everything seemed to be going along just fine. But as often happens, unbeknown to us, a couple of things were happening simultaneously.

In Toronto, David's guys had made a couple of big heroin moves and had decided to get out of heroin and concentrate on designer drugs which would draw a lighter sentence if they were caught. They had one last heroin deal going down in a hotel room somewhere in Toronto.

They didn't know it, but the hotel suite was bugged. During the conversation, they repeatedly referred to someone named Serge in Montreal. They also talked about Chubbs (the nickname I had earned from being able to crack Chubb safes).

Of course, the crew got busted[39]. The police retrieved the wiretaps and heard all about this fellow in Montreal named Serge who wasn't involved in that particular deal, but was obviously part of some very big action.

We were closely connected with both the Quebec mob and the French mob in Quebec, and it so happened that two major crimes cops were having coffee together in a surveillance car when they spotted one of the top Quebec mob guys moving boxes from one van to another. The cops knew it must be something important for this fellow to be doing the manual labor himself, so they immediately put a tail on the second van.

The trail led from Quebec City to Montreal where it met a third van. I got out of that third van, and the police watched while the load was moved to my vehicle.

When they attempted to follow my van, they would have noticed that we were running a caravan[40] with me in the middle, a crash car in front, and a block car behind. All three of us were communicating on

---

[39] Busted - arrested

[40] Run a caravan - move an illegal load of drugs or swag (stolen goods) with a block car behind and a crash car in front

walkie-talkies.

A crash car is reinforced with concrete. If the police put up a road block, the job of the crash car is to sacrifice itself and smash through the road block. The block car bringing up the rear functions similarly, blocking anybody who might come at the middle car from behind.

The police tailing us would also have observed our driving strategies: making lane transfers where our three-vehicle caravan moved in sync from the slow lane to the fast lane, then slowing down to jam up traffic in order to see if anyone was following, paying attention to who moved and who didn't.

Observing all this they might have thought, "Whoever these guys are, they're good. They're experienced. They have got to be top-end criminals, and whatever they're moving is important. We are onto something big here."

Of course, they had pictures of the van, the license plate, and the guy driving it, and it didn't take long to determine that the van was connected to a numbered company. Further investigation revealed a warehouse listed to the same company—a warehouse in which we happened to have a lot of chemicals stored. Naturally, they put a watch on that, too.

One very snowy, blustery, winter night, I came out of the warehouse and noticed a van parked opposite. All the other parked vehicles were piled with snow, but this one was clean, even though its tire tracks had filled in. I knew immediately it was a surveillance vehicle that was clear of snow because it was heated. It also had darkened windows which meant the people inside were probably taking my picture while I stood there looking at them.

I slid into my car and started driving. Picking up my portable phone with the scrambler, I said one word:

"RED!"

Everyone hit the mattresses[41].

The lab we had going stopped dead.

A 5000-kilo shipment of hashish had just arrived; we left that, too, which was a good thing because a separate group of RCMP and DEA agents were sitting on it to see who would pick up that load. They got tired of waiting when we didn't come, and simply confiscated it. It was

---

[41] Hit the mattresses - went into hiding

only when we went back later that we discovered how close the police had been.

We walked away from the warehouses and all the vehicles and went underground for about three months. It was part of the game, part of our contingency plan. The whole crew went up to the Piedmonts, to my five-bedroom chalet with its heated, in-ground swimming pool. We also had a club up there. One side was a disco, the other a high-classed restaurant. We simply closed the club for the summer and used it ourselves, holding goat roasts and pig roasts, calling friends up from Montreal, and opening up the disco for our own enjoyment. We spent the whole summer up there and had a great old time.

ELEVEN

In the fall, we surfaced again and started a new drug lab from scratch. For the first time, I had an active part in the drug lab action.

We purchased a piece of mountain property in Northern Quebec, almost at the mouth of the St. Lawrence River. The property had three lakes on it and two rustic chalet cabins. When you looked across the landscape, you couldn't see the buildings because they were hidden in a natural hollow. It was very remote; we used four-wheel drive Toyotas to get in.

We bought the place so we could fit out the chalets as laboratories and manufacture drugs there during the winter.

We brought in Brainiac, our old lab guy from Ontario. He was busted with Peppy in the 1970s for the very first drug lab in Ontario, and had served his sentence. Now he was out and ready to go back into action.

Since Peppy was busy setting up a drug lab for us in Glen Sutton, we decided we would use Brainiac for this operation and I would go in with J.C., my muscle, my right-hand guy. Together we would do the lab run and bring out the product.

Around February, we went up to the property and got things started. Because we knew we were made[42] on the Code Red operation,

---

[42] Made - the police were onto us

we were a little jittery and took extra precautions to avoid attracting attention. None of the buildings had power or running water so we put generators into the second building for heat. To obtain the water supply necessary to manufacture the drugs, we drilled about three feet through the lake ice and sank a shaft to bring up water. We also installed a vent system in one of the chalets. When you are manufacturing drugs, you have to vent the place because the chemicals involved are highly unstable and could easily combust and blow the place sky-high.

With no heat in one of the buildings, venting systems in both, and minus forty degree temperatures outside, we were excruciatingly cold. We wore big coats and two pairs of long-johns each, and still we were freezing.

There was another problem.

Brainiac was rusty. This was his first lab run in ten years, and since labs were not supposed to be my part of the operation, we decided to do the full load in one run instead of breaking it in half as we usually did. That meant working seventy-two hours straight through without a break.

It was a very high stress situation. As the hours ticked by, we became extremely tired and cold. Not only were we freezing, we were running cookers and petri dishes and trying to get the crystallization process to work in a place that was frigid.

Because Brainiac wasn't quite sure what he was doing, we decided we should do a hit[43] of the stuff to see if we had missed a step or if the batch had crystallized properly. J. C., Brainiac, and I became the guinea pigs.

As if things weren't already tense enough, they got really complicated when J.C. went out into the fields surrounding the property to do some security sweeps.

He never came back.

Brainiac and I looked all over for him, but all we could find were his tracks leading off the property. We later learned that J.C., being very high on the sampled drugs, became paranoid when he saw some tracks in the snow. He was convinced there were people out there watching us, and he bolted off the property. He stole a car in the nearby village,

---

[43] Do a hit - take drugs by snorting, injecting, or inhaling

and took off. He was too high to realize the tracks he saw were his own.

"Something's going on here," I said to Brainiac when we couldn't find any trace of J.C. Remember, it was only a few months earlier that we'd hit the mattresses on the last operation. I wasn't taking any chances. I said, "I'm going to call Peppy, and we're going to pull the pin on this."

I got Peppy on the emergency sidewinder phone. He came up with trucks and a crew and we began dismantling the lab.

"We'll separate the product from the glassware and the lab," Peppy said. "The product is good. Serge, you take the product and follow me. We'll take it to our new stash. Then we'll come back, get the rest of the lab, and clean this place out so there isn't a trace of it left."

To Brainiac he said, "You stay here and start cleaning up. Box whatever you can. We'll be back with another crew in about six hours to finish up."

Brainiac, having tried some of the experimental drugs, ended up as paranoid as J.C., and instead of cleaning things up as Peppy had instructed, he decided to go out into the trees behind the chalets and keep watch on the place in case someone came. He fell asleep in the bitter cold and froze to death.

When the crew came back to clean up and Brainiac wasn't at the chalet, they assumed he had done the same thing as J.C., so they packed up everything and left.

I began phoning Brainiac's family in Ontario to locate him. "Where is Brainiac?" I asked his wife. "Have you heard from him?"

Of course, the police had wiretaps on the phone lines, and once they began intercepting these urgent calls of mine, it wasn't long before they zeroed in on the property.

Months later, Brainiac's bones were found among the trees, picked clean by wild animals. For a while, the police thought I killed him and my phone calls were a ruse to make myself look innocent. Those same phone calls ultimately became a water-tight alibi for me.

By this time, the police had figured out who 'Serge' and 'Chubbs' were. They had also pegged our various contact points, but they still didn't know the identity of my partner. We were just too careful in everything we did.

We were very systematic, very ingrained, very professional. Twenty-four hours a day we never let down our guard. We all had code names, we never talked on telephones, and never ever inside wired buildings. We didn't own telephones just in case we made a mistake or someone phoning us made a mistake. We never used the same payphone twice. You wanted to make a phone call to Toronto? Great. Use a payphone, but never ever use that same payphone again.

We bought one of the first four-wheel Chevy Blazers that came on the market so we could drive along the highway, go twenty miles past our cut-off, then cross the median and double back to see who was following. We were so cautious, we honestly thought the police could not get near us.

At an estate sale, I had purchased a mountain property in the Quebec Townships. The back end of the property was on the Vermont border and the front was near the ski resort community of Glen Sutton. The fact that the backside butted up to the Vermont border was a plus for us because we planned to use it as a gateway for smuggling marijuana from the United States.

The property was the former owner's homestead and included a farmyard that sat on a plateau high up on the mountain, scarcely visible from below. The farm had been a goat farm and still had a dairy on site for manufacturing goat cheese.

The other interesting feature was a parcel of land at the foot of the property that the former owner had allotted as a cemetery. A large portion of his family was buried there. Because of the burial grounds, no one else wanted the property, but it was a perfect place for us to set up another clandestine drug laboratory.

We were doing quite well until the RCMP traced us to the farm. It happened despite our scrupulous care and state-of-the-art equipment.

We had a bank of scanners at the farm that was manned 24-hours a day, but because we had no telephone, the fellow who manned the radios would sneak out every once in a while to call his wife on a public phone about fifteen miles down the road. On one of those occasions, he neglected to take along the electronic listening device detector we used to sweep any cars or individuals that came on the property.

The cops were watching. They went in, found the 'bug' detector, copied the serial number, and left. They soon had a bug custom-made that the detector could not pick up. The next time our man was out, they hid it in the light fixture over the kitchen table.

Now they had us wired. But even so, they didn't learn much because we were so paranoid we hardly ever talked inside buildings. We mostly went outside to talk, and never used real names in conversations, only nicknames.

As a result, the police misunderstood a couple of our sparse conversations and moved in on us too early. They saw us carrying out a refrigerator and surmised we were taking out a finished load of drugs. In fact, we were throwing the refrigerator in the dump.

We were making a batch of drugs, all right, but it wasn't finished yet. It was still in liquid form, not yet crystallized. The police ended up seizing a load of half-done drugs which meant they had some difficulty in charging us. Yes, we were manufacturing methamphetamines, but they didn't have the finished product to use as evidence against us.

The RCMP came in a busload. We had high security with automatic gates and fences, and Bouvier guard dogs that we bred on the property. The police got past the dogs by throwing drugged meat over the fence to put them to sleep.

It happened about five o'clock in the morning. I was in the shower and thought Peppy and Larry were pulling a trick on me. I figured the yelling and screaming about cops was a gag to get me to run out of the shower naked, so I just continued showering.

Of course, it really was the RCMP.

They came in as a Task Force in riot gear with the whole nine yards: black face shields, body amour, and riot guns. We, on the other hand, didn't have a peashooter on the place.

I opened the bathroom door and found myself face to face with an RCMP officer brandishing a riot gun. I immediately slammed the door shut and looked around desperately for some escape route. There was none.

They marched me out and started taking pictures of me in the nude. I looked over at Peppy and they were doing the same thing to him. Then they brought out Larry.

They put us in individual vehicles and transported us separately to Granby in the Eastern Townships of Quebec. We didn't know it, but that same night they made a sweep across the province and simultaneously arrested the other twelve top members of our crew. From their year and a half of investigation and surveillance, the RCMP knew exactly where to find each one of them.

From Granby, the RCMP took us to a small county jail that they emptied out especially for us. Because of our mob connections, they wanted to keep us hidden away and incommunicado. I don't know exactly where the jail was, but we were kept there until they shipped us out to Montreal.

While we were in the country jail, they had to process us, but that was a problem because none of the jail guards spoke English and we didn't know much French. The whole thing was fairly ludicrous.

When they tried to fingerprint Peppy, all they got were smudges of scar tissue.

They asked his name. "Le nom?"

"X."

"C'est vrai? Son nom est X?"

They asked the RCMP: "Son nom?"

"We don't know." They didn't know because we had never used Peppy's real name. They had only heard him referred to as Peppy. It was a long time later that they accidentally learned his identity when they discovered a photograph of him at his girlfriend's place. They took the photo out of the frame and found his name written on the back. Until that happened, they kept him booked as Mr. X.

To me they said, "Occupation?"

I said, "Goat herder."

"C'est vrai? Goat herder?"

By now we were all laughing and making jokes. It was pure jailhouse humor. We sang Willy Nelson's: *'On the road again…goin' places where we've never been…'* And why not? They had us. We were busted, but no one was hurt, nobody was killed. We didn't know quite what they were going to do with us, but we knew they couldn't charge us with a crystal meth rap because there was no finished product. The probability was they would grab us for conspiracy.

We were held in the little county jail for a couple of weeks, then transferred to a central super maximum security lock-up in Montreal City located in the highly secure Sureté du Québec (Quebec Provincial Police) headquarters building.

Nailing us was a major coup for the police. In an article that appeared in a 1996 edition of *RCMP Gazette*, written by RCMP Sgt. Kevin Graham and entitled 'Kitchens of Death,' ours is listed as the most sophisticated laboratory ever busted. We had eight cookers with cups and vent systems.

The *Gazette* report pegged us this way: *"July 1984 Glen Sutton, Quebec — daily capacity of 11.3 kg. This lab was reported as one of 'the largest and most sophisticated methamphetamine labs with ramifications in Canada, the U.S., the Netherlands, and the U.K.*" The RCMP said their own laboratory was not as sophisticated as ours.

But now they had a dilemma. They didn't have the evidence to charge us with possession, but they could press a charge of conspiracy. They said, "There's a new piece of federal legislation just coming into place regarding the proceeds of illegal gains. We are prepared to grandfather[44] your hearing for as long as it takes for this legislation to pass. But make no mistake, we are going to nail you with it. We'll go after separate counts if we have to– Or we can make a deal."

"Okay," I said, "what's the deal?"

"Your partner will get nine years because this is his second lab. You're the co-leader of this outfit and this is your first lab, so we'll give you eight years. We will convict only the top twelve guys and cut everyone else loose. They'll get five years, four years, and downwards. But you lose everything—all the money, all the property, all the numbered accounts. Everything you own is confiscated."

We made the deal.

The spin for us was that we didn't have to go through months of *voir-dire,* effectively eliminating six months worth of legal expenses.

The RCMP investigation had stretched over eighteen months. They had boxes and boxes of evidence, but with the deal we made, they didn't have to go to trial and neither did we. Instead of getting ten years, ten years, and ten years on separate charges, we just copped[45] to one with everything else running concurrently.

No fuss, no muss.

We made two court appearances.

At our first appearance, the courtroom was filled with cameras and reporters. The place was ablaze with flashbulbs popping. We ended up in all the major newspapers. The headlines read: 'Goat Herder: $40 Million Dollar Drug Lab.' We also made the front page of *Allô Police,* a very popular and long-running Quebec tabloid.

It was all fairly sensational. Here we were, connected with the top mob people and the heads of the biggest biker gangs in North America, and all the while, I was still on a national parole.

Some of the people charged with us were prominent business peo-

[44] Grandfather - delay, stall, postpone
[45] Copped - admitted, confessed

ple like our friend who ran for mayor of Autremont and our lawyer whose family member was head of the Young Liberals in Quebec. Everybody tried to hide their face from the cameras.

Initially, we were sent to maximum security in Quebec's Archambault Penitentiary. Peppy, Larry, and I still had outstanding prison sentences to serve, so we were given special attention. Peppy was eventually transferred to St. Vincent de Paul Penitentiary.

Ironically, I went to LeClerc Penitentiary and began my final prison sentence there.

TWELVE

At LeClerc, I was immediately embroiled in a host of problems. For one thing, the guards were petrified because they'd heard I had a contract out on one of them, and from the day I got into LeClerc, they looked for a way to get me out.

I began my nine-year sentence with the same old attitude I'd had before. My persona matched the macho, tough guy tattoos running up and down both my arms.

Within two months I was controlling the drug trade in the prison along with two other crews. I dove headlong into using chemicals and pills myself, which had not been my habit in previous prison sentences. During the last sentence, I had smoked some dope and done a line of coke once in a while, and maybe had an occasional hit of speed, but now I was continually strung out, doing a good half-ounce of pure cocaine every week. And since there was no shortage of drugs in LeClerc, my behavior became completely outrageous.

I reverted to drug trafficking, lonesharking, and violence. Now I had homemade knives and steel bars concealed in my cell. I was threatening the staff and other convicts.

There was one convict, a young wannabe biker and weight-lifter with a big patch tattoo on his back, who figured my dangerous reputation had to be exaggerated. He was too immature to understand that it isn't the man with scars on his face you fear in prison, it's the man who has no scars. He doesn't have scars because he's the one who puts scars on everybody else. Anyway, this guy foolishly decided he could earn himself a reputation by taking me down a peg or two.

I beat him with a three-foot, steel table leg. He went to the hospital. I went to solitary confinement.

The warden said, "I want you to know this. We're developing a new super maximum security unit at St. Vincent de Paul. It will be a prison within a prison for 175 of the most dangerous criminals in Canada. You are going there as soon as it is finished and we hope you all kill one another. I never wanted you in this prison anyway."

"I don't care," I said with a shrug and settled in to wait for the inevitable transfer to this super maximum security SHU or Special Handling Unit.

The warden put me on a secure segregation order (maximum security solitary confinement) where I couldn't come out of my cell unless I was shackled and handcuffed. I was only allowed out for one hour a day. If I went to take a shower, the handcuffs came off but the ankle shackles and chain waist belt remained in place. I exercised alone. I wasn't allowed visits or communication with anyone. No guards or convicts came near me. My food was shoved through a slot in the door.

Not only was I in solitary confinement, I was in deep seg, which is reserved for convicts who are seriously and genuinely feared. Being in deep seg meant guards came to my cell in twos, and then only when accompanied by a supervisor.

In my deep seg solitary confinement situation, I had plenty of time for reflection. I had come into prison this time with a couple of profound realizations. The first was that I was as good a criminal as I was ever going to get, and they got me. What's more, they got me good. Despite all our organizing, the sophisticated bugs, and our state-of-the-art electronic surveillance equipment, they got us. We had the slickest operation of any in my professional criminal career, and they nailed us. I knew in my heart I was never going to get any better than this.

In every case before, I was able to recognize where I could have done something different, maybe made better contacts to get the job done, but not this time. I was at my pinnacle. It was all downhill from here.

The second realization was that for the first time since 1973, I had absolutely nothing. The millions and millions of dollars I had channeled into holding companies were gone. Even my goat farm was gone. It was sold at public auction, I learned with some bitterness, to an RCMP officer for ten cents on the dollar.

Not only had they taken all my money and my assets, they had stripped away my potential for making money. I had come into prison broke; I would leave prison broke.

When you go to prison, it's always nice to have money and a crew on the outside generating some income to maintain your comfort level in prison. The stark truth facing me now was that I was in jail for the first time in my life with no businesses on the street, no properties, no source of bankroll, no operations generating money for me. There was no one outside, period. Everyone was busted with me. We had nothing left, and I was as good as I was ever going to get.

I had been in dire straits before in my life, but I had never given up or admitted defeat. This time, in my heart of hearts, I think knew I had come to the end of the line, and it was probably that realization more than anything else that triggered my outrageous behavior as I started in on this prison sentence.

The Federal penal system was in the midst of a transition at that point. It was short of maximum security spaces because one stand-alone super max facility just outside of Montreal had to be shut down thanks to pressure put on the Canadian government by Amnesty International (AI) and the United Nations (UN) who deemed the facility inhumane. There were no windows in the prison. Guards walked across the tops of cells, and there was no privacy whatsoever. The prison was like one gigantic concrete box.

"You can't lock people up in boxes," AI and the UN said, and as a result, the place was closed down. The administration was in the process of moving the SHUs out of Archambeault in Quebec, Edmonton Max in the West, and Millhaven in Ontario, to stand-alone special handling units. One was under construction in Renouse, New Brunswick. In the meantime, St. Vincent de Paul Penitentiary was being refurbished following a major riot there to function as a temporary SHU until the one in Renouse was finished.

And so I sat.

No matter what prison you are in, or how many people you talk to about prison, everyone describes it the same way: boring. Prison has to be boring. Think about it. Convicts do the same thing every day, three hundred and sixty-five days of the year. Guards tell you when to get up, when to sleep, what to eat, and when to eat it.

Deep seg solitary confinement is especially boring because you have no association or communication with anyone. You are in your cell twenty-three hours a day and there is a forbidden zone in front just in case someone might want to pass you a kite[46], drugs, or a weapon. You have a one-and-a-half inch thick bullet proof glass window in the three-and-a-half inch thick steel plate cell door and a slot below the window through which your food is passed.

What did I do in my solitary confinement cell?

I devoured everything that was readable, though books were in very short supply. With only thirty-five English-speaking convicts out of a total population of 750 in this Quebec prison, the administration was in no hurry to accommodate us with English-language reading material. As a result, I read everything in English that I could get my hands on.

I paced a lot. You learn to pace in jail. You pace, you do exercises and push-ups, you pace some more. It becomes so mindless that you pace automatically. Your mind is off in a million places, but your feet just keep moving.

To put it bluntly, I was bored to death.

It was during my time in deep seg that I began to watch the actions of a certain volunteer who came into the solitary confinement area every week. I would later learn his name was Jim Yorgy.

My study of Jim Yorgy began one day when I happened to look out the window of my six-by-eight foot concrete cell and witness a very strange sight. Off to the side, in a glass-walled room, I watched the guards bring a man in and strip-search[47] him.

It struck me as very unusual. Not the strip-searching. That was not unusual. Strip-searching is an everyday occurrence for prisoners. Sometimes it happens several times a day, especially for violent prisoners who have been known to carry weapons or drugs on their person. The guards strip-search just to harass, and they often got women guards to do it, just to make the process more embarrassing.

No, it wasn't the fact that this man was being strip-searched that drew my attention, it was the fact that he was smiling. And he wasn't a

---

[46] Kite - message, letter

[47] Strip-search or 'skin fan' - guards remove your clothing to see if you are carrying contraband or a weapon

convict.

All my life, I had prided myself on being savvy about people and able to accurately read human nature. As a young man on the streets and a career criminal in adulthood, being able to read people could mean the difference between life and death. I needed to be able to assess at a glance whether or not somebody was going to nine me[48], shoot me, rip me off, or whatever.

In this case, I was baffled. It was the first time I had ever seen someone smile while being insulted and humiliated.

Out of curiosity, I said to one of the cleaners, "Who is that guy?"

"He's a volunteer."

That, too, I found unusual, and it piqued my interest. What was this guy doing here? I wondered. The guards certainly didn't want him in the solitary confinement unit.

Of all places in a prison, solitary confinement is where you are most likely to have suicides and slashings. It is where they regularly have to call in the riot squad to subdue someone with tear gas. People go crazy in solitary. They run head-first into walls. It gets pretty bizarre in there, and this guy was disrupting the routine of solitary confinement. The guards would be afraid he might see things he shouldn't.

But even though they made it very difficult for him, this man obviously had permission from the administration to be here because he showed up twice a week, every week.

The fact that he was a volunteer made me very angry. Why would someone who wasn't paid to do it come twice a week, every week, just to get strip-searched? He was a fool!

I watched him. Each time he came, the man would go to each cell, stop and speak to the man inside for a few minutes, then hand him some magazines through the slot in the door, and move on to the next cell.

What, I wondered, would possess someone to go through this much humiliation and aggravation to speak to convicts in solitary confinement?

It wasn't like I had a lot of other things to think about, so I became quite fixated with trying to figure out this man's motives. The more I studied him, the angrier I became because he baffled me. What the

---

[48] Nine me - cheat me

heck was it with this guy? I wondered.

I started to time his visits. What days did he come? What were his hours?

He would get to my cell, but because I was in deep seg, he wasn't allowed to speak to me or give me magazines. He would stand just outside the forbidden zone and look at me.

I looked right back at him, and of course, I wore my prison face and practised my best Clint Eastwood snarl.

He wasn't intimidated. He just looked back at me and smiled. He seemed like a very pleasant fellow.

I started to get really miffed. First, because I couldn't figure out what he was about and what motivated him, and second, because of his smiling. How could he smile when he was getting all this aggravation from the guards?

I watched this guy for months.

One day, the warden stopped by my cell. "St. Vincent de Paul is ready," he said. "The English population is going there. You're being shipped out with the next load. Your partner is already there. And remember what I said. I hope somebody kills you."

I shrugged. "Yeah, right."

The next time the little man came in, I again watched him go through his routine. This time, when he came to my cell, I decided I would bring things to a head. It would be my only opportunity because the next time he came, I would be gone.

When he stopped in front of my door, instead of letting him go by, I smashed my body against the steel plate door as hard as I could. It made a thunderous crash. I'm not a big man, only 5'8", but I am barrel-chested and slab-muscled. I learned very early in life that my best advantage was to go on the offensive and do the unexpected. I had been known to bite off someone's ear or the tip of his nose. I had a reputation for being a little 'out there' in terms of going on the offensive to put the other person at a disadvantage. That was my intention on this occasion.

Of course, I startled the man, and he jumped back.

I began screaming at him through the slot in the door. "You are an idiot! You've got to be nuts. What is your trip[49]? You come in here,

---

[49] What's your trip? - What's going on in your head?

you let the screws[50] humiliate you and treat you like a dirt bag. They insult you, yet you come here twice a week and hand out magazines and talk to the garbage that nobody else wants to talk to. You're the stupidest man in the world." Of course, my tirade was liberally peppered with the rawest gutter language I could muster, but by this time, I had worked myself into a real lather.

He paused for a second and just looked at me. "You may be right," he said calmly.

If you ever want to end an argument in a hurry, just agree with the other person. I didn't know what to say. He had just reversed the tables on me. Now I was on the defensive. In my experience, this was not how people reacted. I was used to seeing anger met with anger, insult with insult.

The man went on, "I happen to be a Christian. I know about you. Everybody knows about you. You've made some bad choices along the way, but you weren't born to be what you are today."

"You can choose to believe one of two things," he said, "that you are a fluke of nature, an animal that walks on two legs with no purpose, no beginning, and no end, or you can believe that you are a creation. You were created a person of worth and the only thing that makes you a loser is your own choices."

It was not a retiring, schmaltzy kind of remark. It was a little 'in your face,' and it took me completely by surprise. This man was telling me I was a person of worth created by God?

"I happen to believe that God doesn't make garbage," he told me bluntly.

"I know all about you," he added, speaking quickly because he wasn't supposed to be talking to me. "You are one of the most notorious convicts to walk in or out of prison. I know all the things you've done. As soon as you come to a prison, the guards talk about you because you've broken guards' jaws and you've instigated riots. No matter where you go, they talk about how crazy you are and all the gang stuff you've been involved in. But you want to know something? All those things are cop-outs for the bad choices you have made.

"I choose to believe that everyone is created equal, and I choose to believe that everyone is created excellent. From that point on, it is

---

[50] Screws - guards

the choices we make in life that determine what we become. The most important choice in the world is to understand that you are a creation of God."

I was speechless. I just stood there staring at him.

He took a step back, hesitated, then stepped forward again and shoved some magazines through the slot in my door.

I took them without thinking and threw them on the floor in the corner of my cell.

Then he left.

Supper time came and they brought me my tray. As usual, there was no knife or fork, only a spoon which had to be accounted for when they collected the tray.

I took the food and made it into a sandwich. That's what you do in prison. If you get a steak, you make a steak sandwich. I grew to love mashed potato sandwiches.

As I ate my sandwich supper, I kept looking at the corner of my cell where the magazines still lay. I was feeling a little disgusted with myself because I had accepted them instead of throwing a zinger back at him to get the upper hand, the last word. What I should have done, I told myself, was spit in his face and tell him to keep his mouth shut— or words to that general effect.

However I did love to read, and reading material was in very short supply.

Eventually, I went over and picked up one of the magazines. It was a publication of Prison Fellowship Canada entitled *Jubilee*.

Okay, I thought as I continued chewing on my sandwich, it says the magazine is for prisoners. The cover advertised an article called 'New Life Inside.' I was so desperate for reading material, I figured I could take a look at the article.

I opened the magazine, and bang! There, staring at me, was a good friend of mine, Roy Hill. The story was about him.

Roy was from the Parkdale area of Toronto. I grew up with him. I spent time in jail with him. We were friends. This is like Old Home Week, I thought.

I settled back and began to read.

"What?" I exclaimed aloud. "This guy has gone nuts. Roy's gone soft in the head. He says he's a Christian. What's he talking about? He's a professional brawler, a bodyguard. Roy beats up police officers for sport, four and five at a time. He looks like a typical Irish thug—nose all over his face, great big hands, built like a bull moose. What's he doing in this thing? What is going on here?"

Naturally, I continued reading his story.

Roy told about his life, about being brought up in the West End of Toronto in a home filled with alcoholism and brawling.

"Yeah," I said, "I knew all that."

But now, Roy said, his life was different. He was a Christian.

Oh, no, I thought. He's like that Jimmy Cavanaugh guy over in Collins Bay Penitentiary. What's the matter with these people? Have they lost their wits?

At the end of the article, Roy said something that I will never forget. In the last sentence of the article he said, "For the first time in my life, I have come to know total freedom and peace of mind."

That statement stuck with me. Roy was an unsophisticated strong-arm man, an average guy with a Grade Eight education. He was brought up in the School of Hard Knocks. How could someone like him be making a profound statement like this?

My initial reaction was envy. What is total freedom? I wondered. What is that concept? The answer becomes especially important when you're sitting in solitary confinement waiting for transfer to the SHU.

I thought a lot about Roy, and the article, and this peace of mind he talked about. With peace of mind, did you ever stop worrying?

I had always lived my life on the edge like a hunted animal, aware of everything and every movement. I trusted no one. I was constantly weighing people because I had learned the hard way that you could be betrayed by your best friend.

And what was peace of mind anyway?

The transfer came through to St. Vincent de Paul, the temporary super maximum security penitentiary. It was an old prison—a dungeon. They put me in the SHU, the prison within a prison. There were 175 prisoners in there including my two partners who had been transferred ahead of me.

I was surrounded by professional hired killers convicted of seven and eight murders, people talking to flowers, bug-house dangerous prisoners, and convicts doing double and triple life sentences. Every tough guy in the whole province of Quebec was in there, and it was chaotic.

People were getting stabbed, having their bellies ripped open in the showers. Guards were running around with shotguns, and you knew the shotguns would go off if you got into a fight. You were locked up twenty hours-a-day in your cell.

To protect themselves, everyone made whatever homemade shank[51] they could for a weapon. I had a towel bar in my cell mounted on a piece of wood. I took off the wood, drilled a hole behind it to stash my drugs and knives, then put the wood back on and repainted the screws.

The food in St. Vincent de Paul was the worst I had ever eaten in prison. The only way I could get decent meals was to claim I was a vegetarian and needed a special diet. They gave me a little hotplate and some food supplies once a month so I could cook my own food in my cell.

I couldn't get any good English books and there were no televisions, but my partners and I got a connection going for hashish.

I was back in action—but somehow, things had changed. The haunting realization was always there that I was the best criminal I could be, yet I was sitting in jail again at the front end of a nine-year sentence. I was nearly forty years old without a possession to my name.

I was getting worn out.

I would look at the other guys being transferred in from other prisons, and think, "This is a waste." I would look at myself and think, "My life is a total waste."

My future held nothing, and for the first time in my life, I didn't know what to do. I was already considered one of the old guys in prison. When I finished my sentence, would I do it all over again? I'd only end up in prison again. The prospect was not appealing.

I settled down to a life of dull, colorless boredom.

You lose track of time in prison. My birthday often passed without me even knowing it. Days ran into weeks, weeks ran into months, months ran into years.

Being in the SHU made it even worse. You were locked down for the majority of the day unless you were doing one of two jobs: going to school or making mailbags. And you know me with mailbags. There was a long waiting list to get into school, so I just sat there, putting in time.

---

[51] Shank - homemade prison knife

Over the months, I grew quite close to Glen, the kid in the next cell. He was in prison because he got strung out on speed and robbed three pizza joints with an unloaded shot-gun. When he tried to run away from the courtroom, they gave him a fine of $350 and a nine or ten year sentence at Millhaven Penitentiary. In the reception unit there, a guy raped him. The kid went out, got a knife and stabbed the guy, and since there were only the two of them when the guards arrived, and one guy had a knife sticking out of his chest, it was obvious who put the knife there. They gave the kid another ten years, got him classified as a dangerous convict, and sent him to the Super-Max. He was nineteen years old, doing twenty years in jail.

I really liked this kid. He was from Southern Ontario, and it nipped at the fringes of my consciousness that, in a way, I was responsible for the speed that got him into this mess in the first place. I had controlled the drug labs in Ontario, and my speed went into the city from which he came.

I grew to like this kid. We started playing a little chess together through the bars on the front of our cells.

We were on the second tier of cells. I couldn't really see Glen except at night when his cell was reflected in the wall of glass opposite us. However, whenever we were allowed to leave our cells, he and I were placed beside one another, so we talked, we went to the yard together, and in the process, we developed something of a friendship.

Months went by.

One night I heard unusual noises coming from his cell, the sounds of shuffling and fabric tearing. What the heck was that all about? I wondered. I got up off my bunk to see if I could tell what Glen was doing from the reflection in the window.

The kid had ripped up his sheets and knotted the strips together to make a rope. I watched him sling it around the light fixture, put the loop around his neck, and hang himself.

I screamed for the guards to come and cut him down, but by the time they heard me, Glen was already dead.

I was devastated. In all our conversations, he had never mentioned anything about committing suicide. I should have known, I told myself. There were slash marks on his arms, signs of self-mutilation or perhaps previous suicide attempts.

Responsibility for his death hung over me like a shroud. After all, the whole thing started when he was strung out on my drugs.

Would the course of history have changed without that? I asked myself. It's like the question: What might have happened to WWII and the Holocaust if Adolf Hitler had become a successful painter instead of an frustrated amateur? What would have happened to this kid if my speed hadn't been going through Gooch into his city, the Niagara Peninsula, and Kitchener-Waterloo? What if the speed had not been there? Was this one of my bad choices the volunteer had talked about?

I thought about the article on Roy Hill and what Roy had to say about choices and events.

I thought about my life.

What was the sum total of my life? What was my legacy? Was this it—locked up in a super maximum penitentiary, nearly forty years old, doing nine years, without a dime to my name? In my whole life, this was all I had done, and to what purpose? More important, what was the purpose of my life? What would be my epitaph?

One of my favorite books at the time was *A Stone for Danny Fisher* written by Harold Robbins. The book was about a gangster, Danny Fisher, and the story begins with Fisher talking to the reader from the grave. "What is written on my tombstone?" he asks. "What is my epitaph?"

I asked myself the same question: What was *my* epitaph?

What was the sum total of my life?

Zero. Zip.

The answer was sobering. I realized there was no meaning to my life at all and not a thing worthwhile about it. It was worse than that. The end result of my actions was this kid hanging himself.

Roy Hill's comment in the article about peace of mind and freedom continually churned in my head. Then I would think about the volunteer who talked about God and creation, and my mind would go back to when I was a kid, watching the Jesus puppet in church, and my mother telling me about being worthwhile.

"That's it," I said finally, "I can't deal with this any longer. I can't deal with life. I can't deal with myself. I can't deal with who I am. It's over."

I was so disgusted with myself that I decided to commit suicide, too.

Thirteen

Having made the decision to commit suicide, I wanted to do it the hardest way possible. I decided to starve myself to death.

In hindsight, I can see the irony of that. Growing up as a street child, food was very important to me. For years I lived out of garbage cans, ate from bins behind restaurants, fed on stolen garden vegetables and fruit until I made myself sick with diarrhea. Like people who have gone through war or the Great Depression, I hoarded and stockpiled goods. I still do that. It is something I will probably never overcome.

Why did I decide to starve myself to death? No doubt there was an element of punishment involved because for me, the worst possible punishment would be depriving myself of food until I was dead.

Seven days passed without me eating anything and I still wasn't dead. But I certainly was hungry.

I was also deeply depressed. I hadn't been out of my cell for a week.

My partner Peppy came by. "Why don't you come down to the chapel?" he said.

"The chapel?" I exclaimed. "Why would I want to come to the chapel?"

"There's coffee and donuts there," he said. "Of course, there's also a guard up in a cage with a shotgun, but you hardly notice him. Some of the English guys go there. It's kind of relaxing."

I think Peppy was worried about my mental stability and thought

138

this would be a good place for me to chill out.

I wasn't interested. "Are you nuts?" I said. "The last time I was in chapel I got my jaw broken. Forget it. I'm not going to chapel."

Another fellow came by. He was a big black man who was doing a double life sentence in St. Vincent de Paul for killing the man who raped his sister. When the police came in, he killed one of them. He was glued[52]. He would die in jail.

This guy was my boxing partner in St. Vincent de Paul. We did weightlifting and heavy bag together. I quite liked him. (I was big at the time, probably 260 pounds and in dynamite shape, which may be one of the reasons why it was taking so long for me to die of starvation.) In any case, since the kid in the next cell had hanged himself and I had gone on the suicide-by-starvation binge, I hadn't been working out.

My black friend came by my cell. "Serge," he said, "I'm really worried. What's going on with you, my brother?"

I said, "I've got all these questions and no answers. My life is so screwed up that nothing makes any sense. Even living doesn't make sense. I'm just jammed."

"I've never shared this with you before," my friend said, "but the only thing that keeps me sane is the fact that I'm going to chapel and I've become a Christian. Let me tell you something, Serge. I'm doing double life. I'm going to die here. I have nothing to live for, but this keeps me ticking. In a way, I've found such meaning that if I had to do things all over again and get a life sentence just to find out what that meaning is, I'd probably do it again. That's how much it means to me."

When you're sitting with your head in a senseless whirl, at the bottom of the bottom, lower than you've ever been before in your life, and somebody tells you that, you have to listen.

"You go to chapel?" I said.

He nodded.

"What do you do there?"

"We have coffee and donuts."

Great! Didn't he know I was trying to starve myself to death?

"What else do you do?"

"We sing."

---

[52] Glued - done, sunk, finished

Why he said that, I don't know. We used to work out together and then hit the showers. I had heard him sing. He was terrible.

"Come on," I said, "you sing like a frog. Now tell me, what do you *do* there? You can't just have coffee and donuts and sing. That doesn't even make sense."

"Well, there are these people who come in from the street. They're cool. They ask nothing of you. You can relax, take it easy. It's a good way to get out of your cell for a little while, and you just might find some answers, too."

I certainly needed answers.

"But what do you mean, I can find some answers?" I pressed.

"I'm not going to tell you, Serge. I know you too well. You're one of the stubbornest men I've ever met. Just take my word for it. You need to go. Besides, what have you got to lose? You're not eating; you're not working out. When you first started this starvation thing, I thought maybe you were psyching yourself up to go to war or something. But you're not. Come on," he persisted, "I'm going to the chapel. Come with me."

I shrugged. "Okay, tell the screw[53] to crack my cage[54]."

And so I began going to chapel.

For the first two or three times, I didn't talk to anyone. I just observed the crazy Christians.

The 'cool people from the street' were Larry and Sandy Duguay, a couple who volunteered with a Christian ministry called Prison Fellowship. I got to really like them.

Larry went on to become a chaplain at William Head Penitentiary on Vancouver Island, and Sandy took on the position of British Columbia co-coordinator for Prison Fellowship Canada. Back then, Larry worked as a night janitor in a factory and he and Sandy would come to the prison chapel and sing and talk and answer questions. Larry and Sandy had five daughters. I couldn't help admiring this man for being the father of five daughters.

I still had the Prison Fellowship magazine with the article about Roy Hill, so I wrote to the magazine, asking for more. The next thing I knew, they had fixed me up with a couple of penpals. One was in British Columbia, the other in Ontario. I also started corresponding with

---

[53] Screw - guard

[54] Crack my cage - Open my cell door

the magazine's editor, Donna Sterling, who was executive assistant to Rev. Ian Stanley, the director of Prison Fellowship Canada.

All of a sudden, I was into a new way of thinking and a whole new world where people believed differently and had different values. In this new world, people didn't pry; they took me as I was. I had never run into this before in my life.

My British Columbia penpal was a young mother in her twenties with a baby at home. In her letters, she talked about her life out there and about her husband and where he worked. It was all so normal and so very good for me.

The other penpal family lived in Tottenham, Ontario. The mother wrote volumes to me. I would challenge them and question scriptural accuracies. I challenged the reality of truth in Scripture, and the reality of God.

Prison Fellowship wanted to send me some Christian tapes and literature and an English-language Bible, but there was some opposition to that in the French prison. So I wrote to Rev. Pierre Allaire, the head chaplain for the Canadian Penitentiary System.

"These people are crazy here," I wrote. "They won't let me have an English Bible, and they won't let me have any Christian tapes."

He intervened and got me the stuff. In the meantime, a volunteer smuggled in a Gideon New Testament for me.

The prison population began looking at me as if I were losing my wick. I wondered about it, too. Jesus freaks in jail? Bible thumpers? I'd known plenty of phonies who pled hard mouth[55] to the parole board: "Hallelujah, I'm a Christian now. I'm changed. I'm a different man. You can let me out." Unfortunately, every time somebody plays that as a scam, it colors everybody else.

I thought about Jimmy Cavanaugh in Collins Bay, an attempted cop killer in at fifteen years of age and later convicted of a prison murder. He was legit, although some of the guys who ran with him left me with big question marks.

And then there was my black friend who said he was a Christian...

Nine months later I, too, became a Christian. It was December 25, 1985, on the traditional day of Christ's birth. We had a service in the

---

[36] Plead hardmouth - strike an attitude to gain sympathy

chapel. I thought, "This is the day He came to die. The whole meaning of His life and death was so that I could have life. Is it possible that I can have the same freedom Roy Hill has? What is freedom, anyway? For me, freedom has always been just something to lose. If I had freedom, could I look in the mirror again and not be disgusted? Is that real freedom?"

At two o'clock in the morning, I got down on my knees on the cold cement floor in my super maximum security cell in St. Vincent de Paul Penitentiary and made a commitment in my own rough words. It was just God and me.

Nothing happened. Prison gates didn't open; the cell doors didn't rumble. Horses didn't gallop through the corridor; no blinding lights shone down upon me. But somewhere in the pit of my stomach, I knew I would never be the same again. I knew it was for real.

In chapel about two months later, as a public declaration, I let Larry Duguay lead me in repeating the same words I had spoken in my cell. The sweat was pouring off me. I was soaked, but I needed to do it publicly.

Once I had publicly declared myself to be a Christian, I went to talk to my partner Peppy. I said, "You know, I'm legit about this. I'm a Christian, whatever that means. I'm not quite sure yet, but I do know I can't go back to using drugs and being a drug dealer. I can't do that if I'm going to be a Christian, and I want to be one."

Peppy had known me for a long time. He knew I wasn't a wing-nut. He could tell I was serious about this.

"Good luck," he said. "I respect you. If this is what you want to do, that's cool. I'll support you. But remember, if you ever change your mind, I'm here. There will always be a place for you with me."

I was still smoking dope and packing a knife, and I still had a stash in my cell behind the towel rack. I gave the dope and knives to Peppy. "Here," I said, "I'm done smoking dope." And I meant it.

I realized, if I was going to break out of the funk I was in, I needed to get out of my cell more than three hours a day. Remember, in St. Vincent de Paul, the only way you could do that was go to school or work in the mailbag shop.

When they rebuilt St. Vincent de Paul after the riots, they developed the main cell block as a SHU or Special Handling Unit, but there were still a number of old buildings on the periphery, separate from the main cell block. There was a Psych Ward on the grounds in a separate building in a fenced-in enclosure, and inside that was the old school building. It was a highly desirable place to be.

Peppy was already taking classes, so we pulled some strings and got me into school, too.

The teacher who headed up the prison school was a young man named Michael. He was idealistic and fresh out of university. This was his first teaching job, and he truly believed, as did many of the university professors that I would meet later on, that teaching was a vocation, not a job. They made no judgment calls on you; it was all about expanding your mind and getting you an education.

Michael had small-town roots and obviously saw the value of education as a vehicle. In hindsight, I can see that he blatantly manipulated me for positive purposes. He laid out the rules: the only way I could get into this 'soft spot' was if I took some correspondence courses and tutored some of the French convicts in English.

I had enough street French to be able to communicate with the French guys, so I said, "Yes."

Teaching the French guys didn't last long. I was still too volatile. It was only a matter of time before I would have stabbed one of them in the eye with a pencil or something, but by then, I was bound to the correspondence courses.

The only English correspondence courses Michael could get for me came from the University of Waterloo in Ontario. The university put me on probation in a non-degree program. The agreement was that I could only get more courses if I passed the first two.

I paid for the courses myself. It took all of my canteen money.

I really didn't have much faith in myself. After all, what did I know about university level courses? I didn't know how hard they would be or that with a Grade Five education, I wasn't supposed to be able to do them. And how would I know what courses to choose?

Michael made the choices for me. We looked through the course catalogue together. "I think you should take social work and sociology," he said.

"What the heck is sociology?"

"It's the study of people and cultures."

"Okay," I said. "That should be easy."

And social work—? "I've seen all those dimwit social work nuts around here for twenty years. I should be able to do that. Sign me up."

The material arrived: text books and lectures on cassette tapes. I was required to complete the assignments and write a proctored exam.

"This is crazy," I said. "I can't do this stuff."

But since it was the only way for me to stay in school, I went to work. My innate determination, natural tenacity, and my ability to stay focused kept me at it. I finished both courses and wrote the exams. University level exams require a supervisor or proctor to oversee the writing to make sure no cheating takes place, and Michael did that for me.

When the marks came back, they were in the high seventies. I said to Michael, "These aren't my marks."

"Yes," he said, "they are."

"You're scamming me. Phone that university and ask what I really got," I demanded.

He made the phone call and put me on the line.

Those were my marks.

The look of exultation on Michael's face in that moment made me realize that whatever had driven him to become a teacher was fulfilled that day.

For me, the whole experience of achievement was foreign. With my background as a convict, I had never dealt with anyone before who treated me without judgment, who applauded my success, who expended personal effort on my behalf to challenge and stimulate me. It was incredibly refreshing, and I believe it was the first step on the road toward normality, the first easing of the seriously twisted mess that was my life.

Michael treated me like an ordinary human being. He didn't condone what I had done or judge me on what my background and lifestyle had been, or how much time I was doing in prison. He looked beyond all that and connected with my humanness.

I was literally dazed by my own academic success. I hadn't thought myself capable of completing university level courses, much less achieving high marks. This just wasn't me. Arrange a drug deal? Sure. Plan a bank robbery? No problem. Work the ace gaff[56]? Put a crew together? Absolutely. Forge checks? A breeze. Do funny money[57]? Peel a

---

[56] Ace gaff - a tool for picking circular locks like those on laudromat appliances

[57] Do funny money - make counterfeit money

safe[58]? Use a thermo-nuclear lance and walk through a bank vault? In a heartbeat. But academia? Come on. That wasn't my forte.

And yet, I had done it.

I immediately ordered two more courses. Then three more after that.

Every time the course outline came, I was filled with self-doubt. "I can't do this," I'd say. But Michael would reassure me, encourage me, help me, and instruct me through it.

I became hooked on education. I found it thrilling to expand my mind. I had moved from carrying a paperback about Horatio Hornblower and how he fought Napoleon on behalf of the British Navy to acquiring a more intimate knowledge of the world in which those fictional episodes took place. I was beginning to take the articulate language I already had and put it on paper, to use and exercise my brain, to activate my creativity—things I had never done before.

One day they told me I could leave the SHU in St. Vincent de Paul. It was almost a surprise; I had lost all track of time. All I knew was, I had completed four university courses and was halfway through three more.

They transferred me to Cowansville, a medium security institution in Quebec where I had to argue to keep my correspondence courses. Eventually, I became a full-time student in my cell all day long.

It was in Cowansville that I began to learn something about my Native heritage.

I made the acquaintance of an Indian fellow there. We were having coffee together one day and he said to me suddenly, "Can you get us a Native Brotherhood Room?"

I must have looked puzzled because he went on, "The English have a room, the Jews have a room, the Christians have a Prayer Room, but we can't get a Native Brotherhood Room."

I said, "Why are you asking me this?"

"Come on," he replied. "If you could get a Christian Prayer Room within two weeks of coming here, you can get us a Native Brotherhood Room."

He was right. I walked into Cowansville Penitentiary as an open Christian and one of the first things I did was introduce myself to the

---

[58] Peel a safe - break open a safe

chaplain. I wanted to keep the line open for correspondence from my penpals and Prison Fellowship.

I guess my reputation had gotten around, too, because I had hardly been there a week before a group of Christian guys come to me and said, "We understand you're a Christian. We need a room where we can pray. We can't get one. Will you get it for us?"

I said, "I'm just fish here. I'm brand new."

They said, "Yeah, well, your partner's here. All your main guys are here, so we know about you. We need a prayer room and you know how to make it happen."

I went to the administration and asked for a room where the Christians in the institution could gather to pray between seven and nine o'clock in the evening. We got it.

Now this Indian fellow wanted me to lobby for a Native Brotherhood Room. "What are you going to do in this room?" I asked. "Drink? Party? What?"

He said, "Listen, Serge. I grew up on a reserve. I don't know any Indians who aren't drunks. Look at every Indian here. You went to jail for something that involved a lot of money. There's peanuts involved when we Indians go to jail. We fill the prison system, and we're all drunks. We need to get a spiritual elder in here."

"Why are you bothering me with this?"

He looked at me in surprise. "Because you're an Indian."

"What do you mean?" I said.

"You told me your mother is Cree. That makes you an Indian."

I was stunned. I had never thought of myself in those terms before.

"You got the room for the Christians because you're a Christian. Well, you're an Indian, so why won't you get a room for us Indians?"

What could I say?

I got a room for the Native Brotherhood, and next thing I knew, they were inviting me to be part of the group.

I went down a few times and pretty soon I was speaking to the elder and going to their banquets. I learned about smudging and sweat lodges. I found out about the history and culture of the Indian people—my culture, my people.

I discovered that Native people never drank alcohol until the white Europeans came. I learned that Indian parents traditionally raised their children without discipline because in their culture, it was the place of the grandparents and elders to discipline the children. The parents provided all the physical needs, gave their children comfort and love, and taught the child the necessary survival skills, but in the old Native culture, when a child needed discipline, it was the elders who sat down with the child and decided on the discipline or punishment. If the action was criminal in nature or something that hurt the tribe or another individual, the grandparents and elders would meet in council to decide what should be done. Every elder was an uncle or aunt. They gave wisdom, discipline, and teaching.

It was in the Native Brotherhood Room that I also found out about residential schools. It was the first time I had ever heard about it, and I quickly realized that St. John's Training School was part of that whole system.

I thought a lot about my own history with drugs and alcohol, and it was at that point that I decided to learn more about addictions. I started taking social work and sociology courses that zeroed in on the subject of addictions. From those, I learned that alcohol is a poison to which Indians never developed a tolerance. Through more research, I learned about the genetic patterning for predisposition to alcoholism.

In the Native Brotherhood Room, I gained an education about the part of me that was Native. My mother had told me a little bit about her roots; now I realized they were my roots, too. I began to identify with the noble Indian race. It was a very different perspective from the one I'd had before.

While all this was going on, I was continuing with my university courses and practising my Christianity in practical ways that were changing me as a human being. My faith was gradually honing my character, my heart, my values, and my morality.

I could also see changes in my personality and character. I was gentler, more mellow, no longer looking for a fight. I stopped drugs cold turkey and never touched them again. My language changed, and so did my interests. I was beginning to understand those things called self esteem and self-concept, as well as the ramifications of the physical, psychological, and emotional abuse I had endured in my early life.

Through the courses I was taking in psychology, social work, counseling, sociology, and deviant behavior, I was able to understand some of my own past behavior. I was also aware of the influence my roots and my background had on my addictions, my behavioral patterns, and my anger and rage.

My rage was legendary. It often turned me into a robot. According to my guys, in a fit of anger I would lose all color in my face and go deathly quiet. I completely lost touch with reality and knew no fear. It was as if something had possession of me. Now I was striving to understand all that.

And as understanding gradually came, an unusual thing happened. I began to like myself—possibly for the first time in my life.

I also started to plan for the future. I knew I had to earn a living somehow when my sentence was up, but I had no idea what that would be. I didn't like manual labour; I didn't like working with machines or getting my hands dirty or sticky. So what were my options for supporting myself in the future?

Education was a possibility, but for that, I knew I would have to enroll full-time in a university.

I felt strongly that this change I was experiencing as a human being needed to be put into action outside the prison walls, but I had no idea how that would work, either. The concept was totally alien to me. Remember, from the time of my fifty-five-day rampage in 1971 to that moment, I had never been totally free. I was always on parole or in prison serving a sentence. And even when I was outside the prison walls, the life I lived was anything but normal.

I reasoned that if I could immerse myself in academia, I would have a better chance of making the transition. It would be my cocoon as I began to find out what the world on the outside was really all about.

I began to make plans for that day.

FOURTEEN

Through my correspondence with Prison Fellowship Canada, I had acquired a wonderful mentor in the person of Rev. Ian Stanley, the director of Prison Fellowship Canada. He had been placed in the position by the organization's founder, Charles Colson.

Ian and I became close friends. I bounced everything off him. He even traveled to Quebec to visit me in St. Vincent de Paul.

"Serge," he said, "you have to realize that in becoming a Christian, you have caused some major ripples throughout the system."

What he said was true: the news that I was a Christian had spread quickly. It shocked a lot of people because it was completely opposite to everything that had earned me stature as a criminal. As I said before, I was at the top of the criminal hierarchy in terms of the crimes I committed, the people I knew, the reputation I had carved out through my contacts, my violence, and my many years in solitary confinement. Paradoxically, I had also earned a certain amount of respect for being a man of my word and living strictly by the unwritten convict code.

I was known as a big money-maker, something that generates a lot of respect in prison since ninety-five percent of convicts in the prison system have never seen ten thousand dollars in one place at one time in their lives. Sixty-five percent come from below the poverty line. Very few convicts are successful criminals. I was. In addition, I ran with all the other successful criminals. Whether it was Outlaw Motorcycle presidents or top-level crime bosses, I knew them all.

Because of my reputation and status, everything I did immediately became prison gossip. The news spread quickly on the wire, the underground communications system that operates via visitors, phone calls, and the like. There is an old saying in prison: If you want the news to get out, tell a convict.

That is what happened when I became a Christian, and it caused ripples not only among the convicts in the prison system, but among the guards, as well. Most thought it was a scam.

Ian also warned me that the Christian community has a habit of putting people who have had a dramatic life change on a pedestal and making them into Christian superstars. He knew it had taken skill and intelligence for me to rise to the position I had in the criminal world, so it stood to reason that I would be able to articulate the change that was now taking place in my life. Ian was wise enough to recognize that before I started talking about it publicly, I needed time to get myself untwisted, time to adapt to a 'normal' lifestyle, time to get my feet well-planted on the ground. With that in mind, he challenged me to think about which city I would go to when I was released from prison, and what university I wanted to attend.

That was a problem, all right. I couldn't go to Toronto or Ottawa, and I certainly couldn't go to Kingston. I knew far too many people in high criminal circles in all three of those locations.

But what about Kitchener-Waterloo? The only person I knew there was Dr. Fred Desroches in the Department of Sociology and Criminology at the University of Waterloo. I had come to know him through my correspondence courses. I had listened to his lecture tapes and completed assignments which he received and marked, and through the lengthy exchange, we had become good friends. He was under no illusions about my circumstance; my return address was a penitentiary, after all.

I decided that Waterloo was where I wanted to start my new life on the outside, but in order to do that, I had to get back into Ontario. That posed a unique set of challenges, the biggest one being that I needed to be transferred to an Ontario prison. And because my reputation was so well-established throughout that province's penitentiary system, no one wanted me.

I made an application for transfer, but the Ontario region penitentiary board said, "No."

"You've got him," they told Quebec, "you keep him. We don't want him here."

It took a lot of intervention and a lot of persuasion from people at the Ottawa/Kingston level and Corrections Canada Headquarters to over-ride the decision. Even Rev. Pierre Allaire, the national chaplain for correctional services, got involved.

Weighing the teeter-totter in my favor were a number of people at national headquarters who were beginning to realize that this life-change I claimed to have had was legitimate. Their position became: "We know this guy well. If he says something is true, it is. This is not a scam. This man would not claim to be a Christian as a scam."

My transfer to Ontario eventually came down as an order from national headquarters. The decision was made to make Millhaven Penitentiary my entry point in order to qualify me as a federal convict in the Ontario system. From there I would be processed to Warkworth Penitentiary.

It was quite a reunion for me in Millhaven. The officer in charge of reception there was Mr. John Neely. He and I went back a long way. We had been in prisons together since the mid-1970s and in an ironic way, his career had run almost parallel to mine. He rose through the administrative ranks from correctional officer to keeper, to chief keeper, to officer in charge of reception for Ontario, to deputy warden.

I didn't stay long in Millhaven, but was quickly sent off to Warkworth Penitentiary, a medium-security penitentiary located just outside of Campbellford in Northern Ontario. I was only there for a little over a year, but in that short time everything good that I had become came very close to being unraveled.

It was a huge step for me to ask for a transfer to Warkworth. It was a flagship facility, the newest, most modern penitentiary in Ontario. Warkworth incorporated all the new conventions for rehabilitation: living units, pods, and fewer guards who now dressed in street clothes. All these new innovations were borrowed from a European model.

Warkworth was intended for first time offenders—those who were coming to prison for the first time and could still be 'saved.' It was for white collar criminals, too, who had made the mistake of defrauding people of their life savings. Unfortunately, Warkworth was also the place where they put the overflow of sex offenders now that Kingston Penitentiary was full to the rafters.

Putting them in a higher security prison would have been tanta-mount to issuing them an automatic death sentence. As I've said before, in prison culture, it is every convict's sworn duty to kill sex offenders or at the very least, to run them out of the prison. In fact, if you knew a fellow-convict was a sex offender and made no effort to kill him, you were liable to be killed yourself, or severely beaten.

No one of my criminal status or reputation had ever been in Warkworth before, and since sixty to seventy percent of the prison population was sex offenders, everyone—staff included—was scared stiff of what I might do.

It was a big step for me, as well. I was going into a penitentiary where there were sex offenders, pedophiles, people who had raped and abused children, knowing I could not treat them as I would have done in my past life. These were perpetrators of vicious and ugly crimes. One guy had put his baby in a microwave oven. If I were ever sent back to a regular prison for some reason, I would be killed for not dealing with these sex offenders according to the unwritten convict code.

But there was no real choice to be made. Warkworth was the only place I could go if I wanted to continue my course of education. And I did want to continue, because without it, I would have no ability to earn a living, to have a new life, or to put into practice what my faith told me I had to be as a man.

From the first day I arrived at Warkworth, the staff and inmates did everything they could to persuade me to leave. I was taken directly to the head of preventative security and the chief keeper who said very bluntly: "Nobody wants you here." They showed me a box full of kites, hundreds of little notes of protest from the convicts saying they were afraid for their lives, and threatening to go on strike if I came to the prison.

"Listen," I said, "I don't care if you want me in this prison or not. It's not my decision. This is a national headquarters decision. You can argue it out with the commissioner of penitentiaries, but until you start finding dead bodies lying around, just let me be."

They gave me a very hard way to go, beginning with keeping me in the reception unit twice as long as they should have. Generally, an incoming convict is kept in reception for six to eight weeks. During that time you are assessed and put through various tests. You don't mingle with the mainline population; you don't have recreation opportunities. In fact, you have very little freedom at all. You are not allowed access to the common room or any perks in your cell.

The administration doubled the time in reception for me, and I was forced to spend it in a cell with three other men.

When they finally let me out, they put me in the most restrictive cell block in the prison with the toughest living unit supervisor. Worse, they refused to give me work which made for some very difficult days. I was confined to my cell all day long with nothing to do. The reality was, I was in a minimum security facility with less freedom that I'd had in the super maximums.

Nor was I earning any money, something I needed to do in order to pay for my university courses. And there, too, the administration was dragging its feet. They refused to clear the way for me to order in my courses. The guards complained that I, a convict, should not be allowed to have university courses when they had to pay for their kids to go to university. I guess they thought the system was paying my tuition. In fact, I had paid my own way all along.

When they finally did make some movement on getting me the correspondence courses, they said, "You can't do them in your cell."

"Why can't I?"

"Because you should be going to the school."

"The school won't let me have university courses."

"That's because you don't have your high school yet. Why don't you do your high school? Besides, if you get a job, how do you expect to do classes and a job at the same time?"

That seemed a moot point since nobody in the prison was willing to give me a job. They had probably seen so many twisted people in their work, they truly believed I was beyond untwisting. But they weren't taking into consideration the change in internal morality and ethics that comes from faith, or the mind-expansion that comes with education, or my stubbornness.

There was a young woman on staff named Sandy. She was in charge of the recreation program. I went to Sandy and said, "All I want is to do my university courses in the daytime and work at an evening job, but nobody in this place will hire me. Nobody will cut me any slack." I told her about the various initiatives I had been involved in during my prison career: inmate committees, and running sports projects and whole sports departments.

"I know how to do professional umpiring and refereeing for floor hockey," I said. "I'm a weightlifter, a boxer— You wouldn't go wrong bringing me into your department, Sandy. I promise you, you won't suffer any grief from me. I know the word is out that I'm going to take over the place with drugs, but that won't happen. I am the real thing."

A couple of other people, including Peppy's younger brother, who had been in Warkworth for a couple of years, talked to Sandy on my behalf. "Serge is a good guy," he told her. "Can't you cut him some slack?"

Sandy went out on a limb for me, and took a mountain of flack from her co-workers and the head of social development in the process. "You're crazy," they said. "You're setting yourself up. You're going to find bodies in the gymnasium. You're nuts for doing this."

But she gave me the position anyway, and as I promised, I did a good job for her.

It was an interesting time. I handled all the recreational activities for the prison, set up an ice cream parlor, worked in the Sports Shack, organized their teams, and did all the other things I knew how to do.

The work provided a much-needed normalcy to my days. I was able to work on my university courses out in the yard shack or the sports shack, and I could also study in the gymnasium office. It was a great relief not to be jammed for twelve hours a day in my cell.

But the challenges weren't over. The rest of the staff gave me nothing. Sandy had to fight to take me to a hockey game with the rest of the crew. I didn't get passes; I didn't get three-day leaves. Everything I applied for got shot down. They even dismantled the John Howard Society group in Warkworth so I couldn't become the chairman of it. That, despite the fact that Graham Stewart, the national chairman of the John Howard Society, came to protest the decision.

But the worst was yet to come.

About four months before I was released from Warkworth, I got into a beef with a crew of pillheads, a group of tough young guys who would never have challenged me in my previous life.

I was in the sports department, doing my job there, and an issue came up over floor hockey and my refereeing. These guys were in the floor hockey playoffs, and were coming to games pilled up and hungover. The beef was that they wanted me to give penalties to the other team, but not to them. I didn't work that way.

As the playoffs went on, they got angrier and angrier until the four of them jumped me in the equipment room and beat me almost to death with goalie sticks.

My old instincts of self-preservation rose to the surface and I refused to go down. In defending myself, I took a couple of them to hospital with me, but I got the roughest end of the deal.

I was in critical condition and fell into a coma. When I came out of it, I found my leg cuffed to the hospital bed. They immediately put me in handcuffs and shipped me back to Warkworth in a paddy wagon even though my jaw was shattered in the front and vertically splintered, three teeth were knocked out, and both eyes were swelled shut. I had sixty or so stitches in my head plus two cracked ribs and a possible broken collar bone, and I was a mass of bruises.

The doctor's parting words as we left the hospital were that I might have a brain lesion. They fully expected I would die.

"What's a brain lesion?" I mumbled.

"We think you may have an open cut on your brain."

"Then why are you sending me back to prison?"

"It's not our choice," the doctors told me.

Back at Warkworth, they put me directly into solitary confinement.

Ian Stanley from Prison Fellowship and some people on the street heard about my predicament and contacted a lawyer and Graham Stewart with the John Howard Society. With a great deal of difficulty they were able to get me moved out of solitary confinement about a week later and put in the hospital wing of the prison where I was locked in my room.

Eventually, after five or six weeks, I recovered. They discovered I did not have a brain lesion. What the doctors saw may have been a blood clot or a shadowing on my brain. My jaw was so badly shattered my front teeth couldn't be saved so they pulled them out and immediately fitted me for a dental plate.

As it became increasingly apparent that I would recover from the incident, the prison administration was in a quandary. What were they going to do with me? By now they were aware I had done nothing wrong, so they couldn't transfer me out of the penitentiary. They suspected, however, that if they released me into general population, I would seek retribution on the pillheads.

It was a thorny issue, but after Sandy and several other staff people went to bat for me, the four who beat me up were locked in solitary confinement and then shipped out to other penitentiaries where they met with no end of trouble. A couple went to Collins Bay and had to be put in protective custody because my friends there wanted to kill them. The others ended up in protective custody in Kingston Penitentiary.

I found the whole experience at Warkworth extremely puzzling. I was cleaned up, not doing dope anymore, a practicing Christian minding my own business and doing my job running the sports programs and a lot of other stuff. I wasn't causing anyone any grief; I had even earned a university diploma, though the penitentiary wouldn't let the university give it to me. So why was all this happening to me? I was being persecuted unbelievably, primarily by the guards who couldn't seem to get past my reputation. Granted, I had been an evil man; I had instigated prison riots, assaulted guards, was even accused of prison murders, but all that was in the past. I was a different person now. Couldn't they see that? Couldn't they see that my behavior was totally different now?

Right up to the day I left prison for the last time, the guards were still convinced I was pulling a scam. "He'll be back," they said. "You just watch." As far as they were concerned, it was all an act.

Many years later, I appeared in court on behalf of John Hogan, a lifer who was invoking the faint hope clause. John was the youngest member of our former crew and I felt somewhat responsible for his beef. He had killed an informer in a drug ring, and it seemed to me that part of what he did was at my feet.

John and another convict, Tony Genovese, were transferred to Warkworth some months before my hellish experience with the pill-heads. They had both come to a sense of faith thanks to the influence of John Neely, the officer in charge of reception at Millhaven Penitentiary. I got them involved in the recreation crew, and in many ways, we were able to change the mindsets of a number of people at Warkworth.

It was several years after I was released from jail that John Hogan contacted me about representing him at a faint hope hearing.

I said, "I'll make you a deal, John. If you will follow the route I have taken, if you will get an education through correspondence courses, I will pay for them."

Fortunately, it was a couple of years before he took me up on the offer because I couldn't have afforded it at the time. But I stood good on my offer. I paid for his university and John eventually graduated with a B.A. in sociology, a diploma in social work, and another diploma in addictions. He is now in Great Britain working with young people in the system over there.

When you're doing a maximum life sentence with a minimum of

twenty-five years, you can apply for a faint hope clause hearing after fifteen years. This is what John was doing.

I went to testify for him, as did John Neely, because John Hogan was legitimate.

On the stand, I spoke at length about the legitimacy of the change in John's life. "I wouldn't be offering to pay thousands of dollars for his university education if it wasn't real," I told the hearing. "The man John killed was not a citizen, but a biker, an informer. John poses no risk to the public. He deserves this chance."

Later that day, I sat across the table at lunch from a former guard from Warkworth. Now retired, he was also there to testify. As he looked at me, his eyes filled with tears.

I was taken aback. "What's wrong?" I asked.

"For years I truly believed you were nothing but a con artist," the man replied. "Until I heard you on the stand today, I would have bet everything I owned that you were scamming. You know, there are still guards at Warkworth today who believe you're scamming. I believed it, too, and I want to apologize for what we put you through."

It was a shock to realize that ten years after my release from prison, guards were still waiting for me to return.

The attitude of the staff in Warkworth back then had a profound influence on the way I approached the parole board when the time came for my own early parole.

I said to my classification officer, "When I go before this parole board, I don't want you to say one word about me being a Christian. My spirituality stays out of it. I'm making good progress in my education, and I have plans to go to university. In eighteen months, they'll have to let me out on parole for my year of supervision, anyway, so I'm going to ask them to let me out now on supervision. The very fact that I'm sitting in this place is proof that my mentality has changed. I have been here with all these sex offenders who are mollycoddled by the guards as if they were honorable citizens, and I have done them no harm. That alone should be proof my mentality has changed."

The early parole was granted, and none too soon. I don't know how much more abuse I could have taken without reverting to my former behavior.

On August 26, 1988, I left prison for the last time. Ian Stanley and Donna Sterling, my friends from Prison Fellowship, came to get me.

The first thing I did after checking out of Warkworth Penitentiary was to get down on my knees and kiss the ground.

It wasn't until we were an hour and a half on our way that I realized I had left my $186 at the prison. We had to go back because that money and two changes of prison clothes were all I had in the world.

Fifteen

My parole from Warkworth Penitentiary had a condition: I must first secure living accommodations that met with the parole board's approval. That stipulation was put in place because everyone except my classification officer believed I was scamming.

Just to be on the safe side, the parole board gave me a three-day pass during which time I was to find a place to stay after I was released. I felt an urgency to get the arrangements made so I would be out of prison in time to start the fall term at the University of Waterloo.

I was hoping to book in at the House of Friendship in Kitchener. It was a hostel/drop-in centre/soup kitchen run by a Mennonite charity with a house on the property that was used as a federal half-way house. Of course, my first preference was not to be in a federal half-way house on day-parole, but that seemed to be the reality.

To my chagrin, a week before I was to go out on the three-day pass, I discovered the House of Friendship had decided to get out of the half-way house business and there was nothing in the city to replace it.

That threw me into a state of near panic. Without a place to live, there would be no parole for me.

"What happens if I can't find a place to rent?" I asked Ian Stanley during a panicky telephone conversation. "I don't have any money to put up front for rent, and I can only put down a small deposit. What happens if they won't take me at the student residence at the university? I'm euchred[59]. I'm nined[60]."

"Let me make a few phone calls," Ian said. "Maybe we can find a Christian family who has a place to rent."

He made a call to a minister friend of his, George Meyer, to see if George knew of any place where I could stay.

It so happened that George was away for the week, but his wife Sandy answered the phone.

"Sandy," Ian said, "I have a man who is being released from prison and he needs a place to stay. I will personally vouch for him. Do you have any ideas?"

"It's odd that you should ask," Sandy replied. "I was just talking with a woman from our church this week. She and her husband have a ministry of renting a room in their basement to a university student from out-of-province. Bill and Juliana generally rent to Christian kids, but the girl they've had for the past four years just left to go back West. Why don't I call them?"

"Please do," Ian urged her.

Bill and Juliana were supposed to have been away on a holiday, but at the last minute, Juliana had a feeling they should stay home. As a result, they were there when Sandy telephoned and explained the situation.

"We've never had any experience with this sort of thing," they said. "We usually take young people from good Christian homes. What do we know about dealing with someone coming out of prison?"

"However," they went on, "we're willing to meet him. Tell Reverend Stanley to send this fellow over for supper."

We arranged for a supper date on the last day of my three-day pass. I still wanted to look around and see if I could find something on my own.

And so, in late August of 1988, I boarded a bus for Kitchener-Waterloo on a three-day pass. It was the first pass I had received since coming to Warkworth.

I first went to the university and applied to get into student accommodations. Of course, with my history, that flew like a lead balloon. Ironically, the dean of student accommodations who turned me down flat that day ended up sitting next to me on the platform when I got

[59] Euchred - done, sunk, finished
[60] Nined - sunk, dead

my first President's Award for Outstanding Achievement. But in all fairness, I can't say I blame the man for his decision. I was forty years old and coming out of twenty-some years in jail. He could hardly be expected to put me in a dormitory with a bunch of teenagers.

I also checked for accommodations with the Student Union and the university newspaper. There were places available, but I didn't have enough money to make a down payment on anything. As it was, I would have to take out a student loan in order to make it financially.

By the time I went to dinner with Bill and Juliana, they were my last and only hope. All my other avenues had been shut down. I didn't tell them that, even though it was very hard not to get down on my knees and beg them to take me in. I didn't want them to feel any pressure.

It was not an intense dinner. We talked. I told them a little bit about my heart and tried to be as truthful as I could about my background.

Afterward, I went out in the backyard and played with their dog Taffy so Bill and Julianna could discuss the situation and pray about whether they would have me in their home. It seemed like hours, but I'm sure it was no more than twenty minutes before they called me back in.

"You can move in here," they said, "and we don't need a deposit."

I was ecstatic. "That's just wonderful," I exclaimed. "You won't regret it."

I couldn't believe it. For me this was a confirmation that there was a God and that I was on the right track. This was where I was supposed to go. There were so many pieces in this puzzle of mine, but they were all falling into perfect place—just in time.

Much later, Bill and Juliana told me they were scared to death. They had no idea what they were getting themselves into or whether or not they were making a wise decision. But they talked and prayed about it, and finally agreed to give me a chance.

With firm accommodation arrangements in hand, I returned to Warkworth, secured my parole, and walked out of prison for the last time one week before university registration. I was immediately thrust into a whole new, scary world.

It was bizarre. Seven days out of the penitentiary where I had lived in a solitary cell, and here I was in this university with a thousand students milling around me, people constantly moving, running in every direction. I was completely overwhelmed by it all.

That first day at university is etched in vivid and painful detail in my mind. Students had to stand in line to enroll. When I got to the front of the line, I was suddenly confronted with all this paperwork that had to be filled out, forms to be completed for classes and student loans. The girl behind the counter began asking me questions and I froze.

"Later," I mumbled. With sweat pouring off me, I raced to Professor Fred Desroches' office.

"What's wrong, Serge?" he inquired. "You're white as a ghost."

"I was standing in line and people were pushing me and touching me," I said. "I'm not used to it. You don't do that in prison. If you put your hands on someone or jostle them, there's a knife coming. All those kids were moving in close and giving me no space. I couldn't handle it."

It was true. I never stood in line in prison. As one of the convict elite, my clothes weren't even washed in the regular laundry; someone pressed them for me. I didn't eat with everybody else. I had people scrub my cell. You could say I received royal treatment in prison and now here I was among all these crazy nineteen- and twenty-year-olds who were pushing and jostling and butting into line.

Fred got me calmed down and I went back the next day to enroll. I arrived very early in the morning so I would be at the head of the line. What a traumatic experience!

I found the complexity of the process completely bewildering. The campus, though one of the smaller ones in Canada, seemed gigantic. Just getting from building to building was a challenge.

The first week I picked up my student loan at the bank. That was a nightmare. Despite my university courses, I still had a Grade Five education and my only preparation for life on the outside was a pre-release program Ian Stanley from Prison Fellowship Canada had supplied. Student loans? Signing papers? Having money shipped from here to there? I had no clue how to go about it.

Once my student loan came through, I went to buy a meal plan. I got in line and the fellow asked me, "Which one do you want?"

"What do you mean, which one?"

"You have to pick one of three different meats."

Duh—? You don't make choices in prison. You take what they give you. Now I had decisions to make.

Eating the meals presented an even bigger challenge. I would sit down at a table with some other students, all of whom were probably twenty years younger than me. What could we talk about? I had no conversational skills and certainly no aptitude for making small talk. These kids and I had nothing in common, no point of reference. What was I going to tell them? Where I came from? I was from the Inner City; they come from towns. They had supportive families; I never did. Did I tell them I was fresh out of prison....? Or that I spent twenty years on drugs?

During my last months in prison, I began accumulating all the documents I would need to start a new life on the outside. There were so many things I had never considered before. I had no legitimate ID. I didn't have a birth certificate. I didn't have a social insurance number because I had never worked and had never paid personal income tax.

I had to hire a private investigator to locate my birth record. By this time, I had made contact with my mother by mail and asked her a few questions regarding my birth. It was through her that I learned the name of the church in New Brunswick where I was baptized. The investigator found the baptismal record, but there was no surname on the certificate, only a first name: 'Joseph Serge.' It was a tremendous surprise to learn that my first given name was Joseph.

One line down it said: "Bastard."

Because there was no surname listed, I took my mother's surname, LeClerc, as my own and made application for a birth certificate.

Then I applied for a social insurance number. Even that was not straightforward. You don't just walk in with your prison record and say, "This is who I am. Please give me a social insurance card." It was especially complicated because my birth was never registered with the government.

"Where are you from?" the people in the government office asked.

"I'm from Canada."

"Oh? Prove it. Let me see your birth certificate."

"I don't have one yet."

"Well, we have no record of your being born in Canada, so we won't give you a social insurance number. There must be something fraudulent going on here. How can you be forty years old and never have worked or filed taxes?"

I finally got that settled when the province of New Brunswick gave creditability to the baptismal certificate and issued a birth certificate. Receiving it in the mail was a most memorable event.

Then I was told I needed a health card. That meant standing in line in a another government building and facing another barrage of questions.

It was the same story: "What do you mean, you're forty years old and you've never had a health card? Then give us your social insurance card."

"I don't have it yet, but I'm working on it."

Eventually I would need a driver's license, but in those early days on the outside I didn't have a car, so I had to use the city bus for transportation.

The first time I got on the bus, the driver pointed to the fare box. I didn't know what he meant.

"Put your fare in there," he said.

I didn't know you had to pay to ride a bus. I handed him a five dollar bill.

"I can't provide change," he said. "You have to deposit the exact fare."

"How much is exact fare?"

He told me.

"All I have with me is this five dollar bill and I'm not putting it in there."

The driver let me ride free that first day.

We had gone several blocks before I realized the bus was taking me in the opposite direction from the university. I made my way to the front and said to the driver, "I want to go to the university."

"Well, you're on the wrong bus," he said. "You want bus number so-and-so."

Number—? I didn't know the buses were numbered. I thought you got on a bus and it took you wherever you wanted to go.

"How do I get to the other bus?"

"You'll have to stay on this one until we've completed the route. I'll tell you where to get off so you can catch the bus you need."

Eventually, I found the bus heading for the University and got on.

"Transfer–?" the driver asked.

Everything was so foreign to me. I was trying to figure it out on the go without looking like an idiot and without bending under the pressure. I was a stranger in a strange land, and it wasn't an easy place to be.

I had spent most of my former life in a deviant sub-culture where up is down and down is up. It is a world apart with no point of contact with mainstream society. The value system is totally different. So is one's societal and world view. Morality is different. The way one earns a living is different. Where the rest of the world is twisted one way, you are twisted the other way. Living for me had consisted of aliases, false addresses, and no identification. As a result, making the transition from prison to mainstream society after almost thirty years of being a deviant, a criminal, a drug addict, and a convict, was a long and difficult process. So was learning to cope and survive.

I can well appreciate why so few people with a background like mine make it when they try to rejoin the real world. Not only was I a stranger in a strange land where I was struggling desperately to become untwisted without snapping, but I was consumed with self doubt. I knew how to be a drug dealer, but could I do this? Could I be normal? Could I learn enough about this world to live in it normally? It wasn't an issue of low self-esteem, but rather a question of existence. It was the whole question of co-existing and managing in an unfamiliar situation.

Needless to say, it was a very lonely time.

I started going to the university gym to work out. Everybody stared. I guess they had never seen anyone with so many massive tattoos. The young people were all using new, modern gym machines that I had never encountered before. I didn't know how to use them, so I worked out with dead weights.

Everyone else on the campus wore blue jeans. I hadn't had a pair of blue jeans for twenty years—not since my biker gang days. For most of my life, I wore a suit and tie. As a kid, they called me The Poser—someone who dresses in the latest disco styles. Now I felt I needed blue jeans in order to fit in with the college crowd.

Bill and Juliana worried about me. They knew I was struggling. I would wake up in the middle of the night in a cold sweat from what I now know were panic attacks. At two in the morning I would get dressed and go out for long walks, sometimes in blinding snowstorms. Everything felt claustrophobic. It seemed to me the walls were moving in and crushing me.

Many times I was tempted to simply give up. How, I wondered, would I ever fit in?

I was desperately lonely. Other than Bill and Juliana, my pastor, Ian

Stanley, and Fred Desroches, the only other person I knew in Kitchener-Waterloo was Gooch, the president of the Hell's Angels biker gang. He used to be one of my customers, so our relationship was good.

A month or so after my release from prison, I had dinner with Gooch. I wanted to let him know I was attending university and going straight.

"No doubt you've heard about me," I said.

He nodded. "Is it true?"

"It's true," I said. "I'm attending university. I'm not in action and I don't want to be in action. I just wanted to let you know that I'm in your town and if you see me on the street, let's just wave to one other."

Gooch was disappointed because he had hoped to use me, but he respected my wishes. The hardest part was turning down the car he offered.

Another former cohort was J.C. who was a partner with Peppy and me for twenty years and headed up our Ontario operation. J.C. and I went a long way back, to the Junction days, in fact. We were very close and had what I would call a heart-felt relationship. I was there for him when someone deliberately ODed[61] his brother. I got a gun for J.C. and accompanied him when he went to shoot the people who did it.

When I got out of prison, J.C. wanted to help me out, and several months after my release, he sent me some money and some clothes. He said the clothes didn't fit him anymore, but I know most of them were purchased brand new for me. The gesture might have been his way of persuading me to come back and work with him, but J. C. died soon after while testing a load of high-grade heroin. The heroin was too rich, and he realized he needed to get something into himself quickly to counterbalance the effect, so he took some cocaine and went to sleep. (Heroin is a downer; cocaine is an upper.) It was too much for his system. J.C.'s heart just stopped beating while he slept.

His death was very hard on me because he was the last tie with my past. His passing cut the connection completely and forced me to put every ounce of my energy and effort into making a go of this new life. I have often wondered, had J.C. lived, would he eventually have worn me down during the really tough spots of my life—the times when I genuinely questioned whether I could untwist enough to make it in this new life? I'd like to think I would not have gone back, but there were some very serious struggles, and J.C. and I were very close.

---

[61] ODed - overdosed on a narcotic

Sixteen

My mentor, Ian Stanley, and I met every week or so for dinner. The counsel he gave me during those encounters was wise and direct. He repeated what he had told me before. "People of your reputation and stature don't generally become untwisted," he said, "and I'm afraid if people hear your story and learn about your background, they're going to set you up on a pedestal. Pedestals are shaky. They can get kicked out from under you very easily."

"Serge," he said, "you have spent your whole life twisted, living in a parallel universe. Before you begin telling your story, you need to get your feet firmly planted on the ground. You must feel comfortable in your own skin. You've got to learn the rules, the structure, and the boundaries of this new world. Please, do not let yourself be used, or pushed, or pulled in different directions. And whatever you do, do not allow your ego to become inflated by other people's admiration."

He also warned me there would be people who judged me on things like my tattoos: a big peacock with tail in full display that I got when I was 13, a green-eyed wolf, a tiger, an eagle, and a ferocious-looking Viking.

My parole officer, a man from the Salvation Army, said virtually the same thing as Ian. "I recommend you don't reveal anything about yourself for the first year," he advised. "Just be quiet, and complete this first part of your journey. Learn how the world operates. It's a bit like climbing the Alps. Think of yourself as being at a rest stop part way up."

So, to the best of my ability, that is what I did.

A key person in my struggle to gain some type of normalcy in my life was Mohammed who ran an ethnic food store in a small three-shop plaza across a field behind Bill and Juliana's home. The route I took to university every day went past the shopping plaza, and this store, the Universal Market, caught my attention.

One day I stopped in to buy a pop. I looked around in fascination. The store was stocked with a wide range of Middle Eastern and Oriental foods and had displays of exotic and bizarre things like chocolate-covered locusts.

I found myself stopping often and lingering to examine these wonderfully strange things. I noticed that the owner was Middle Eastern and his wife was Oriental.

After four or five visits, the owner and I struck up a conversation. His name was Mohammed. As time went on, our conversations got longer and longer, and I learned that he was a Kurd. I had never met a Kurd before, so I was intrigued.

"What does that mean—you're a Kurd?" I asked. "What do you mean you have no country? Where did you come from and how did you get here?" I wanted to know everything about him.

Mohammed came from the Kurdish triangle around Turkey, Iraq, and Iran. He talked about Saddam Hussein, the politics of the area, the persecution endured by generations of Kurdish people, the genocide, and how many of his family members had been wiped out in the genocide.

Inevitably, religion came up in our conversation. He was Muslim; I was Christian. We talked about that and discussed the similarities: the fact that we were both people of The Book and believed in the same Jehovah, God the Father, and Abraham. He gave me a Koran, which I read. He told me about the difference between radical Islamic thought and what he believed as a moderate Muslim and a Kurd.

Mohammed had a little kitchen at the back of his store, and I was introduced to Muslim food and Ramadan. It turned out he was one of the leading figures in the Muslim community which was constantly doing whatever it could to help free the Kurdish people.

Since I had no other social life, many nights found me at Mohammed's store. The friendship I developed with Mohammed and his family was putting me in touch with the normal world. I became comfortable in my own skin and gradually began coming to terms with myself as a new, untwisted human being.

By now, Mohammed knew my background and what I was doing in Waterloo. Some of the things I shared on purpose just to see what the reaction would be.

One day he asked if I would help him behind the counter. So here I was—a criminal on parole, this ex-con whose specialty was ripping off store tills—working the cash register, giving change, and interacting with customers.

Mohammed came into my life at a point when I really needed someone. He was non-judgmental and totally accepting. Perhaps the close kinship we developed was because, in many ways, he was as much a stranger in a strange land as I was.

The other person who played a huge role in helping me adjust was Dr. Fred Desroches, professor and department head of Legal Studies and Criminology at the University of Waterloo. He was single at the time, and it was with him that I started doing the social thing in the real world.

We both love blues music, so every Friday night Fred and I would go to the local blues club, or we'd meet at The Bombshelter, a pub that was popular with students. Fred knew I didn't drink, so he would join me in sipping on a glass of soda water with a slice of lemon. Invariably, students came over to talk to him and I was included in the conversation.

At one point, Fred asked me to lecture for him in class, and as I began to reveal some things about myself during those lectures, I grew more at ease with who I was and who I had been. I found that, much like teachers, professors, and academia in general, students are very accepting and non-judgmental.

Soon I was lecturing for other professors as well. All of this helped me to learn to socialize, to have conversations, to have points of reference for conversations.

In many of my professors, I found the same dedication to teaching that I had first recognized in Michael in St. Vincent de Paul, in Fred Desroches as he worked with me through my correspondence courses, and in Peter Carrington and others from whom I took courses. They didn't seem to care what I had done or that I had been in prison. They were there to teach and bend and stretch my mind.

Academically, I was doing phenomenally well and my marks remained high. I was an honor student on the President's Honor Roll. My professors enjoyed having me in their classes because they knew they could count on plenty of feedback and healthy debate. I earned my marks by critiquing and contributing my personal point of view. Students began coming to me after class to ask, "So what did you think about today's lecture?"

As I gradually learned to live in the world, I found it to be wonderfully stimulating intellectually. I soaked up knowledge like a sponge. I loved it. It was so liberating to challenge my mind. It was freedom like I had never known before. As my body was freed from prison, so my mind was being freed from the shackles of ignorance where I couldn't use language, where I dared not debate for fear I would be stabbed.

One of the most difficult moments for me at university was when I was informed I needed to take a statistical analysis class. I immediately went on a campaign to have the statistics requirement removed. I fought hard against it, wrote letters of protest, even went to the dean declaring that, as a sociologist, I didn't need statistics. I argued that people are individuals, that I saw no need for statistical analysis. I didn't want it, didn't need it, wanted no part of it, shouldn't have to do it.

Of course, I had to take statistics, but I raised such a kafuffle that the department held a special summer course in statistical analysis for a dozen of us and pulled in a gerontologist to teach it.

I had all the books like *Stats for Dummies,* and I had even arranged for two people plus a hired tutor to help me get through the course.

The very first day, the professor drew a mathematical formula on the board with some numbers and a squiggly line. "Does anybody have any questions?" he asked.

I put up my hand.

"Yes, Serge?" he said, without even turning around.

"I don't understand what you've just done up there," I said. Remember, I only had Grade Five level arithmetic.

"This is a formula."

"Yes, I understand that, and I understand that it is a mathematical formula, an equation of some kind, and you're going to get an answer at the end of it. What I don't understand is the squiggly line you've put in there."

"That's square root," he said.

"Okay," I said, "so what is square root?"

"What do you mean, what is square root?"

"That's what I want to know. What is square root? Why don't you write the word square root?"

"This is the sign for square root."

"Why would you want to put a sign there?"

"Because it means the divisor of a number that when squared gives the number."

"Then why don't you just put the number there?"

"Serge," he said, "come and see me after class. I have some mathematics books you need to get."

They got me through the class. I think I got sixty-three percent. It was the lowest mark I'd ever gotten in my life, and I sweated bullets all summer to get it.

Eventually, I got a job on the university campus. I needed the money. I had taken out a student loan, but after paying my room and board, my tuition, and buying a meal ticket, there was nothing left.

I had never worked before and had no real experience, so getting a job was not easy. Ultimately, the university intervened and I was hired to do telemarketing at the Alumni Centre. The job paid me five dollars an hour for eight hours a week.

A few months later, I saw a job advertised for weekend counselors at a home for developmentally handicapped children. There were three adult males in the home and the ad was specifically looking for male counselors.

I went to see the lady in charge. I leveled with her about my background, told her what I was doing now, outlined the courses I had completed in my education, and supplied some references.

I got the job, and in time, became a supervisor in the facility. In hindsight, I realize how very brave this woman was to hire me when I had no work experience whatsoever. Obviously she saw something in me that was genuine, and I am grateful that she gave me a chance when she needn't have and shouldn't have.

Needless so say, getting the counseling job was a huge break for me. It allowed me the opportunity to have a little better income and, more importantly, to know that I was contributing, that I was helping someone else, perhaps someone even more dysfunctional than I was. It made me feel as if I were finally giving back, finally having worth and being productive instead of being a blight or a drain on society.

But there was still so much to learn about 'ordinary' life. Given my past, I had obviously missed many experiences that most people consider commonplace. One of them was camping.

Some of the male staff where I worked were avid campers and fishermen, and they decided I should go with them on a camping trip to Algonquin Park. To me, Algonquin Park was like the Great White North. It was a twelve-hour drive from Toronto.

The plan was to go canoeing. I had never camped. I had never canoed. I didn't fish. I didn't swim. And what did I know about wild animals?

After much prodding, I agreed to go. "Okay," I said, "I'll go camping, but here's the deal. I don't do anything. If we do this portaging stuff—? You'll do the portaging. You'll set up the camp and the tents. I will take care of the food. I'll buy the groceries and cook the meals. That will be my contribution to the camping trip."

Since I knew absolutely nothing about traditional camp fare, we ended up with what could only be termed gourmet outdoor cuisine—instant everything. My camping partners thought they'd died and gone to Heaven.

I took along a stack of books (I was never without books) and while the other guys were out in the canoe doing whatever it is people do in canoes, I stayed back at camp reading my books under a shady tree and cooking the gourmet food.

The day came when my friend Ian Stanley said, "It's been more than a year now, Serge. You're adjusted. You're working and paying your rent; you've got a year of university under your belt. Maybe it's time to do a little more."

I said, "Okay."

"Is there anything you'd like to do?"

"I wouldn't mind taking out a membership in my church."

With Ian's encouragement, I went to see George Meyer, my minister.

"Before the congregation votes to take me into membership," I said, "I've got to let them know about my background and share who I am so they can make an informed decision."

It was the first time I had ever shared my story publicly. Needless to say, it was a very emotional experience for me and for everyone listening. They had come to know me from my faithful attendance at church every Sunday. It was very, very difficult for me to reveal to them the person I had been in a previous life.

There were many tears shed that day, and I was granted full church membership.

I was feeling a growing urgency to give back more to the society I had so ruthlessly plundered as a career criminal. I decided the best way to do that was to offer my time as a volunteer.

I got turned down by sixteen different groups.

Even with my pastor at my side, I was turned down.

I believe it says something that I didn't give up. I could understand why the different organizations wouldn't take a chance on me, and I didn't blame them. Nor did I take it personally. I realized it wasn't about me, but about the circumstances, and in hindsight, I think I probably needed the waiting time to become healthier and more untwisted.

One day I went with George to Anchor House, a juvenile drop-in centre run by Ray of Hope Ministries in Waterloo. The organization received a *per diem* from the government to operate three such drop-in facilities.

There I met the program director, Jon Hill. He and I would become dear friends.

"I would love to have you work here as a volunteer," Jon said, "and I think it would be great for our young men to meet someone with your life experience, to have one-on-one interaction over the pool table and hear your story."

And so I began to donate my time at Ray of Hope. I later came on staff as a shift supervisor, and eventually sat on the board as assistant chair. I also established the first Prison Fellowship Canada volunteer program at Anchor House where volunteers could come in and work with the young people.

Of course, all the while, I was attending university, working on my bachelor of arts degree and taking courses like psychology, social work, identification and treatment of child abuse, juvenile delinquency, criminology, juvenile justice, law and order, regulating deviance, sociology of mental disorder, sentencing as a social process, and the like.

The academic process for me was stretched out somewhat because I was in an educational co-op system that offered two options. After your first year of university, you could do four months of study and four months of work, or you could do eight months of classes and eight months of work. I chose the eight-month option because I wasn't eligible for any government grants. I also figured it would be wiser to build up my résumé with eight months of work experience rather than four months.

As well, I needed the extra time to decide what I did or did not want to pursue as a career. I was leaning toward sociology, and I definitely knew I wanted my work to be centered around youth. My preference was a faith-based, non-profit charity because I perceived there would be a stronger, deeper dedication to the cause in such an organization. I already had some experience with that through Roof, a drop-in centre for street kids that a woman named Katy and I had started in Waterloo, and Oasis, a similar faith-based centre.

The bottom line for me was the fact that I understood the spiritual need of these hurting young people because I was once one of them. I knew what it was like to be in deep pain.

About that time, a group of police officers approached me. "We've heard about the good work you're doing in Kitchener-Waterloo with Roof and Oasis," they said. "We're wondering if you would do us a favor."

Me—? Do the police a favor? This was certainly a switch.

"There is a school we're having problems with," they went on. "It's an upper-middle-class school with a lot of rural kids coming in, and there is a big drug problem. Would you come and give them a talk?"

Outside of my church, I had never spoken to an audience before, let alone an audience of high school students. For that matter, I had never even been inside a high school before in my life. But I found myself on the platform, pinned by the spotlights, surrounded by a horseshoe of bleachers filled with 1700 students.

Had I known beforehand there would be so many present, or that I was expected to speak for fifty minutes, I would probably not have gone. I had no idea what I was going to say, other than why these teen-agers ought not to do drugs.

I took a deep breath and began. "Okay," I said, "let me share some stuff with you. I want to share some of my ideas and opinions, and tell you your options."

Then I just let it flow. I talked about me, about my mistakes, about the fact that no matter how many mistakes you make in your life, you can turn things around. I talked about drugs and where they took me. I talked about why a person does drugs—not to feel good, but to stop feeling bad. I talked about parents from the point of view of the street kids with whom I was working, and how easy it is to think your parents are your enemies when in fact, they love you deeply. I talked about my own life and my feelings.

I talked about how they were not animals that walked on two legs. I told them they could choose to believe they were a fluke of nature or a creation of great value. I said, "The secret of life is to keep yourself excellent because you were created excellent, and you need to make choices that will keep you excellent."

I talked about my own insecurities and struggles. I talked about what I had learned in hindsight about my own life. I talked about attitude.

I talked the way I still talk today. I talked with passion, from the heart.

It was a defining moment for me and the launch of an international speaking career that would allow me to address millions of young people in schools throughout North America.

After the assembly, many of the kids came to talk.

I felt good. For the first time, I felt that maybe my life hadn't been a total waste after all, and that from the chaotic mess something good might come. I realized that my previous life had given me wisdom—albeit gathered from bitter experience. I realized that people would listen because I'd been there, done that.

SEVENTEEN

Word got around, and soon more people wanted to hear my story. I found myself in demand to speak at high schools, youth rallies, summer camps, and all manner of different organizations.

One evening, after giving a talk to a Full Gospel Businessmen's chapter, a man in the audience came up and handed me his card.

"My name is Ron Hall," he said. "I operate a place called Turning Point Ministries, and I would be very interested in talking with you about it. I understand you're scheduled to speak at a meeting in the St. Catherine's area. Could you make some time to meet with me? I have a proposition that might interest you."

Turning Point Ministries was a non-profit charity that ran about ten different ministries including Turning Point Girls' Home and Turning Point Men's Farm, both long-term residential facilities for young people with addictions; crisis pregnancy centers in St. Catherines, Brantford, London, and Leamington; an emergency shelter for battered women in London; and a number of other outreach programs.

Ron's proposition was this: Would I be interested in coming onboard as his assistant for an eight-month work term? My primary job would be to assess the organization's existing programs and make recommendations for possible improvements. Since I had no history with the organization or the people involved, he felt I could be objective in my assessment. The other thing Ron wanted me to do was initiate promotion, public relations, and fundraising strategies for Turning Point

Ministries.

I found the offer exciting. It gave me the opportunity to operate in a leadership role and hone my skills as a program analyst, to analyze what they were doing, see how they were doing it, and maybe tweak it to higher efficiency. There was intellect involved in the work. I would get to see how a well-run organization with many different programs and venues functioned.

Ironically, the aptitudes I needed for this job were closely connected to the skills I had already demonstrated in being an organized crime figure and in pulling together the Exceptional People's Olympiad. I felt completely comfortable with the prospect because I would be doing things I already knew how to do. Now, however, I was doing them for good rather than for evil or nefarious reasons.

I was eager to accept Ron's offer, but there was a hitch. I would have to get my parole switched from Waterloo to St. Catherines. That caused some consternation at the St. Catherines parole office because they had never dealt with a high profile criminal like me before. I didn't quite fit what they were used to. I was a notorious convict, described by the RCMP as Canada's Most Dangerous Criminal. I had a background of major drug dealing and organized crime. I was coming in for an eight-month work term, not living in a half-way house, and working as the assistant executive director for a respected province-wide organization. It was all a little disconcerting for them.

The bottom line was, parole services didn't want me in St. Catherines and they gave me a tough way to go, proposing all sorts of restrictions.

I said, "You can't put these restrictions on me. I'm not just out of the penitentiary, I'm a proven commodity. This is a good job offer, and you're proposing restrictions that won't allow me to do this job."

One of the restrictions was demanding I get a travel permit twenty-four hours in advance anytime I wanted to go further than twenty-five miles from St. Catherines. Since I was speaking all over the province and assessing organizations a hundred or more miles away, this was completely out of the question.

In the past, I would have blown my top over such an outrageous demand, but I was determined—as I had been from the moment I walked out of prison—to take the high road no matter what. I had made a vow. Now my position had to be: "Okay, you're being unreasonable, but I won't be. We'll work this process through. I don't care how difficult you try to make it, how many restrictions you put on, I'm going to do this."

I remember my first parole officer, the Salvation Army man, apologizing to me. "Normally," he said, "I wouldn't have you reporting to me three times a week. You'd only be checking in once a month. But this order comes from the highest level. I know how difficult it is for you to get here. You have to take a bus, and then walk three blocks."

I said, "I don't care if you want me to report to you five days a week, or every day, for that matter. I will do whatever you want me to do. I'm not going to cop an aggressive attitude[62], I'm not going to be adversarial. I understand where these orders are coming from. The system has known me well for thirty years. They know I've never completed a parole before in my life, and they have all kinds of reasons to suspect me now."

This new attitude of mine clearly reflected my new-found faith and the change that had happened in my life. Sometimes it surprised even me.

'What would Jesus do?' sounds like a hackneyed saying, but in many ways, without it being holier-than-thou or a presumptuous spiritual thing, that's exactly how I dealt with the issues that arose in my life. I asked myself how Christ dealt with His adversaries and the situations imposed on Him. I kept trying to put myself in the place of Jesus, the Man. How did He respond to conflict? to put downs? to adversity and negativity? I kept repeating to myself, "He always took the high road. He always took the high road."

Part of the change in me stemmed from the fact that I now accepted responsibility for who I was. I was learning to develop a conscience—not an easy thing when you have to look back on the evil person you were and all the evil things you did. I had to come to terms with the fact that I was the author of every one of my evil actions. That meant working through a lot of issues.

The biggest issue was guilt. Dealing with that almost drove me over the edge. It wasn't guilt over just one thing, or a series of little things in a week. It was coming to terms with an entire lifetime of evil acts that I had done as a man.

It took me years to get through the self-recrimination and to come

---

[62] Cop an attitude - adopt an aggressive or confrontational attitude

to terms with questions like: How can I have a sense of self-worth after all the terrible things I've done? How can I keep from giving up on myself, my faith, this new person I'm trying to be with a new code of ethics, a new standard for living, and a new way of being?

Going through that process was harder than the twenty-seven months I spent in solitary confinement. I sweated bullets over how anyone else could forgive me when I had so much difficulty forgiving myself. More important, how could the Creator forgive me for all the hurt and destruction I had caused His other creations? And what about the hundreds and thousands of young minds and bodies I had poisoned with my drugs? How about the acts of violence? the people I hurt? the families I tore apart?

One by one these issues came to my mind, things I hadn't thought about in years. My memory dredged up the years when I worked as a heel man[63] with Hughie. We would go into apartments and condos and I would take kids' piggy banks out of their bedrooms. I didn't care about the money; I just collected the banks. It was a big joke. Now the faces of those children, as they must have looked when they came home from school and found their piggy bank missing, haunted my mind.

I visualized the faces of people finding their jewellery, their family heirlooms, the big televisions they had maybe saved for a whole year to pay off, gone because of me. I had to deal with all that ugliness. It was like a never-ending reel that played over and over in my head.

It would have been much easier not to think about it, but I knew that in order to become healthy, I had to confront every bit of my past. I could not hide; I could not pretend.

Many people in prison have an epiphany of some sort that changes them, be it age, burn-out, fear of prison, or a faith experience. When they leave prison, they hide from their past; they don't let anybody know about it. I made a decision that I would not do that. Instead, I vowed I would pay back society. It became a clarifying issue for me. I knew I would never be able to undo the damage and destruction, but I could at least acknowledge it, and maybe pay back enough to tip the scales on the other side at least a tiny bit.

Putting my past out there for all to see also gave me the passion to

[63] Heel man - prowl man who is a daytime sneak thief looking for opportunities to steal

pursue my chosen course. I knew very early on that the salvation of my soul was God, but for the salvation of my humanity, I had to challenge the government on wrong social policies. I needed to be a social advocate for disadvantaged youth, battered and pregnant women, people with addictions, and high school kids. If I did not do that, I knew I would never be able to live with the tremendous weight of guilt I carried.

This process I was going through is called *habilitation*. As I've said before, the correctional system erroneously aims to *rehabilitate* convicts, but the word *rehabilitation* means 'to change to a former state.' That is where the problem lies. To be rehabilitated, I would have to be restored to the child I was before the age of eight. After that, I became twisted and completely dysfunctional because of my twenty years of addictions, the corrections system, and my life as a street kid where I learned to live by a very different and skewed set of values.

Did I need to be rehabilitated to my former dysfunctional state? Absolutely not. I needed to be *habilitated, renewed, reformed* in the sense of becoming untwisted so as to bring order to the broken pieces. I needed to develop a proper perspective on the world, a new view on life and on myself.

For me, a significant part of the untwisting process was my education. I was very well-read, and my vocabulary was immense. I didn't always know how to pronounce words because I had never heard them spoken, but I did know what they meant and how they applied. It was this broad-based knowledge that enabled me to embark on my educational journey.

To be perfectly frank, I began the journey with purely selfish motives. At the beginning, I had no intention of ever using my education to help humanity; I just wanted to find out who I was and how I had become so twisted. Everything I studied had to do in some way with me and my life's experience. I soaked up courses on juvenile delinquency, criminology, sociology, studies on the culture of poverty, the culture of suicide, dysfunction, and drug addiction. To everyone else, it seemed I was studying from a social work/counseling/ psychology perspective, but it was all designed to look at me. I hated analyzing myself, but I was desperate to find out what made me tick.

I knew I was twisted; my faith showed me that. But what had made me so twisted? What was the reason for the unbelievable blind rages that seized me and zoned me into complete disregard for the inevitable physical punishment or even the risk of death? There were times in my life when I would continue fighting even after being stabbed and beaten, having bones broken and my face smashed, with no acknowledgement whatsoever of the pain. I was like a machine. So where did this level of complete psychosis come from? Where did the rage and the hate originate? More importantly, how could I come back from all that and become normal?

The untwisting journey was long and arduous. It advanced inch by inch with each scrap of understanding, each new insight into myself. I often think of the process as being a little like peeling an onion. I had to remove the skins layer by layer and then examine each of those layers in order to understand the dysfunctional person I had become. For the sake of my psychological health and well-being, determining how many layers I could safely remove before going deeper was a delicate balance.

Complicating the process even further was the fact that I was trying to adapt to a completely alien world without the usual response mechanisms. In the past, I had predictable mechanisms in place to respond to conflict, stress, even social encounters. Now they were gone. I couldn't scream at people or punch them out. I couldn't hide myself in drugs.

Had I been able to work through the untwisting process without interruption or opposition, it might have been easier, but I didn't have that luxury. In the midst of the struggle to understand myself and all I had been, I was also dealing with insults, rebuffs, and gossip.

One particularly devastating incident occurred when someone started spreading a story that I had been arrested with marijuana. Here I was, just beginning to speak at schools, when all of a sudden a whole group of schools cancelled their bookings.

I phoned one of the principals. "What's going on?" I asked.

"You can't expect us to have you in our school when you just got busted with marijuana in your vehicle," he said indignantly.

"What are you talking about?"

It turned out there was another convict, a formerly illiterate fellow who had turned himself around, learned to read, and was now going around speaking in schools on behalf of literacy. He was stopped on the highway with marijuana. This fellow lived about an hour and a half from me and had a French name, though it was not at all similar to mine. But because he was an ex-con speaking in schools, everyone assumed it was me.

Of course, the gossip spread like wildfire and seriously damaged my credibility. It was more than a year before I got that put to bed. I was only able to endure the episode because I had worked through the guilt mechanism. My faith said all that was behind me. My God had forgiven me, and if other people couldn't, the problem was with them, not with me.

Understanding my twenty years of drug addiction was a major priority. For two whole decades, I had lived on the edge of a precipice. I used drugs at such a phenomenal level that people used to come and watch me inject because they couldn't believe the amount I could tolerate. I did drugs to the point where, on one occasion, I had blood oozing out of my nose and eye sockets from burst blood vessels. At one point, the bottoms of my feet were burned because of the high concentration of chemicals in my blood. I did drugs in stereo—injecting in both arms simultaneously. I'd be so high I couldn't get up off the chair for an hour, but immediately afterward, I would hit a bunch of narcotics and seconals to drive myself down the other way so I could start it all over again just to experience the rush.

Why did I do that? It had nothing to do with the high, or the thrill the drugs produced. What I have come to understand is that I didn't become an addict to feel good; I became an addict to stop feeling bad. Everyone has an empty hole inside them that needs filling. Some of us try to fill the hole with gambling, drugs, pornography, or alcohol. Addiction happens when something captures your mind, soul, and spirit to the point that you don't do it to feel good anymore. The pleasure is long gone and you almost cringe doing it, but you are driven to continue because you have this deep, black hole inside that screams to be filled. It is not the craving for the drug; it is the deep need to fill that hole.

Once this understanding crystallized for me, I was able to see how the drive to fill that empty hole lured me into a lifestyle of violence and danger. I was desperate for meaning, for identity and purpose. I was willing to do anything to achieve it.

At times it was extremely hard for me to follow my new-found code of ethics and morality, my faith, my perspective of the world, and more importantly, my perspective of myself within the world as a functioning, productive citizen. Probably the saving grace for me was that I was progressing with great speed and alacrity on the academic front. For the first time in my life I was excited about living. Everything about learning was a joy.

I remember my advisor telling me I needed to take a language at university.

"What do you mean, take a language?" I said. "I don't even speak English properly."

"You don't exactly have to learn to speak a language," he explained. "You could take a course in Greek or French civilization, or something like that."

"Okay," I said, "I'll take French civilization." I knew from reading books that democracy had its beginnings in French civilization and that the French Revolution led to democracy in the United States.

I took two semesters of French civilization from Professor Pierre Dubé. One day he said to me after class, "I can't believe you, Serge. You always sit up front; you never miss a class. You're always asking questions, and you're at the top of the class in grades. You are soaking all this up like a sponge."

I was. I couldn't learn enough about architecture, painting, art, furniture, the Baroque Era. I loved it all. I had an insatiable thirst for knowledge. I was loving life. I enjoyed it so much I don't believe I ever once stood back to see what I was accomplishing. I didn't dwell on my grades. In fact, I made it a point to be so well prepared for my exams that the night before, I would go to a movie. My assignments were always in two weeks early.

I graduated in 1989 with a diploma in general social work. It was earned while I was still in prison, but the administration wouldn't allow me to receive it until I was released. In 1991, I earned a Bachelor of Arts degree in sociology and two years later, I was awarded a double honors degree with a major in sociology and a minor in social work.

My thesis was on drug dealing, something I knew a good deal about, having been a drug dealer at the beginning of the drug culture in Canada, and a manufacturer and distributor of designer drugs. My thesis work went far beyond the degree requirement. My advisor, Fred Desroches, used my thesis as the premise for a book on drug dealing from the perspective of a generic drug dealer. We worked together closely on the writing of that book.

Because of my firsthand experience in various areas of addictions, criminology, psychology, and social work, some of the professors at the University of Waterloo invited me to lecture in their classes on such things as drug dealing and addictions, the 1971 Kingston Prison Riots, juvenile delinquency, the cultural development of poverty, and similar related topics. I had lived it and done it all, and was able to blend personal experience with academic theory and insights.

All of this contributed to the expertise Ron Hall of Turning Point Ministries saw in me.

Following the eight-month work term with Turning Point, I returned to university for eight months, but continued to work with the organization on a part-time basis.

Before I finished my thesis, Ron Hall left Turning Point and to gether, he and I founded Maranatha Ministries. Our goal was to serve other charities. Through presentations and workshops, we offered guidance and assistance to charities like crisis pregnancy centers and prison ministries regarding fundraising and on-going financial development. We also provided help designing promotional material and developing effective programs.

Ron and I acquired an old dairy building in Brantford and started a food bank that supplied various shelters and soup kitchens, crisis pregnancy centers, plus a Teen Challenge Farm.

At the same time, I was busy in a number of different directions. I sat on the board of Dove Ministries, a shelter for battered women, and was assistant chair for Ray of Hope Ministries. I also did a lot of speaking and found myself organizing youth rallies where I would speak and Peter Kun, a dynamite singer, would provide the music. We held these rallies in many different places—sometimes on haywagons, even in the middle of fields. People came, put up tents, and we had a grand old time.

Speaking at camps led to becoming a national representative for Circle Square Ranches, a branch of Crossroads Christian Ministries.

Eventually, Ron and I set up a counseling service. I already had the necessary credentials to do so, and Ron took the courses he needed to qualify. He specialized in marriage counseling and my specialty was addictions counseling. We set up two offices, one in Waterloo and one in Brantford.

Together we developed Career 7 Associates, a business within Maranatha Ministries that offered consultancy work and motivational speaking. It was through Career 7, that I met my future wife, Noreen.

It was also through Career 7 that my speaking career really took off. It earned me a good enough living that I was able to begin paying off my student loans. Not long afterwards, Bill and Julianna's son Glen and I became co-owners of their house.

Bill and Julianna were retiring and wanted to move to Hanover in Northern Ontario. Glen and I had become good friends over the years. Glen and his wife were divorcing and their son was coming to live with him, so Bill and Juliana said to me, "Why don't you and Glen buy our house? You can have the downstairs, and he and Chris will have the main floor."

"That would be great," I said, "but I don't have any money for a down payment. I'm still paying off my student loans."

Bill and Julianna came up with an arrangement whereby they would provide the down payment as a gift, and Glen and I would come up with the mortgage money for the rest of the purchase.

It was a very compatible arrangement. I renovated the downstairs for myself with a big bedroom, a spacious living room with fireplace, and a counseling office. I used the kitchen upstairs, and Glen and I spent many evenings in the upstairs livingroom, watching sports together.

Eighteen

During the summer of 1992, I was invited to do a week of speaking presentations at a new church plant in a working-class area of Ontario. Towards the end of the week, the pastor asked if I could meet with a fellow named Bob. He was a teacher in an inner-city school in Toronto and a recovering alcoholic.

I said I would.

Bob and I spent a couple of hours together, and at the end, I gave him my business card.

Some time later, Bob was in the office of Noreen Hardwick, the principal of the school where he worked. While he was there, a telephone call came from her son Mark's parole officer. Mark had missed another appointment and this time, the officer said, the police would have to arrest him.

Bob could see from the expression on the principal's face and her body language that something was terribly wrong. "Is there a problem?" he asked.

Noreen wasn't in the habit of discussing her personal affairs with her teachers, but this day was different. She told Bob about Mark, her only child, who was into crack cocaine and whose life had spiraled downward so far in the past three years that he was now facing a jail sentence. She told about accessing professional assistance within the system and finding no effective help for Mark.

"I don't know what to do," she said. "Nobody can help me."

"I know someone who might be able to help," Bob said, reaching into his wallet and pulling out my card. "His name is Serge LeClerc. Would you like me to call him?"

The chances of finding me at home were about one in a hundred. I loved what I was doing and had become something of a workaholic. You could find me anywhere else, but very rarely at home. This time, when Bob called, I was there.

I have a hard time saying, "No." That may be one of the problems with developing a social conscience; you want to leave a legacy and pay back at least a little for all the damage you have done. So when this fellow asked if I would be willing to help Mrs. Hardwick, I said, "Yes."

"Put her on the phone," I told him.

My first impression of Noreen was that she had a very sweet voice.

"Where do you live?" I asked.

She told me.

"I'm going to be speaking first thing on Monday morning at a high school not far from where you live," I said. "I'll come to your house around 10:30. You be there, and have your son there, too."

Noreen agreed, though not without some trepidation, I would later learn. Who exactly was Serge LeClerc, she wondered? And why did I think I could help her son when no one else could?

Noreen was under a lot of stress. The fact is, much of her life had been lived in stress. What gave her release and meaning was teaching, even though it wasn't her first career choice.

When she finished high school, Noreen told her father she wanted to be a social worker.

"No, you don't want to be a social worker," he countered. "People don't like social workers, especially the people you're trying to help. People don't like you going into their home and poking around and taking their children. You should be a teacher. You'd make a good salary."

So Noreen became a teacher.

She married young—at twenty —to a fellow she believed would be a good husband. After twelve years of marriage, they adopted Mark as a baby. Seven years after he came into their home, the marriage broke down in divorce. Noreen devoted herself to her young son and her career, both of which she loved with a passion.

Special education was her forte. She opened the first class in Ontario for children with learning disabilities. From there, she went on to become a special education consultant. Armed with extensive experience and a masters degree in education, she soon became coordinator of all the elementary and secondary inner-city schools in Toronto. A dedicated advocate for the successful schooling of all children, Noreen also lectured for many years on an evening class and summer school basis in all areas of special education at the University of Toronto, York University, and Brock University. In addition, she was a popular public speaker.

Mark was about seventeen when the central office of the Toronto School Association asked Noreen to take on the principalship of a particularly difficult inner-city school in Regent Park. It was a difficult job made more difficult by Mark's escalating drug use and rapid downward spiral into crime.

Everyone in the system knew that Noreen was divorced and that she was having problems with her son. Her colleagues were aware that he was fast derailing and they all wanted to help. When Mark stole Noreen's car and wrecked it, one of her superintendents stepped up and referred her to a friend to get it fixed. Others offered advice and recommended professionals whom they believed could help. Nobody had.

Like most advantaged kids (and this is what a lot of people do not understand about the drug world) Mark had disposable income to purchase his drugs. Inner-city kids, on the other hand, use crime as a vehicle to escape the culture of poverty. Many inner-city kids living in poverty come from dysfunctional homes characterized by alcoholism, divorce, lack of education, and the like. It is what criminology calls *anomie*, a floating state of alienation and lack of value, realizing they are not going to meet the standards and goals considered normal by mainstream society. They begin to internalize alternative values and perspectives, and look for illegitimate opportunities. They don't just wake up one day and decide to become criminals or drug dealers; they learn it through their culture and the mindset they develop. In order to learn illegitimate methodology to commit crime, people generally have to live in a culture that presents a wide selection of illegitimate opportunities.

Drug dealing is the easiest vehicle for crime. All you need is a supplier; you can easily find a market for it. In this case, the market is middle-class kids. And if one kid is in a middle-class high school, he will soon bring you thirty more customers.

It is no mystery why dealing drugs is the vehicle many impover-ished young people use to achieve some form of success. It allows them to acquire the recognized status symbols: the leather jacket, the ready cash, the car, the jewellery. All they're trying to do is break out of the culture of poverty, realizing that the normal stream for life success does not exist for them.

When middle-class kids get strung out on drugs and find they have used up their disposable income (their allowance and their lunch mon-ey), they begin to victimize and steal from the people closest to them: their parents, their siblings, their grandmother. They get away with it for a while because people in these sorts of families don't generally count the money in their wallets. They aren't wise to fraudulent scams, and therefore, do not keep their PIN numbers secure. They will often say to a family member, "Drop by my bank and pick up some money for me. Here's my PIN number."

Middle-class kids don't know how to steal because they haven't had illegitimate opportunities. They haven't developed the mindset of ano-mie where they see the whole world as their prey. Instead, they resort to a number of scams that victimize family. One is to take a parent's cheque book and write themselves a cheque, forging the parent's sig-nature and adding a note like 'Happy Birthday' at the bottom. Most people only scan their bank statements at the end of the month, and if the child can get to the mailbox and intercept the statement and the cancelled cheques first, all the better.

This was one of the things Mark was doing. He also stole Noreen's credit cards. He would go to Canadian Tire, buy an expensive piece of equipment, then return it later for cash. Another source of money for him was stealing and selling valuable Royal Doulton figurines and jew-ellery that Noreen inherited from her mother. He also stole her car.

Mark was doing all the typical things that middle-class kids on drugs do, and he was at the point of being out of control.

The telephone call from Bob and my subsequent conversation with Noreen struck a responsive chord in me. I didn't know if I could help, but I sure wanted to try.

I ended up staying at the Hardwick home for most of the day. It didn't take long for me to determine that Mark was not a bully nor a fighter; he was just a very troubled young man with a deep drug prob-lem.

I confronted him with his drug use. I told him what would happen if he kept on the path he was traveling. I predicted he would be in prison within a few months, and I described what he could expect there.

"What do you know about it?" Mark jeered.

So I told him some of my story.

Mark ran out of the house and back in several times. It was terribly hard for Noreen to stand by and listen and watch this whole process without interfering, but I believe she knew it was their last resort. Noreen has her own take on the encounter and tells it this way:

When Bob told me about this Serge person, I really didn't think he would be able to help us. I had already been everywhere. I had been to the shrink; I had pursued all the traditional avenues within the system. I had done everything I knew to do, and nothing worked. It was all profoundly traumatic.

I'd even had a nervous breakdown over it that kept me off work for five months. I was now back at work, but I still cried all the way to work every day in the car and all the way home again.

I was skeptical, but I was also desperate, and when Bob asked if he should phone this Serge fellow, I said, "Go ahead." I was too emotionally distraught to pay much attention to the conversation.

Suddenly Bob said, "Serge wants to talk to you."

I took the phone and heard a brusque, no-nonsense voice say, "I'm going to be in Mississauga next week. Give me your address."

I did.

"I'll be there at 10:30 in the morning," he said. "You be at home. And keep your boy at home."

I said, "I will."

"Don't forget. You stay home. And keep your boy home."

The night before Serge's visit I made sure the house was spic and span. I baked muffins to serve with coffee, and even prepared a pot of chili just in case he stayed for lunch. The next morning I was up early, laying out my best silver and my nicest coffee mugs.

At 10:30, a little Nissan pulled up in front of the house. A man got out. He was wearing blue jeans and a leather bomber jacket, and with his beard and moustache and little round yellow John Lennon glasses, he looked like someone from a biker gang. I wondered what on earth I had gotten myself into. He looked exactly like so many of the men I saw every day on the streets of Inner-City Toronto.

He rang the doorbell and I answered, offering my hand. "Please come in," I said. *"Can I take your jacket?"*

He took off his jacket, and my heart sank. He was wearing a black t-shirt with 'Drink & Die' across the front, and his bulging arms were covered with huge tattoos. Now I knew for sure he was a biker.

"Where's your son?" he asked.

I called up the stairs. "Ma-ark, Serge LeClerc is here."

Mark appeared and came down the stairs slowly. When he reached the bottom, I proceeded to introduced them.

"Mark, this is Serge. Serge, this is—"

But Serge wasn't there. He was already in the livingroom. He turned to Mark and demanded, "Who do you think you are, treating your mother this way?"

"It's none of your — business," Mark shot back. "That's between my mother and me."

"No, it isn't, because your mother has asked me to come here," Serge countered in a voice louder than Mark's. "Now I'm going to ask you the question again? Who do you think you are, treating your mother this way?"

The next six hours were mostly a blur for me. I could see that while Serge was talking to Mark and confronting him about his crack cocaine use and his criminal activity, he was also watching Mark, making a clinical assessment. And Mark, overwrought as he was, was making his own assessment of this bizarre situation and the larger-than-life individual who had the audacity to challenge him in this way.

"I know you're on drugs," Serge told Mark flatly. "You can get away with deceiving some people. Maybe your mother believes you're not using, but I don't believe you. And I'm going to tell you something else. Within a few months, you will be in prison. Let me tell you what they do to nice boys like you in prison."

It was extremely hard for me to watch my son go absolutely nuts. I couldn't handle the confrontational nature of the exchange. It gave me a terrible headache, but I knew what was happening that day was very important. Mark told me later that he hated Serge, but he really liked him, too.

Around noon, I served lunch at the dining room table. We had the chili I had prepared the night before. During the meal, Serge started talking to me, asking me about myself and what I did for pleasure. I said I enjoyed gardening, decorating, and doing my school work.

He called me the next day. I said, "Why are you phoning me?"

"Because you are in crisis with your boy," he said. "I think I should come back and help you set up a plan for him."

So we went through that process. Mark was still getting into trouble, not going to school. It broke my heart because he'd had such an enriched life with all the educational advantages a kid could have. He was in French immersion, he traveled, kayaked, skied, and played the French horn. When he started giving all that up, I knew he had a problem.

Then Mark stole another credit card from me and Serge said, "Noreen, you have to stop this right now. Let him know he has to stop this with you. Your son will continue to victimize you, and you can't let that happen. You are enabling him by allowing this pattern to continue. He must be held accountable for his actions. I'm going to take you down to the judge and you're going to have him charged."

That's when the mother instinct really kicked in. My father had always told me you never, ever put your family in jail. If your brother steals from you, you learn to hide your money, but you don't put your brother in jail. So here I was with my son, my only child…

I let him be charged because I knew it was the only way to get this stopped.

I ended up taking Mark on as a client, for lack of a better term. It turned out that I knew his probation officer and between the two of us, we were able to get him into a nine-month secure custody program in a long-term residential treatment centre. It was either that or jail.

Normally, at this point, I would have turned the case over to someone else, but I didn't this time. I remained involved, visiting Mark, advocating for him, representing him, and working with Noreen to get him established in the treatment program. The reason I stayed was because, in my professional opinion, the program we put him in had a weakness. It generally dealt with disadvantaged youth rather than kids like Mark. I felt the transition and the after-care was weak, and that the family input in the programming was non-existent. Because of the reputation I had established in addictions counseling, I was able to say, "No, this is what we're going to do," and I continued on with Noreen, acting almost in a parental role.

Through this process, Noreen and I had many in-depth conversations about our work, and it didn't take long for her to recognize there was a place for my services within the school system. It was also evident that we shared many common interests and world views, including those on inner-city poverty and young people in trouble or in custody.

I began working as an in-service consultant and advocate in many Toronto schools where Noreen and I established week-long residential programs that were held in both elementary and secondary schools. These were unique projects where I would stay for a week in an inner-city or alternative school, the kind of place where students went when they were kicked out of the other schools or living on their own. Some were pregnant; some came to school with babies; some had drug problems and were trying to pull their lives together. Most were alienated from mainstream life. I would stay for a week at a time in those schools and hold teacher in-services, teach classes on law, family studies, and the justice system, and do full assemblies and community nights. I set up an office in the school, and during noon hour, or when I wasn't teaching, students had access to me for one-on-one counseling. I also set up a hotline for the parents to talk to me about their kids who were in the school.

Because of my past experience in both the East End and West End of Toronto, I turned out to be something of a celebrity in these inner-city schools. When we did a community night in Cabbagetown, for instance, there were kids hanging from the rafters. They all wanted to come and see this guy from Cabbagetown who'd made it, this guy who broken out. Many came because I had done time with their dad or their uncle.

Noreen and I also developed a cutting edge curriculum program that was years ahead of its time. The in-depth material focused on transitioning young offenders coming out of custody and going back into the school system. It addressed the transition, advocacy, after-care, and retention. The project involved many, many months of preparation and scores of meetings with superintendents, trying to persuade the Toronto Board of Education to accept this innovative new model.

Noreen and I found we worked well together, and we became close friends. She was an excellent cook, too, and I love to eat.

On one occasion, Noreen said to me, "If there is ever a social event I'm invited to, would you be my escort?"

I said, "Sure. I'd be happy to do that."

Some time afterward, Noreen went to China on a month-long education exchange. Before she left, she offered me the use of her cottage on Lake Simcoe. She said it was her way of reimbursing me for the work I'd done on Mark's behalf. Any other time, I would have charged a fee for my services, but in this case, I hadn't charged anything.

I accepted her offer and headed up to the cottage for a time of rest and relaxation. I invited Ron Hall to join me for part of the time.

Noreen actually owned two cottages. One was an older building where she had a boat stored. She asked if, while I was at the lake, I would mind going over and bringing the boat back. So there I was, this inner-city kid who had never been in a boat before in his life, saying, "Yeah, sure, I'll go get the boat."

The first thing I did when I got there was drive around the lake in my car to find out where this other cottage was. My plan was to hire a cab to take me there so all I had to do was go to the boathouse, start the motor, and drive the boat back across to the other cottage. Simple, right?

Wrong.

I got in the boat and began cruising across the lake, but by the time I reached the other side, the boat was half-full of water. I thought nothing of it and simply tipped the boat over on the beach to get rid of the water.

An evening or two later, Ron came. We decided we would take the boat and go across to Orillia for dinner. Unfortunately, with two of us in the boat, it began taking on so much water that we were soon bailing for all we were worth.

We made it to the dock in Orillia, but as I got out of the boat, I said to Ron, "This boat is sinking, Ron. It's full of water. We'd better empty it out or we'll never make it back."

An old fellow came over and watched us bail for a while. Then he said, "Did you put the plug in?"

"The plug—?" I echoed. "Why would you have a plug in a boat?"

"All boats have plugs," he said patiently. "That's so if they fill up with water, you can drain them out."

When I got home after the week at the lake, Glen said, "Hmm-mm... Cottage? Boat? That's kind of interesting."

In due time, Noreen came home from China. She had several gifts for me. I brought them home and showed them to Glen.

"That's a lot of presents," he remarked. "Let me get this straight. Before this woman went to China, every time you went to work with her you came home with casseroles and things. Then she goes to China and gives you her cottage. Now she comes back from China with all these presents. Let me tell you something, Serge. One present? That's a thank you. Two presents? That's a thank you with fondness. Three presents? That's a thank you and this is getting serious. Four or five presents, she's getting designs on you, my friend."

Being about as thick as a board and pretty naïve when it came to romantic relationships, I said, "Nah... She's just grateful and kind."

"Serge," Glen said, "you've been in prison too long. This is more than just a friendship."

"No," I insisted, "this is just a friendship."

Sometime later, Noreen invited me to spend the weekend at the cottage with her. I said, "I can't do that. You're going to be there, too."

"There are two bedrooms," she said. "Why don't you come? You can read and relax, and do whatever you want."

"Well, then, fine," I said, "I'll come."

It was during that weekend, across the dining room table, that Noreen revealed to me that while she was away in China, she realized that the feelings she had for me were more than friendship. "Serge," she said, "if I were ever to have an intimate relationship with a man again, I would like it to be with you."

"O-oh, you would, would you?" I blurted.

I was stunned. I didn't know what to say. Hadn't I just convinced myself and Glen that there was nothing more than friendship between Noreen and me?

I had to go away and think about this for a while.

It was quite a psychological adjustment. In my head, I truly believed I was meant to be a bachelor. Since leaving prison, I had been in a couple of relationships that hadn't panned out and I figured with all those years in jail and my history as a drug addict, I just wasn't husband material. I didn't think I knew what it took to be a good spouse. I didn't believe I was meant to be married.

Nine months later, Noreen Hardwick and I were married. Actually, we got married twice.

We had planned to be married during the summer of 1993. I thought it would take that long to get everything in order. Besides having an office in the house I co-owned with Glen, I also had an office in Brantford, about an hour and twenty minutes away. As well, our organization had the foodbank in Brantford which Ron and I operated from a converted dairy, and I was speaking all over the place.

In fairness to Noreen, who had resumed her position as coordinator of inner city schools in Toronto, I knew I should move to where she was, rather than her to me.

Glen and I put the house up for sale and it sold much faster than I anticipated. Part of the deal was immediate possession.

Suddenly I had nowhere to go.

"We're engaged," I said to Noreen, "but I won't move into your house until we're married."

"Fine," she said, "then let's get married."

That's what we did. We got a license; I used Ron Hall as my best man even though Noreen had never met him. Noreen had the inner-city advisor, Marnie Somers, (whom I had never met) stand up for her. We were married at the First Homestead which is now used as a chapel in Etobicoke, Ontario.

Then I moved in.

Our second wedding was held on August 26th. One of the reasons for the second ceremony was that Mark wasn't able to attend our first wedding because he was still in his recovery program. This second wedding was a private affair in the garden of our home with about a hundred and fifty guests. Mark was involved. Peter Kun, who often accompanied me when I was on the road doing youth rallies, provided the music, and Brian Inkster did the ceremony. He was a chaplain at Barton Street Jail. I had known him for a long time, but he had never done a wedding before he married us.

We chose August 26 for our wedding day because it was such a special day for me. August 26, 1988, was the day I was released from prison for the last time.

NINETEEN

Marrying me meant a number of adjustments for Noreen. For a long time, she avoided talking about my time in jail. She referred to it as being 'at camp.' I said, "Noreen, you have to stop calling it camp. It was prison. I was in prison."

Meeting people from my past was also an education for her. There were several who wanted to go straight, get an education, and build a new life. Two or three of them came to me for help.

On one occasion, before Noreen and I were married, I was working with two former drug addicts and long-time offenders, mentoring them, assisting them financially, and helping them get established in school.

I often talked about these 'projects' to Noreen. She wanted to meet them, so I invited these two men over to her house for dinner.

At one point during the meal, Noreen said to me, "Sergie, would you please get the bread from the kitchen?"

The men's jaws dropped. "Sergie—! Sergie—?"

Noreen looked startled. "What's wrong?"

"Sergie—?" they repeated. "If anyone in prison had called him Sergie, he'd have killed them," and the two roared with laughter.

Following our marriage, I continued with my speaking schedule and through that, was asked to make a presentation at a school for troubled boys. A family in my church had a son in the school; he was into drugs and having other difficulties. They offered to pay my fee if

I would go to the school and speak to the boys.

I said I didn't want the money; I would do it for nothing. My visit to the school resulted in the headmaster offering me a job. "We're losing a lot of potential students," he said. "They don't want to come here because of the drug problems that exist, and we have nobody to address the issue effectively. Of our one hundred and twenty-five students, I'm sure fully one-third have addiction problems. Would you consider joining our staff? Unfortunately, we wouldn't be able to pay you a lot of money for the work."

I discussed the proposal with Noreen.

"It would get you off the road," she remarked. I was still speaking up to one hundred and ten times a year and making good money, but a hectic schedule like that is not acceptable when you're a married man. Besides, Noreen was winding down her career and looking to take early retirement in a year or so.

"I believe this is the sort of work you would really like," she added. "The school is about an hour and a half away, but the driving is good."

I accepted the position with the Creative Centre for Learning and Development, but we made the arrangements through my consulting company so that I could continue speaking and doing promotional work on the side.

Noreen retired. We sold our home in Toronto, and moved closer to the school. I worked there for seven and a half years, all the while remaining on the roster of two speaker bureaus. I had honed my skills as a specialized counselor around the issues of substance abuse, and besides acting as a consultant in that capacity, I also set up counseling services in the boys' school, and at Rocklyn Academy, a private school for troubled girls that Noreen and I established with another couple. One of my areas of expertise was programming and designing program delivery for youth with addictions, focusing on preventative and community-based initiatives.

At no time did I try to push myself on anyone as a speaker. It was reminiscent of my wanting to be a volunteer and getting turned down sixteen times. I had the philosophy that everyone had a right to first satisfy themselves that I was authentic, because I was definitely an exception to the rule. I had *habilitated* in spite of the system, therefore, I could understand how people would be distrustful. I let it be known that I was willing and available, but I waited for people to come to me.

I wanted them to feel comfortable doing it.

Eventually, my speaking caught the attention of a local Crime Stoppers chapter and the president invited me to speak at a conference for Crime Stoppers in Ontario.

In many ways, it was a stretch for me to do this. It was a stretch for the police, too. I'm sure they investigated me thoroughly beforehand through CPIC, the Canadian Police Information Centre, the repository for all criminal record data. There was certainly plenty for them to find.

I had never spoken at a Crime Stoppers conference before, but I believed in what the organization was doing. I knew how crucial it is to socialize young people into morality, values, and ethics—exactly what the Crime Stoppers program tries to do. It was also what I was endeavoring to do through my presentations in schools. I felt we were creating a milieu of morality and values, and encouraging young people to break the silence and do the right thing.

After that first conference, everything seemed to snowball. I was invited to speak at an international Crime Stoppers conference in British Columbia, then at another one in Wyoming. Through these conferences, contacts were established with various police forces across North America, as well as with the Royal Canadian Mounted Police in Canada.

The most unusual presentation of my entire speaking career was in Newfoundland where I was invited to be the keynote speaker and presenter at the Policeman of the Year Awards. Law enforcement personnel there embraced me wholeheartedly, gave me lunch, and took me on a tour of the RCMP headquarters. Later, I presented the award for Policeman of the Year. How ironic is that, when not many years before I was on the RCMP's Most Wanted List?

I toured the whole province of Newfoundland speaking on behalf of Newfoundland Crime Stoppers and the RCMP, and through it, made a strong network of close friends.

I also spent a few days with the district commander of the Northwest Territories, flying around in his plane, touring the Territories with him. We became good friends.

Wherever I speak, I share my life story. What makes it unique is not that the story is so unusual—plenty of people have experienced the first part of my life—but after doing the first part, very few have done the second.

I'm sure many who hear my story don't quite believe that everything I say is true. Some surely think I am exaggerating my criminal record. If they do, they are wrong. I tell the story exactly as it was. I have never hidden my background. My full résumé was, and is now, on my website. I am up front about everything. I want people to see the fruit of a changed life, the completion of a five-year parole, the earning of a university education. It is very important to me that people understand, just as it was important when I married Noreen for her to understand that though I was a very evil man at one time, the man she married is not that same person.

The work I did with Crime Stoppers took me to a new and different level. It took me to the place where I was able to begin looking at creating a positive epitaph for myself, an epitaph that might in some small way make up for the mountain of damage I had caused in my lifetime as a thief, a criminal, and a drug dealer.

Coming to that point was no easy thing. I had broken every one of the Ten Commandments—more than once. That's not something most human beings do in their lifetime, and I had to forgive myself. It was an essential part of the arduous journey of untwisting.

Given my lengthy criminal record, one of the snags that often came up when I was invited to speak in the United States was getting proper clearance to cross the border. On one occasion, I was booked to speak at a large conference in Washington, D.C., but I had to cancel the appointment because official clearance did not come through in time.

Another time, I was asked to go to Indiana to appear as an expert witness on a death penalty trial for a nineteen-year-old boy who killed a shopkeeper while in the psychosis of speed addiction. He was strung out on crystal meth. The family knew me, and I had done six months of counseling with the boy. The authorities wanted to give him the death penalty.

In many American states, capital murder trials are divided into two separate phases. The first part is for conviction, determining whether the person is innocent or guilty. The second part is the sentencing trial where they consider whether or not to impose the death penalty.

This was the death penalty phase of this young man's capital murder trial, and as a polysubstance abuse expert, I was asked to testify.

The young man's lawyer called me. "You are the foremost expert in this field, and you know this boy intimately. The State wants to kill him. Will you come down and be an expert witness?"

I said I'd be happy to do that, but I almost didn't make it.

To get me across the border, they had to get a U.S. senator in-volved. They had to put paperwork in place at Niagara Falls so that I could cross the border there and fly from Buffalo to Indiana. It was a tight squeeze. When you're operating on a fixed trial date, there isn't a whole lot of flex.

By the time we got through all the red tape, I said to myself, "This is nuts. The only thing stopping me from crossing the border to do these things is the fact that I have a criminal record. I need to get my-self a pardon."

Now understand, I didn't want the pardon to hide what I was or what I had done. I needed a pardon to take my criminal record off paper so I could go anywhere a door was open and my expertise was needed. In this particular case, my expertise and testimony literally meant the difference between life and death for that young man in Indiana.

When I got back home, I went to a lawyer and told him I wanted to apply for a pardon.

He laughed.

"Nobody with your criminal record has ever been granted a par-don," he said. "Pardons are not meant for men like you. People like you die in prison. They never go straight, and they certainly never apply for pardons. Man, you've got organized crime on your record, you've got a $40 million drug lab, you've been a career criminal—I'm telling you right now, they're not going to give you a pardon. Besides, it will take a lot of work and maybe five or six years of your life. Are you prepared to invest that kind of time, money, and energy?"

"Yes," I said, "I am."

Shaking his head, he prepared the application.

I mentioned the incident to a friend of mine who had been a po-lice chief for twenty years. I told him I had applied for a pardon, and that I expected it to be a very long process.

My lawyer was right. There was a lot of rigmarole involved. Every place where I had ever been arrested—every city, every province, every police division, every police force, every RCMP detachment—had to be contacted. Each one had to sign off and state their opinion and po-sition regarding this application. I also had to be cleared by the RCMP and the parole people for the five years immediately following my last incarceration. I had to have fingerprints taken. It's a tedious process that involved a good deal of protocol, legalese, and copious paperwork.

But I went through it all.

What I did not know was that following my conversation with my police chief friend, he put out the word throughout the law enforcement community. People from Crime Stoppers Canada, Crime Stoppers International, police chiefs, sheriffs, RCMP superintendents and inspectors, law enforcement officials across Canada and the United States—all of them wrote letters of reference on my behalf and sent them to the Canadian government. Each one basically said, 'This man is the real deal. Here is what he has done to make restitution. We will validate him.'

When the officials in Ottawa saw all these strongly supportive letters flooding in, they granted the pardon. Instead of taking five or six years, as my lawyer predicted, it took two.

In August of 2000, my lawyer called. "You've got a letter here from the Government of Canada and the National Parole Board," he said. "You'd better come down to the office. We'll open it together. But remember what I told you. Expect a 'No.'"

I drove to his office.

The lawyer opened the envelope and drew out the document. He screened it first because it was full of jargon and legalese.

After a moment he looked up. "You won't believe this," he said. "This is unbelievable. I have never seen anything like it in my life. Your application went before the House of Commons and the Government of Canada has passed an Act of Parliament to give you a full national pardon. I can't understand how this happened. It is completely unbelievable!"

It was only later that I found out about the letter writing campaign on my behalf.

Needless to say, I left the lawyer's office in a state of euphoria. As Noreen and I drove down Highway 401, we asked one another, "How do you celebrate a pardon? Is there a protocol? Do you have a party? Whom do you invite?"

We laughed and joked about it, but receiving that pardon was immensely important to me. It was unparalleled as a personal validation for the work I was doing. I no longer had to prove anything. People recognized that I was real. I was a good man. The words that came out of my mouth were substantiated by my character. The pardon said I did more than talk the talk. It said I walked the walk.

TWENTY

By 2002, I was beginning to think about retiring.

The truth is, I was worn out. When you have an addictive personality, you tend to do things in excess, be it gambling, drugs, alcohol, sex, pornography, or work. In my case, it was work and the difficulty I had saying, "No."

Being a work-driven person, I had been going full throttle, carrying a caseload of forty clients for years, supervising a department with a staff of five, and all the while keeping up a full speaking schedule.

I was exhausted.

Noreen had taken early retirement; we were comfortable. I was drawing substantial fees for my speaking appearances and figured if I did a dozen or so engagements a year, I could make enough money for the two of us to live on. That would give me the luxury of spending more time with my wife and perhaps taking on some charity projects.

Our biggest decision was where we would retire. The Sunshine Coast of Spain was high on our list of considerations.

A year before my planned retirement, I made a trip to Saskatoon, Saskatchewan, at the request of two friends I had come to know through Crime Stoppers. Drew Byers was the past president of Crime Stoppers Saskatoon, and Dave Scott was the chief of police in Saskatoon at the time.

Drew and Dave wondered if I would pay a visit to the prairie city to meet with a group that was establishing a faith-based, residential recovery centre for young men with addictions. My friends asked if I would do some speaking in the area to give the project a little promotion, and, as well, meet with a couple of committees to see if their programming was on track.

I said, "Sure, I'll come for a couple of weeks."

I went to Saskatoon, spoke to a number of audiences, and had a series of meetings with the Prairie Hope group. I felt the project was a good one, and certainly much-needed in the province.

Then I went home.

Not long afterwards, I got another call from Drew Byers. "We're looking for an executive director for Prairie Hope," he said. "Can you suggest anyone?"

"Yeah," I said, "I know a couple of people. I'll contact them. Why don't you send me the job specs and I'll pass them on?"

The conversation went on a little longer, and in the course of it, Drew asked, "By the way, Serge, what are you doing these days? Do you want to come out here and do some more speaking?"

"Oh, I don't know," I said somewhat vaguely. "I'm sort of taking it easy these days."

Drew immediately picked up on the 'sort of.' "You mean you're not with the school anymore? You're free?"

It wasn't long before I received a letter from the board of Prairie Hope with a formal proposition asking if I was interested in applying for the position of executive director.

I phoned back and declined.

A month later, they called by telephone. "We have this search committee," they said, "and your name keeps coming up. No one else seems to fit the bill quite like you do."

"We want to be very honest with you, Serge," they added. "If we can't get the right person to head up this project, we're going to scrap it."

The committee was having all sorts of difficulties getting the centre off the ground. One was finding an appropriate location. A wonderful river-view property had been donated, but some of the residents in the area were opposed to having a rehabilitation centre in their community and launched a 'not-in-my-backyard' protest that included intimidating other potential neighbors. They won that round. The Prairie Hope committee was unable to get the land properly zoned and, as a result, they lost a good deal of the money they had already invested in the project.

"If something doesn't happen very quickly," the board said, "the project is going to die. You have all the right skills, Serge—the ability to communicate and the expertise and insight into addictions. We would really like you to come out here and listen to what we have to say."

I told them I would talk to Noreen.

About the same time, Ron Nikkel from Prison Fellowship International flew down from Washington, D.C., to ask if I would be the keynote speaker at a Prison Fellowship International Conference. Charles Colson, the founder, would be in attendance and they wondered if I would do a workshop on leadership.

"And by the way," said Ron, "we're looking for someone to resurrect Prison Fellowship Canada. Are you interested? It would be a national position and you could assume the national directorship in a year or so."

At first glance, that offer seemed the more tempting of the two. I could work out of our home, and the salary they were offering significantly exceeded that of the group in Saskatoon. All my expenses would be met; my schedule was my own.

I said to Noreen, "I'm thinking this isn't a bad deal. It's nothing at all like having forty kids on my caseload and managing a department."

Noreen was oddly uncomfortable with the idea. She had watched me come away from speaking engagements in prisons and seen the effect it had on me. Talking to kids in prison tears me up inside because I identify so closely with them. Noreen didn't want me in that milieu. She felt that, over time, it would have a detrimental effect on me. She also felt that anything to do with prison was part of my past, not my future.

We decided to go to Saskatoon and give the opportunity there a closer look. Noreen came along to be part of the interview process. I wanted to have reinforcements in case I had to say "No" to my friends Drew and Dave.

The plan backfired.

They placed the offer on the table. We went back to the hotel to discuss it and pray about it.

Noreen said, "I think we ought to come here. You've talked a long time about leaving a legacy, about balancing the scales. Well, Serge, this province has a massive drug problem and it doesn't have a long-term residential substance abuse treatment program of any kind. You know the statistics: Saskatchewan incarcerates more children per capita than anywhere else in the industrialized world. The prison population per capita is the highest; the drug problem is the highest. In terms of alcoholism, Saskatchewan's average doubles the national average. Drugs and alcohol are the number one killer of kids below the age of twenty-five in this province."

"With your Aboriginal background," she went on, "you are ideally suited to this position because this province has the highest Aboriginal population in the country. You can speak effectively, and you have great insights into what needs to be done. I think you should accept the position."

I told the search committee I needed more time to consider the offer.

There were several things to consider. Accepting the job in Saskatoon would mean leaving Mark in college back in Ontario; it would mean saying good-bye to our church and our friends. It would mean selling our Fonthill home which we had just spent four years renovating and landscaping. We had also spent two years doing the same thing at our Lake Simcoe cottage. Besides, Noreen and I were getting ready for retirement.

I have never heard God speak in my head saying, "Serge, go and do this, or do that." I take a more pragmatic view of things. I recognize that we live in a tactile world where it is very evident what one ought to be doing if one truly honors the 'Do unto others as you want them to do to you' rule. We are instructed to feed the hungry, clothe the naked, and visit those in prison. For me that is living out what Jesus the Man did. His vision of how we should treat one another is spelled out very plainly in the Sermon on the Mount.

I also believe that God opens doors of opportunity, but you have to be in the hallway to see them. I have made it a policy in my life to be in the hallway wherever possible so that I can see what doors of opportunity God wants me to go through. I believe He also closes doors, and that circumstances dictate which door you need to go through. It involves examining the circumstances, pinpointing the need, and determining how you can best serve humanity.

Being a practical sort of man, before making my decision, I went to see my friend George Glover, the National Director of Teen Challenge Canada.

Teen Challenge began in the early 1960s with a young country pastor by the name of David Wilkerson who was fresh out of bible college. Being rather idealistic and not clearly appreciating the world into which he was walking, he went to the inner-city of New York with the idea of beginning a ministry there.

Wilkerson soon became involved with a young gang leader named Nicky Cruz. That was the genesis of Teen Challenge, a long-term, faith-based, residential substance abuse recovery program which now operates in eighty-two countries of the world with more than six hundred programs. Teen Challenge came to Canada around 1975.

Teen Challenge is acknowledged as one of the most successful recovery programs in the world, something that has been substantiated by in-depth, long-term studies conducted by four major universities in the United States. It claims a seventy-plus percent success rate longitudinally (the studies followed students for up to seven years after graduation from the program).

I realized that what the committee was trying to set up in Saskatchewan was basically the Teen Challenge program under another name.

"George," I said, "you're familiar with the Prairie Hope project in Saskatoon because the organizers visited the Teen Challenge Farm in Ontario before they ever began developing their plans. They have asked me to be the executive director, but before I say yes or no, I need to have a plan in my head. I can't go there, find a place, get it zoned, raise the funds, hire a staff, get the PR done and the program going all at the same time. I know this is an unusual request, but would you allow me to use the Teen Challenge program and send my staff here to the Teen Challenge Farm to be trained?"

I was going out on a limb here because I had no real connection with Teen Challenge myself, but George knew me well. He knew my integrity, and my way of thinking and being. Because he sat on the Teen Challenge International Board, George offered to speak to Dave Wilkerson about the arrangement. He did so, and in the process, was able to reassure them of my character and guarantee that the program would not be misused in my hands.

He came back with permission to use the Teen Challenge protocol with one proviso: "You can count on our help if you—*and only you*—take the position."

It was a deal.

With the promise of the Teen Challenge curriculum in hand, I contacted the Prairie Hope Search Committee and told them I was prepared to accept the position of executive director. I said I would begin in May of 2003.

Not only did I use the Teen Challenge program material and have my first four staff members trained at the Teen Challenge Farm in Ontario, but the organization also donated the first two vehicles for the Saskatchewan project and gave me invaluable assistance and support thereafter.

It soon became evident that it was ridiculous for us to continue as an independent program, so we began the process of transitioning into Teen Challenge Canada. One year later we officially became Teen Challenge Saskatchewan.

I spent the first couple of months in Saskatoon on my own, living at Drew Byers' home until I found a nice rental house. Then Noreen and our two dogs came to join me.

I found office space for the organization and inherited a part-time 'Girl Friday,' $17,000 in the bank, an abundance of good will, and a lot of good people who were already sold on the project.

Here we go, I thought.

But it wasn't quite that easy. The resistance we met in establishing Teen Challenge Saskatchewan came as a shock to me.

We attempted to purchase three different properties before we finally acquired one near the town of Allan, Saskatchewan. All three times, there was a very strong negative response from the community in the form of threats, name-calling, secret meetings, not to mention insults from the provincial government and rebuffs from established health and addictions services. It threw me for a loop. I wasn't prepared for this kind of resistance. I didn't realize that we would be a political embarrassment.

Noreen and I were traveling somewhere in Montana on our way from Ontario to Saskatchewan when I received a call on my cell phone. A public meeting had been called to share the vision of our proposed program with the community around the piece of land we were trying to buy. We wanted to explain what the program was all about and assure residents they were in no danger. Instead, the residents held a secret meeting and informed Debbie, my Girl Friday, that they had taken a vote and the special zoning we required would not be allowed. They gave no reason, no explanation.

This was the third place we had been unsuccessful in purchasing. I couldn't understand the animosity. I found it deeply discouraging, and so did the board. I believe they were ready to give up.

As my personal life story has shown, rolling over and giving up is not part of my make-up.

We went searching again.

I was working with Archie Balon, a realtor whom I had met through my work with Crime Stoppers. Among other things, Archie was the chair of Student Crime Stoppers under Drew Byers and chair of the local Habitat for Humanity project. Bottom line: he was heavily involved in the community and one hundred percent behind the Teen Challenge project.

Archie and I spent months criss-crossing the province looking for potential properties on which to establish the Centre. I hadn't expected the process to be so adversarial. The moment people heard what we wanted the property for, the opposition began. They called us names, swore at us, threatened us, warned they would dump manure on our driveway.

On this one particular day, Archie and I were coming to the end of a very long day of searching. We had driven seven hundred kilometers. Part of that was an exploration trip to Prince Albert, a community about one hundred kilometers north of Saskatoon. None of the properties we had looked at seemed right.

As we were approaching Saskatoon, Archie said, "You know, Serge, there is a property near Allan that came up on the listings last night just after I got home from our last trip. It is so new it hasn't even been multiple-listed yet. The farm is in an area we haven't investigated, and it sounds like it might be just what we're looking for. I know this has been a long day, but would you like to go and have a look at it?"

"Why not?" I said.

Of course, that was the property we bought. It was ideal for us— ten acres of land thirty-five minutes from the city in the middle of nowhere, the perfect location for an addictions recovery program. We had absolutely no neighbors.

The property had not one, but two houses on the yard, and an in-dependent water source. It had outbuildings, too — a barn, a quonset, garages, and storage buildings, all of which were invaluable to us.

What's more, the sellers, Andy and Sandy, were thrilled to have their property going to an initiative like Teen Challenge. The acreage was part of a homestead farm that had been in the family for eighty

years. One of Andy's brothers died on the property in a farming ac-
cident. Another lived in one of the two houses on the property and
committed suicide as a result of alcohol abuse, so Andy and Sandy
could not imagine the homestead being used for anything better than
a rehabilitation centre for young men with substance addictions. They
especially loved the fact that we were going to use the original house as
a dormitory.

We purchased the property, and given our past experiences, applied
with some trepidation to have it zoned.

The reeve of the municipality, Jim Gray, said, "Speaking on behalf
of this community, I want you to know that we are proud to have you
here. This is a good work you're doing. It is necessary. I have studied
your material and it makes good sense. I will personally push the zon-
ing through. We will find a way."

The property was zoned under an education and religious designa-
tion. The whole process was complete in two weeks.

We acquired some staff and started getting the word out that we
would be open for clients in a couple of months. Our plan was to have
everything we needed in place before we opened.

Almost immediately, we had four young men on the waiting list,
but when one of them committed suicide, I said, "I'm not waiting any
longer."

We opened our doors even though we needed more staff and all
we could offer were mattresses on the floor. The four staff people
were already in Ontario being trained, and I told the boys to bear with
us, the beds were coming.

The program is the same as any other Teen Challenge program
across North America—twelve to fourteen months in length. It is
faith-based, very professional, and long term. The philosophy of the
program is this: You have made the choice to enter into a relationship
with a disease. It is the only disease of its kind in the world from which
people do not want to get well. But if you have entered into the rela-
tionship, you can also make a choice to leave that relationship. We do
not believe, as some programs do, that you are in recovery for the rest
of your life. We believe you have come to a place of recovery and can
become a *recovered* addict as opposed to a life-long *recovering* addict.

Students learn to live again once they have made the choice to leave
the relationship with the addiction. The choice no longer becomes the
issue. Remember, people do not do drugs to feel good, they do drugs

to stop feeling bad. The program helps them get to a place where they stop feeling bad. The goal is for them to get high on life and stay that way.

I end my story with Teen Challenge because I believe this is my crowning epitaph. The work that is being done at Teen Challenge Saskatchewan is making a huge difference in scores of peoples' lives. Long after I am gone, it will continue to make a difference, as will my on-going work with my other favorite organizations like Crime Stoppers, Prison Fellowship, New Life Prison Ministries and the like.

As I look back on my life, I am grateful that God found a way to use my life's experiences for good. It is because of my own addictions, my time in prison, and my past experiences, that I am able to share the passion and vision of what Teen Challenge does and will continue to do.

Many good people have come alongside in this work that changes peoples' lives in a radical and permanent way, in a way that gives them back a life.

Today I am just an ordinary man striving to be a good and peaceful person. I go to work each day; I tend my garden. I go to garage sales; I walk our dog. I travel here and there, watch TV, answer e-mails, and enjoy my life with my dear wife. I continue to love public speaking and, as always, I have a supply of good books nearby.

GONE TO GROUND

Selected Poems & Essays

JACQLYN THORNE

with photographs by the author

GONE TO GROUND
Copyright © 2016 JACQLYN THORNE

To order additional copies of this title, please visit your local bookstore, Amazon.com, or the author's website, www.creativejourneywoman.com.

ISBN-13: 978-0692730249
ISBN -10: 0692730249

DEDICATION

For my mother,
who read me Longfellow
and set out to make me a poet
right from the start.

CONTENTS

ACKNOWLEDGMENTS

Heart-felt thanks to my friend Maria Wulf, who gave me the courage to begin sharing my words at last, and the welcome opportunity to do so. I would also like to thank my writing teacher, Jon Katz, for his support and guidance, my writing group, and all my friends, my homemade family and fellow travelers, for their support and encouragement through the years. Everything is possible with love.

FOREWORD

In 8th grade I wrote my first official poem for an English class. Entitled "Quiet Calamity," it was about the inner turmoil I felt at the time, a conflicting combination of isolation and chaos that resulted from years of difficulties in my family. It was both a statement and an emotional release for me, and I still recall composing it to this day.

My teacher, Mrs. Chipley, typed our class poems up on crisp white paper, and published mine alongside those of my classmates in a clear plastic sheet binder. Every student received a copy to take home, and I waited anxiously to get mine into my hands.

I remember how proud I felt seeing my written words on the page, sharp and black, and somehow more important and meaningful when reproduced by someone else, when read by so many others.

Mrs. Chipley later gave me quite the compliment, telling me how far beyond my young years my verses were. She told me to keep writing, poetry, essays, stories, whatever I wanted. And despite a few bumps, hurdles and dry spells during my life, I really have not stopped since.

Writing and poetry have become, I believe, my way of asking questions, the hard ones and the easy, as well as my attempt to understand the answers. Most of the poems, essays, and photographs included here are rooted in the deep, spiritual connection I feel with nature and the physical world around me. I have learned (and continue to learn) to live my life within their framework, looking always to these sources first for guidance.

I haven't published any personal writing since that first poem back in grade school. I'm excited now to finally share my work with you, and hope among my words here you will find some to carry with you, to remain connected, stay grounded.

Gone to Ground

weathered stones
rough in my palm
scrape and peel,
carving their way
down to my bones

stiff thorns break
my thin pale skin,
blood flows, ready
to meet the air,
kiss the ground

silken soil slides
through my fingers,
under my nails,
down to the quick
never to come out

going down now
into the ground
again, taking up
my place, kneeling
here on this earth

finding a heaven
lies in the dirt
the rock, the wet
and sky, as above
so with me below

Low Fallen Sky

one foot in front of another
through the fields I walk
under a low fallen sky;
snow drips down around me
first to arrive on the scene

one step after another
as heaven above me
sheds its weighty crown;
below on earth I wander
adrift on a dry grassy sea

meant for now to roam here
untethered, anchorless
through this cold gray dream

No One Could See

hidden among lambs
lying in green grass,
carefully camouflaged,
waited my soul—
a wolf adorned in
pale sheep's clothing;
no one could know,
not even me,
what would unfold,
rise up from the grass,
emerge from shadows,
come crying to life
when my skin came off

but I felt a roaring
spill out of my chest,
rolling and burning,
chilling all the world:
no, you will not
take me back down
to the ground again,
I will not hide anymore
among sheep,
share their skins;
no more concealing
who I am,
deceiving myself,

wool over my eyes—

the wolf at the door
howling now, is me

Don't Draw the Blind

don't draw the blind–
I want to watch
the sun set behind
gray leaden hills,
the black line of trees,
as clouds curl up
and away, whispering
goodnight to the day

I want to see it all,
look behind the veil
at what day hides
down deep in her heart,
what she dreams of
when she heads off
into slumber, slowly
drawing in the night

I will stay here
vigilant, listening for
the last gasp of light,
whether soft or loud,
watching a clear ribbon
of sky, just underneath
her heavenly skin,
showing itself at last

Made My Bed

every morning I make up the bed,
press down the rumpled pleats,
fluff my pillows in their cases,
tidy up the tangled sheets

I wish it were such simple a task
to straighten up my life;
tuck in heartbreak, pull up sadness,
cover over pain and strife

some choices lay like linen sheets
whose creases will never come out,
no matter how much I tug or iron
or try to smooth them down

nagging small reminders,
they are marks I'd rather forget;
but there is no avoiding struggle
once the wrinkles are set

so I learn to live with consequences,
make peace with all the mess,
resolving to try with each new day
to leave one wrinkle less

Waking the Other

sleep ends broken,
stirred hard awake
by devils, sighs
feeling their breath,
warm on my neck,
whispers in my ear

abandoning my bed,
out I slip quietly
so silent, deafening
pulling back sheets,
covering up my trail
through a deep night

floating disembodied
across the cold floor,
growing ghostly,
heading out, heading in,
seeking comfort
only solitude provides

pressing on, touched
with courage, finally
unafraid, eager to dare
facing darkness on
it's native ground,
opening my eyes —

finding, to my surprise
my soft, steady heart
beating soundly over
conquered devils,
defeated enemies,
victorious and awake

Grasshopper

a tiny grasshopper came
to visit me
as I sat in the field

he climbed my leg
and paused,
to share the sunshine

together we welcomed spring
and the new day

Picking Up Sticks

leaves long raked and gathered,
now spring comes, and the trees
shed their winter bounty;
making my way beneath their bows,
sky blue, clouds shifting above,
I pick up sticks —
last of winter's bones

an endless sea of dry brown fingers,
some long and unbroken,
others crushed near to nothingness;
some fat, some thin
both forked and straight,
tiny souls unique as snowflakes,
fallen to the forest floor

for each one plucked
another presents itself;
walking all day, I could never
gather them all up,
there will always be more,
for the trees stand long and tall
and their burden is now mine

should I stop, give up my task?
admit defeat, and let nature
take it's own course?
or should I persist in trying

with each one collected
to make some small difference
in the whole, unending mess?

staring ahead at my fate
maybe the point, I come to see,
is not to get them all,
or to simply leave them be,
but to enjoy the day –
sun and sky and billowy breeze
and this chance to walk among the trees

contented then, I gather the sticks
and put them all in place;
a pile for kindling winter's woodstove,
some to spark fall campfires
and edge the summer garden,
some left for spring's small birds
to build their tidy nests

no need to hurry or worry for lack,
there's always another branch
on it's way down
to meet the downy grass,
kiss the wet, cold dirt
and lay patiently, waiting
to be discovered

Bits and Pieces

I carried the shifting weight
up the stairs,
down the hall,
to the attic door;
I set it down,
looked all around
for some secret space
on the floor

other loads lay all around me
gathering dust,
holding secrets,
packed away long ago;
no spot left bare,
no room to spare,
for this new burden,
no place to go

what now? I asked the darkness
take it back?
open it up,
scatter the contents around?
throw some here,
toss more there,
leave bits and pieces
on the ground?

only silence greeted me;
no voice said 'yes,'
or cried out 'no,'
I stood without reply –
so I took my box
and turned the lock,
resolved, with no place
left to hide

Sinking In

this house has stood
so long, alone
beneath the tall trees,
stretching up
toward the sky

now settling in,
sinking down
into the ground
that it once
had only rested on

bones are shifting—
time and pressure
leaving their marks
yet never quite touching
it's stony heart

here I sit, inside
counting my scars
feeling their weight;
now I understand,
I am home

Something In the Air

This morning I took a walk through the fields for the first time in quite awhile, feeling somehow different, lighter, than I have in a long time. The air and sky didn't feel as heavy; it wasn't nearly as cold. Birds were singing, busily visiting the feeders. Even my chickens were interested in coming out of their coop. I released them to peck and putter in the relatively snowless yard before I left with my dogs, Hannah and Gordie.

It felt almost like spring.

We started out across the lower field, heading toward the pond. The field is thick with grasses every summer, but almost always wet, too. My house is built on the side of a hill, and all the water that runs down ends up there. When he comes to mow for hay twice a year, the farmer's tractor leaves big ruts around the perimeter. They stay there until the ground thaws in the springtime.

Today when I saw them, frozen gullies now full of ice, I remembered that soon, one day, it would be warm again. Everything green will come back.

We crossed the cobbled together footbridge that marks the path to the pond. It's made out of an old metal ladder I tossed on the ground and covered with boards I found under the barn. It doesn't sound very impressive, but it's better than the crumbling, nail-spiked pallets that were there before, left by the people who previously owned the farm. I put my rubber boot down on one of the exposed nails just last year. Luckily, it slipped cleanly right between my toes.

After that, I decided the rotten pallets had to go. I cleaned

them up (they gave way easily), and set the new bridge down in an afternoon.

This morning the pond was an icy sheet, the dock with it's swimming ladder frozen in place. The pond is small, but deep and always cold, being spring-fed. The few times I've actually been swimming in it, I felt cold and warmer currents moving alternately past my body in the water. It felt very strange, and made me think of all the unseen things far below me, the soft bed of leaves and mud resting at the bottom.

Today, nothing appeared to be moving. But beneath the still white surface, I knew the fish were waiting, metabolisms slowed to a standstill, along with turtles and frogs buried in the muck. Although invisible, they were all still there, waiting to come back to life.

I headed out to check on the three hives of bees. They are wrapped in black tarpaper with a piece of foam board insulation placed in the tops to help keep heat in. So far all the extra precautions seem not to have been necessary. The winter has been mild, and I have gone out before to find a bee or two emerging from the hive, heading out to do her business somewhere nearby in the dried grass.

I put my ear up to the side of the hives, listening. I could feel more than hear them, the vibration of their buzzing deep inside traveling through the wood and Styrofoam walls.

I am always cautious when I do this not to make too much noise against the paper or jostle the hive. Although they are mostly dormant, a bothered bee could come storming out and try to sting me. If she got me, more would most likely follow. Then the dogs and I would be running across the field, ducking through bushes and branches as we went in the effort to

dodge them.

I know this because it's happened before, to my boyfriend (who mostly takes care of them), and to myself. And to the dogs who should know better by now than to get too close.

The hives have not survived the past few winters. It will be a joy and a relief if this year will be an exception, if all the efforts made to protect and feed them, prepare them, will come to fruition. It would mean hope. Which is why when I felt the bees inside this morning, alive and buzzing, my heart started humming right along with them.

Leaving the beehives behind, the dogs and I walked out to the open fields, barely covered by snow. Thin sheets of ice masked some spots on the ground, the wet and melted places. We know where they tend to be now, so it's easier to avoid them. The wind wasn't rough on us, and I felt again the mildness of the air. Peaks of blue sky came through the dull gray clouds, and I even saw shadows on the ground for a moment or two. My lab Hannah ran and ran, working her young legs, while Gordie stayed close beside me.

They were happy to be out; me, too. I knew it was good for us all.

Ready to head home, we turned and walked the path along the old apple orchard. Fooled by the weather, a few trees were already beginning to bud, rough and fuzzy nodules forming. "Not yet," I told them, "be patient. We still have more winter left, so keep quiet, just in case we're not out of the woods yet."

I realized I have felt the same way myself the past few weeks, cautious but wanting to be optimistic, hoping the dark days would soon be done. But knowing deep down, they may not be.

Still now, I felt brighter, my burdened lessened, hopeful and

almost peaceful.

As we returned to the yard, I saw so much life gathered there. More birds had arrived at the feeders, from big doves down to tiny goldfinches, feasting. The chickens were out scratching in the dry leaves, picking small blades of newly green grass with their dainty beaks. One had even dug herself down and was enjoying a dust bath underneath an old cart, something I thought never to see until summer came again.

They were making the most of the day, relishing whatever new feeling they perceived in the air. The one that I, clearly, had been experiencing, too.

On my walk this morning, I realized again that all these creatures were under my care, including the land around me. That by coming here to this place, I had agreed to steward all of it, as well as I could, from the trees to the fields, to the water, and to all the animals and smaller things that lived in and around it. That we all lived here together.

It was a responsibility and an agreement that was meant to help me as much as them. And no matter what sad or otherwise troubling thoughts lay in my mind, the little world around me was still there waiting, needing me to pay attention, to tend to it just as much.

And it, in turn, was eager and willing to give me solace, share peace, as it always has, if I just went out and simply took a walk, breathing the same air once again.

One Last Bright Day

one day more of sun
hard in my face,
along my arms,
before it disappears;
one last chance
to sink my fingers
into the earth,
dig down deep
and squeeze—
holding tightly
to what remains

this last bright day
pressing roots, soil
and soul into place;
one last moment
to feel a promise
of life and hope,
know it will return
anew, green and sweet
again come spring;
now though, to bed

Two Lives Now

I found a fallen sparrow
among the green grass,
the unfortunate victim
of a mirage in the glass;
still and so small,
he lay in a tumble
of soft brown feathers,
his plumage quite humble;
he seemed not to suffer,
I hoped and I prayed,
and promised to find him
a suitable grave

then a snake I encountered,
lame and so stricken,
seeing him writhe
my stomach grew sickened;
crushed near to death,
still unkindly alive,
biting his own flesh
in some primitive drive;
so I found a stone,
and took careful aim—
bringing it down,
I ended his pain

retrieving my sparrow,
I brought them together,
smooth scales and light feathers,
to mingle forever;
two lives now to bury,
weighed on my heart
once separate, now equal,
both fragile and short –
one lived high in the trees,
the other along the ground;
no more sunning or sliding,
no more sweet, cheerful sounds

so I laid them to rest
beneath a young maple tree,
at peace side by side,
now silent and free

JACQLYN THORNE

Wet Dog

wet dog, happy
in the sun

fresh from swimming
in the pond

shakes herself,
and smiles at me

Lost at Sea

swimming in the sea,
learning the ocean
has no end, no edge
no boundaries,
none the eye can see

below live mountains
and deep, dark valleys,
far away continents
close in, stop the spread;
they are lost on me

around me now, instead
endless lapping waves,
stretching out, away
to the distant horizon;
no compass point
or stars in the night sky
guiding me on to shore

floating here, waiting,
hoping the tide alone
can carry me home

Inside Out

don't look now
but your insides
are showing up
out here–

your soft, sweet heart
is on display
for all the world
to share

your gentle soul
overflows,
your skin
cannot contain it

out it comes
to meet the sun,
blinding us all
with love

The Keep

for years I only wanted quiet,
to utter not a word,
for a wall of silence
to surround me
and protect me from the world

it kept me safe, this fortress,
built with my own two hands;
it's walls were thick,
the gate shut tight–
no enemy roamed the lands

now these walls are crumbling,
stony silence breaking down,
giving way to words,
giving up the fight
against the voice I've found

Hibernation

if I could hide my soul
away from winter's chill
I would do it,
and be grateful
for each day spent
in quiet darkness, asleep

but out the window
all I see is the long, slow gray
of a deep winter day,
where the sun
seems ashamed
to show its face for long

here I lay, and pretend
that I am a bear
curled up inside
my own dark cave,
awaiting spring,
for my eyes and soul
to open again

Red Squirrel

a red squirrel sits alone
screaming in the tree,
trying to be bigger
than he knows himself to be

I have come too near
this home that he holds dear;
squinting up, I see
what I'm supposed to fear

his russet body hides
among the dry brown leaves
telling me to go—
but then it's him who flees

Be Still Now

in the quiet
warmth of sun,
resting here
tranquil, at ease
with the world
moving fast,
always around me–
holding on

no frantic rush
to go again;
centered, calm
still as water
unmoved by
current or breeze,
surface pristine
placid, peaceful

reflected down
deep inside me

Just In Time

ringing fills my ears —
foggy sleep fading,
wake up, wake up
right now, not in
five minutes or ten
or two, this here is
the moment

eyes sticky still
with dreams, sleep
stumbling through
gray early light,
pulling back a veil,
curtains opening
revealing the sky
simply on fire

dawn slowly burning,
the sun unleashing
a raw red power,
opening it's eye,
turning it's gaze upon
this brand new day,
scorching clouds
setting seas ablaze

one minute more,
a second further along
spent asleep, dreaming

it would be done,
finished without me –
the greatest show
on earth, over

Black Cat

black cat scratches
at my sleeve,
calling for attention
she so dearly needs

from her throat
a purr begins—
it seems she knows
I will give in

to rub her head
or soft black back,
to share her warmth
which never lacks

content, she sits
upon my arm;
now her claws
do little harm

green eyes close
to rest awhile;
her success
has made me smile

What the Tractors Taught Me

Last night a friend and I went to the Holiday Tractor Parade down in Greenwich, New York. It turned out to be a lot cooler and more fun than I thought it sounded like at first. Judging by the turnout, it's becoming quite an event. Next year they will probably sell tickets.

Greenwich is near the border with Vermont, set in a rolling landscape that is rich and very green, great for farmers and artists alike. It is kind of unique in that it has managed to remain a truly agricultural and farm-friendly town, while at the same time supporting a thriving arts community. It's exactly the kind of place that would bring a lighted tractor parade to life, and have a huge crowd of people come out to see it.

I, however, am not a big Christmas person. Yes, I'm one of those people. I have a hard time with lights going up early, Christmas decorations lining store shelves and music all over the radio when Thanksgiving hasn't even happened yet. So it felt a little early to me to be putting on a holiday parade, and certainly way too early for me to go to watch one.

But, I have to admit, I had a really good time.

Farms large and small and organizations that support them from around the area rolled out tractors, hay wagons, and a few pieces of farm equipment I couldn't identify loaded down with Christmas lights. Though I didn't count them, I'll bet close to a hundred tractors paraded down Main Street last night. They were dazzling, fun, and very festive. Even a borderline Grinch like myself couldn't stop grinning from ear to ear, snapping pictures as each one passed by, more colorful than the last, caught up in the magic of the lights.

With one big caveat– it started to rain about halfway through. Just a bit at first, which wasn't bad. A light drizzle, no big deal. I was kind of prepared for that: umbrella, hat, water-repellant coat in hand. It wasn't even cold, close to sixty degrees. Everyone, including me, was probably happy to celebrate that fact alone. Normally we'd all have frozen our rear ends off standing out on a street corner in November at night up here, watching tractors roll by.

Instead we got drenched. A gusty wind started blowing in, and the umbrella wasn't a whole lot of help after that. My jacket soaked through where it stuck out from underneath the one my friend and I were sharing, and rain spattered my glasses. I had to stop taking pictures because my hands grew too stiff and wet, and my precious phone was, of course, in danger of drowning.

Unable to bear up under the weather any longer, my friend and I started walking back to her house. She lives in town, so it wasn't far. We wove around and swerved through the remaining crowd, people still lined up valiantly on the street as tractors continued rolling along, raising our umbrellas as needed so as not to knock anyone in the head or poke them in the eye. We managed to see the last tractor, Santa being towed on his sleigh, before turning down a side street to avoid the mass exodus behind us.

Most people were a lot less prepared than we'd been. Sixty degrees in wind and rain starts to feel a lot colder when you're soaked through. I imagine there will be a rash of colds and chills a few days from now after last night. Some headline will probably read, "Family of four gets flu, sues Greenwich Tractor Parade."

On our walk back, wet, cold and rather grouchy, I started complaining to my friend about how the rain had kind of ruined

everything for everyone, for me at least. I griped about how I would like to have stayed, taken more pictures, not gotten soaked to the skin. Having at last embraced the festivity of the night, the spirit of the holiday season to come, I had been denied. It had literally rained on my parade.

My friend, ever the optimist now, said that she believed that was exactly what would make the night more memorable, for me, for her and everyone else who came to watch the parade. That it is the anomalies, not the ordinary, that stand out, that make memories stay more with us.

I didn't agree much at the time, but I considered the idea a lot more on my drive home. More this morning when I got up, thinking of what to write. My friend said I could take her idea and write about it, which I am. But I'm giving it back to her, too.

I think it's possible that she's right, at least partially so. I think extremes of either joy or pain, miracles and tragedies, the unique, the different, the anomalies, do imprint themselves on our minds more profoundly than the day-to-day. They stand out, shake us up, make us question or reevaluate our expectations. Maybe that is what nature intended, maybe that is just part of how we learn, how we are meant to remember.

Not that my rained-on parade was a tragedy. Quite the opposite, really. But the whole evening turned out to be not what I expected. It didn't start out that way, with my Christmas grumpy pants pulled up high, and it didn't end that way for me, either. Between the rainbow of lights and roaring tractor engines, the rain and wind, and the conversation with my friend on our walk home, the memory, I know, will stay with me.

Warm and dry now, I can recall the disappointment as well as the magic of the evening. Both mixed up together, weaving their

way through my consciousness. An anomaly, as my friend called it, by the contrast of the experiences. It certainly makes for a good story to tell, and a memorable one, I think, to share.

A Walk at Night

I walk by night
with little fear,
my step so light,
with none to hear,
except the wind
and the trees

a moon rides high
and lights my way,
clouds brush by
but never stay,
soft and quiet
as smoke

I pause to feel
night breeze on my skin,
and listen deep
to the stillness within –
silence comes
to greet me

if only the shadows
made a sound,
they could tell
of what I found
along my path
through the dark

The Silence

here I am,
breaking through—
walls fall down,
crumbling doubt, fear
like dried leaves
under my foot

but I cling
tethered still,
to one true knot
choosing never to untie,
never let it go,
unraveling

keeping it close,
bound up
instead of pain,
makes me whole,
unites my spirit,
means safety

picked apart,
released,
chaos follows
like night from day;
I would go with it
into nothing

leave me be then,
let me hold it
sacred, unknown;
no more questions

in my silence
lies freedom

Tossed Away

crumpled between two hands,
how crisply did I fold,
a paper heart so fragile,
worn thin and weak and old;
I felt my world collapsing,
twisting down upon itself,
compounded by compliance
with every blow I felt

one last satisfying squeeze
sent this tiny, brittle ball
flying toward the waste can,
but instead bounced off the wall;
in a deep, dark corner
I finally came to rest,
to lay in quiet solitude,
unwelcome memory of a mess

my edges uncurled slowly,
and filled up full with dust,
forgotten and abandoned,
but I didn't make a fuss;
I learned to love the silence,
finding comfort on my own,
making peace with demons,
learning to be alone

something still remains inside,
a great mystery to find —

something raw, half-remembered,
a thing pure and unrefined;
so I wait here in the darkness
and when the time is right,
worthy hands will find and unfold me,
bringing all my gifts to light

Like a Stone

my heart hangs heavier
in my chest
with each passing year;
one by one, losses come
taking all
that I hold dear

this skin I'm in
grows tougher, thicker
than it used to be;
my vision, though weary
now is greater
than the world I see

my soul has weathered
hard like a stone
lying on the shore of the sea;
my eyes turn gray
as storm clouds,
gazing back at me

Heavy

the weight of my heart
has finally spread
up into my head–
heavy and dull
it throbs, and robs
me of my rest

too long, it says
too much, too much
this weight I cannot bear
alone, and so
now here with you
it's burden I must share

no sleep for us,
no resting now,
together we must find
a way to walk
through this life
and leave the weight behind

A Restless Dark

I heard the voice
in my sleep
awakening at night,
calling me back
from dreams—
listen up, it said
don't shut your eyes
and ears
to the restlessness within

you've much to say
words to speak,
let the conversations go;
set them free,
stir up memories,
peel off scabs,
show your scars,
bare your bones,
bury the dead

no rest for the wicked
or the weary,
only truth
can bear such weight;
miles to go now,
long miles,
before you sleep
this night

The Relic

old friend now,
I find you written,
still there awake
lingering, after
so much time;
unseen, blazing
I feel you always—
phantom, ghost
gentle reminder,
leftover lover
memory, journey
to another time,
another place,
some other me

our first meeting
pained me well,
but there you were
newborn, fresh
the only scar
I ever gave myself;
I need you close,
longing never
to forget, neglect
a lesson learned;
you won't let me —
we stick together,
skin on skin,
hand in hand,
keeping promises

Promise

a patch of dry ground
among the wet—
safe haven for
the new grass to grow

the sun shines down,
and I nearly drown
in the warmth
and promise of spring

This Country Life

My now mostly overgrown farm of hayfields and dense woods once belonged to more industrious types. The place was surely grander then, some 200 years ago, and served a far more functional purpose than I have so far set for it. It's as if I'm living in the shadow of human beings much harder working than myself, an idea I find both fascinating and a bit intimidating.

And one I'm really trying to work out for myself: What is my purpose here? Should I stay? And if I do, what, if anything, do I do with it all? I continually ask the spirits around me (I'm sure they're there) for any input or advice they'd care to suggest.

So far all the response I've gotten was, "get some chickens."

I've been told by people who've lived in Hartford for generations that my home was once the main house for a farm of a few hundred acres belonging to the Maynard family, stretching from one horizon on the southern end to another on the north, nestled between two hills on the east and west. Before any other houses sprang up on the road, before electric poles and phone lines went in, before asphalt was even invented, my house oversaw it all.

It's hard for me to imagine back that far, that my home was actually standing well before the First World War.

Beans and potatoes were apparently the main crops here then; there is evidence in one of the back fields of the soil depletion, where only thick, woody wildflowers and alpine strawberries grow now. They are things that love poor soil, and stones, and baking under constant heat and sunshine.

Piece by piece the land was sold off, and the farm gradually shrank to the roughly 40 acres it is now. Other houses and utility

poles eventually brought civilization to the road, and my once isolated farmhouse was drawn into the bigger world at last.

Back in the 1970s, the last Maynard married a Batkay, and the place became the Wii Vegetable Farm. They continued to grow beans and potatoes, but on a much smaller scale, and grew other crops like rhubarb and asparagus, as well as ornamental flowers. There were three huge greenhouses out back for starting seeds and transplants, where now only the bony, silver skeleton of one remains.

Pressed into the concrete threshold of that last greenhouse is an imprint of four hands locked in a circle. I imagine it's the hands of the Batkays and their children, but I don't really know. Every time I see it, it makes me stop and think and remember that I'm not the only one who has ever been here. Nor will I (most likely) be the last.

But am I meant to be a farmer? Am I ready to plant my hands into some concrete like those before me did and leave my mark on this place? I honestly don't know. I had dreams of that once, on a large scale. But the winters here are so hard and long sometimes, I don't know how committed I ever could be to that life.

I see myself as more a steward of the land. I enjoy the open fields, walking my dogs through them under the wide-open sky, watching the real farmer in his giant old John Deere tractor mow their grassy bounty every year for hay for his dairy cows, knowing that (even indirectly) I'm supporting a local industry that's struggling to survive. I love the lumpy hay bales, and keeping watch over them for the brief period of time as they cure, before the farmer takes them home.

And I like the space –though it can seem more like emptiness

sometimes. So I feel the urge to fill it, too, with horses or sheep or goats, maybe even a cow or two of my own. I long to see them grazing out there in the afternoon sunlight.

I'd like to walk up to them with carrots or small apples from the old trees out back, and feel the rough tickle of a muzzle as they took the treats from my hand. It's a happy memory from childhood, that feel of a sudden warm breath on my palm, followed by the soft lips and whiskers of my horse. It's a memory so keen it makes my chest tight, the thought of having a horse in my life again.

The thought of rows of lettuce or kale, however, while possibly income-producing, doesn't have quite the same effect.

If I had more animals, I think the occasional loneliness of this country life would be lessened. They would keep me present, grounded but moving at the same time, even in the dregs of winter when I want nothing more than to be gone from this place. The animals would make me stay.

But fields of crops, I'm not so sure. Crops can get eaten, blighted, frost-killed. And I don't think I'd ever feel quite as committed to them. My vegetable garden is enough to manage as it is, thank you. Though I am rather itchy to get out there and start digging these days.

So as spring arrives and the rebirth of all things follows along with it, I'm thinking again about trying to make something of my life here, of strengthening my ties to this place that once called to me so deeply. I'm contemplating a few changes to the house itself, adding some creature comforts that would bring more warmth and convenience into such an old and all-too chilly place, things that would help it become a more inviting home and get my soul through the darkest, bleakest times of winter.

My mission, I think, should I choose to accept it, is to preserve this place for myself, for others, for coming generations. To have help to do that, to bring more life here, would go miles and miles toward creating a life here for myself, one that I want to live. I think it would make a world of difference.

Then maybe I would go out one bright morning and place my palm in the circle the Batkays made, and join my own hand to theirs in silent agreement, saying, "Yes, I'm with you. Lets see what the future brings, together."

Fire and the Light

wind steals the breath,
heat and heart, from my home
pulling, pushing it's weight
through the fine cracks,
those wrinkles of time,
crawling through old timbers,
peeling away the cocoon—

lathe and plaster sigh,
give up, give way
give in to their ghosts,
blowing across empty fields
from the north, the east
heading ever onward, restless
wandering, seeking their end

chasing away fire, and light
towards the cold dark of evening

The Stranger

walking now,
into a den
of sleeping lions –
treading softly,
eyes, ears alert
awake, waiting
for one to stir,
raise its gaze,
follow my step
and rise up,
mouth hungry,
swallowing me
down whole

many eyes open,
watching, silent
letting me come
further along;
deeper, bolder
with every step
I grow, passing
teeth, claws
soft fur, breath
finding only
patience, permission
acceptance

still unsure,
curious, hopeful
feeling my breath,
looking down
to see my skin –
warm brown fur,
my every step
so like theirs,
claws and teeth
all my own;
I lay down,
turning over,
belly soft, bare

resting here, quiet
among sisters
brothers, my kind
no longer wary;
knowing now
I am welcome,
I am home

Bits of Stars

lowliest grain
to highest heaven,
we journey out
to find ourselves—
seeing all,
yet knowing nothing,
we stumble often
along the way

fragile creatures,
we are promise,
filled with hope
and such despair;
climbing high,
then quickly falling,
losing ground
while gaining speed

we miss so much
but always linger,
finding it hard
to turn away;
bound to greatness
and to fault,
strength and weakness
struggle on

light and dark,
they meet within us
creating the spark
of life itself—
brains to bones,
all we are, is dirt
and bits of stars,
shining darkly

Bed of Coals

turning over dust
to find smoldering
deep down, buried
beneath an ashen shroud,
bright hearts burning,
awake and alive

what a surprise,
digging up the grave
of what I thought
was over, ended
a fire long gone out,
learning life remains

cautious now, careful
placing one by one
the fuel to feed these
tender coals, still warm
awaiting the moment
sparks might fly

watching, hopeful
yet nothing comes,
no light from darkness;
all seems lost, wasted
until a tiny ember
catches fire—

alight then, suddenly
flames growing, kissing
smooth dark glass;
eager, hungry hearts
at last reborn,
beating faster

New Womb

lay me down
into the ground
when I am done;
till my bones
into the black soil,
dig deep, dig true
not shallow,
down to where
old stones turn
alongside the worm

let the new trees
find me there
roots taking hold,
taking their fill,
branches spreading,
sowing their seeds,
growing tall, strong
standing firm
against the wind,
holding fast to life

to feel the earth
forever around me,
a new womb
sprung from the old,
taking me back
carrying me home;

all things return
to their origin—
circles close in,
only to open again

ABOUT THE AUTHOR

Originally from Missouri, I came to upstate New York twenty years ago and fell in love with the green, rolling landscape and ever-changing seasons. I make my home now in an old farmhouse in the lovely Adirondack foothills. Surrounded by forty-odd acres of pasture and former vegetable fields, I write, take photographs, paint, garden, work on the house, and take care of my small menagerie of animals, which includes dogs, cats, bees, and chickens. I haven't quit my day job yet, and work as a medication resource nurse at a local hospital.

If you enjoyed this collection of poems, essays, and photographs, please visit my blog at www.creativejourneywoman.com to follow my work and other creative projects.

Made in the USA
Middletown, DE
10 June 2016